CHILTON'S Repair and Tune-Up Guide

Volkswagen

1970–77

ILLUSTRATED

Prepared by the

Automotive Editorial Department

Chilton Book Company

Chilton Way
Radnor, Pa. 19089
215—687-8200

president and chief executive officer **WILLIAM A. BARBOUR;** executive vice president **RICHARD H. GROVES;** vice president and general manager **WILLIAM D. BYRNE;** managing editor **JOHN H. WEISE, S.A.E.;** assistant managing editor **KERRY A. FREEMAN;** editors **Ronald L. Sessions, Martin W. Kane**

CHILTON BOOK COMPANY   RADNOR, PENNSYLVANIA

Copyright © 1977 by Chilton Book Company
All Rights Reserved
Published in Radnor, Pa. by Chilton Book Company
and simultaneously in Ontario, Canada
by Thomas Nelson & Sons, Ltd.

Manufactured in the United States of America

34567890   654321098

Chilton's Repair & Tune-Up Guide: Volkswagen 1970–77
ISBN 0-8019-6619-1 pbk.

Library of Congress Catalog Card No. 76-57319

ACKNOWLEDGMENTS

Chilton Book Company expresses appreciation to Volkswagenwerk AG Wolfsburg, the Arnolt Corporation, and
the Ford Motor Company for technical information and
illustrations.

The editor wishes to give special thanks to CVW En-
terprises, Exton, Pa., Devon Motors, Inc., Devon Pa.,
Group Seven Imports, Phoenixville, Pa., Arrington and
Ritter VW Service, Avondale, Pa., Foreign Car Service of
Willow Grove, Willow Grove, Pa., and Volks Tool Supply, Houston, Texas, for their contributions to the technical accuracy and clarity of the information herein.

Photos by Martin W. Kane

Although the information in this guide is based on in-
dustry sources and is as complete as possible at the time
of publication, the possibility exists that the manufacturer
made later changes which could not be included here.
While striving for total accuracy, Chilton Book Company
cannot assume responsibility for any errors, changes, or
omissions that may occur in the compilation of this data.

Contents

iii

Chapter One

General Information and Maintenance

How To Use This Book

This book has been written to aid the Volkswagen owner perform maintenance, tune-ups and repairs on his automobile. It is intended for both the novice and for those more familiar with auto repairs. Since this book contains information on very simple operations (Chapters 1 and 2) and the more involved ones (Chapters 3–8), the user will not outgrow the book as he masters simple repairs and is ready to progress to more difficult operations.

Several things were assumed of you while the repair procedures were being written. They are mentioned here so that you will be aware of them. It was assumed that you own, or are willing to purchase, a basic set of hand tools and equipment. A skeletal listing of tools and equipment has been drawn up for you.

For many repair operations, the factory has suggested a special tool to perform the repairs. If it was at all possible, a conventional tool was substituted for the special tool in these cases. However, there are some operations which cannot be done without the use of these tools. To perform these jobs correctly, it will be necessary to order the tool through your local VW dealer's parts department.

Two basic rules of automobile mechanics deserve mentioning here. Whenever the left-side of the car is referred to, it is meant to specify the driver's side. Likewise, the right-side of the car means the passenger's side. Also, most screws, nuts, and bolts are removed by turning counterclockwise and tightened by turning clockwise.

Before performing any repairs, read the entire section of the book that deals with that job. In many places a description of the system is provided. By reading this first, and then reading the entire repair procedure, you will understand the function of the system you will be working on and what will be involved in the repair operation, prior to starting the job. This will enable you to avoid problems and also to help you learn about your car while you are working on it.

While every effort was made to make the book as simple, yet as detailed as possible, there is no substitute for personal experience. You can gain the confidence and feel for mechanical things needed to make auto repairs only by doing them yourself. If you take your time and concentrate on what you are doing, you will be amazed at how fast you can learn.

Tools and Equipment

Now that you have purchased this book and commited yourself to maintaining your car, a small set of basic tools and equipment will prove handy. The first group of items should be adequate for most maintenance and light repair procedures:

Sliding T-bar handle or ratchet wrench;

⅜ in. drive socket wrench set (with breaker bar) (metric) (including a 36 mm socket);

Universal adapter for socket wrench set;

Flat blade and phillips head screwdrivers;

Pliers;

Adjustable wrench;

Locking pliers;

Open-end wrench set (metric);

Feeler gauge set;

Oil filter strap wrench;

Brake adjusting spoon;

Drift pin;

Torque wrench (0–150 ft lb type with half-length adaptor); and, of course, a hammer.

Along with the above mentioned tools, the following equipment should be on hand:

Scissors jack or hydraulic jack of sufficient capacity;

Jackstands of sufficient capacity;

Wheel blocks;

Grease gun (hand-operated type);

Drip pan (low and wide);

Drop light;

Tire pressure gauge;

Penetrating oil (spray lubricant);

and a can of waterless hand cleaner.

In this age of emission controls and high priced gasoline, it is important to keep your car in proper tune. The following items, though they will represent an investment equal or greater to that of the first group, will tell you everything you might need to know about a car's state of tune:

12-volt test light;

Compression gauge;

Manifold vacuum gauge;

Power timing light;

A dwell-tachometer; and a uni-syn® gauge (for twin carb Type 2 models).

History

In 1932, Ferdinand Porsche produced prototypes for the NSU company of Germany which eventually led to the design of the Volkswagen. The prototypes had a rear mounted, air-cooled engine, torsion bar suspension, and the spare tire mounted at an angle in the front luggage compartment. In 1936, Porsche produced three Volkswagen prototypes, one of which was a 995 cc, horizontally opposed, four cylinder automobile. Passenger car development was sidetracked during World War II, when all attention was on military vehicles. In 1945, Volkswagen production began and 1,785 Beetles were built. The Volkswagen convertible was introduced in 1949, the same year that only two Volkswagens were sold in the United States. 1950 marked the beginning of the sunroof models and the transporter series. The Karmann Ghia was introduced in 1956, and remained in the same basic styling format until its demise in 1974. The 1500 Squareback were introduced in the United States in 1966 to start the Type 3 series. The Type 4 was imported into the U.S.A. beginning with the 1971 model.

Type numbers are the way Volkswagen designates its various groups of models. The type 1 group contains the Beetle, Super Beetle, and the Karmann Ghia. Type 2 vehicles are the Delivery Van, the Micro Bus, the Kombi and the Campmobile. The Type 3 designation is for the Fastback and the Squareback sedans. The Type 4 is for the 411 and 412 sedans and wagon. These type numbers will be used throughout the book when it is necessary to refer to models.

An explanation of the terms suitcase engine and upright fan engine is, perhaps, necessary. The upright fan engine refers to the engine used in the Type 1 and 2 (1970–71) vehicles. This engine has the engine cooling fan mounted on the top of the engine and is driven by the generator. The fan is mounted vertically in contrast to a horizontally mounted fan as found on the Chevrolet Corvair engine. The suitcase engine is a comparatively new engine and was designed as a more compact unit to fit in the Type 3, 4 and 1972 and later Type 2 engine compartments. On this engine, the cooling fan is mounted on the crankshaft giving the engine a rectangular shape similar to that of a suitcase.

Model Identification

Type 1 Beetle (left) and Super Beetle (right)—1973 shown

Type 1 Super Beetle Convertible (Model 15)

Type 1 Karmann Ghia Convertible (Model 14)

Type 1 Karmann Ghia (Model 14)

Type 2 Campmobile (Model 23)

Type 2 Van (Model 21)

Type 2 Bus (Model 22)

Type 3 Fastback (Model 31)

Type 3 Squareback (Model 36)

Type 4 411 Station Wagon (1971–72 Model 46)

Type 4 411 4-door Sedan (1971–72 Model 41)

Type 4 412 4-door Sedan (1973–74 Model 41)

Type 4 412 Station Wagon (1973–74 Model 46)

Serial Number Identification

VEHICLE (CHASSIS) NUMBER

The chassis number consists of ten digits. The first two numbers indicate the model type, and the third number gives the model year. For example, a 2 as the third digit means that the car was produced during the 1972 model year run.

Chassis number location on dashboard (Type 1 Karmann Ghia shown; others similar)

Chassis number location under rear seat (Type 1 Karmann Ghia shown; Types 3 and 4 similar)

Chassis number location behind front passenger's seat—Type 2 only

Chassis number location on left-hand engine cover plate—Type 2 only

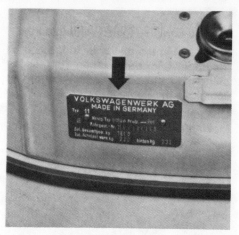

Chassis number location in luggage compartment—Type 1 Super Beetle shown; Types 3 and 4 similar

The chassis number is stamped on a metal plate. On Type 1, 3, and 4 models, the plate is located in the luggage compartment, on the frame tunnel under the back seat, and on the driver's side of the instrument panel (visible through the windshield). On Type 2 models, the plate is located behind the front passenger's seat, on the left-hand engine cover plate, and on top of the driver's side of the instrument panel.

VEHICLE CERTIFICATION LABEL

The vehicle certification label is a decal affixed to the left door jam. It indicates that the vehicle meets all U.S. federal safety standards as of the date of manufacture. The label also gives the chassis number of the car. Beginning with the 1973 model year, the label lists the gross vehicle weight rating and the gross axle weight rating. The gross vehicle weight rating is useful in determining the load carrying capacity of your car. Merely subtract the curb weight from the posted gross weight and what is left over is about how much you can haul around. The gross axle weight rating is a good guide to the weight distribution of your car.

MANUFACTURED BY **VOLKSWAGENWERK AG**   08/71
THIS VEHICLE CONFORMS TO ALL APPLICABLE FEDERAL MOTOR
VEHICLE SAFETY STANDARDS IN EFFECT ON THE DATE OF MANU-
FACTURE SHOWN ABOVE.

Vehicle certification label—1970–72 (Type 1 shown)

This additional line applies only to the Campmobile ——————

MANUFACTURED BY **VOLKSWAGENWERK AG**	09/72
INCOMPLETE VEHICLE MANUFACTURED	08/72

THIS VEHICLE CONFORMS TO ALL APPLICABLE FEDERAL MOTOR VEHICLE SAFETY STANDARDS IN EFFECT ON THE DATE OF MANUFACTURE SHOWN ABOVE.
GVWR LB 4961
GAWR LB 2227/2800   TYPE MULTIPURPOSE PASSENGER VEHICLE

Vehicle certification label—1973–77 (Type 2 shown)

The vehicle certification label is constructed of special material to guard against its alteration. If it is tampered with or removed, it will be destroyed or the word "VOID" will appear.

ENGINE NUMBER

The engine can be identified by a letter or pair of letters preceeding the serial

Engine number location—Type 1 and 2/1600 (1970–71)

Engine number location Type 2/2000 shown (Typical of Type 3 Type 4 and Type 2/1700, 2/1800, with suitcase engine)

number. Engine specifications are listed according to the letter code and model year.

On all Type 1 models, and on 1970–71 Type 2/1600 models using the upright fan engine, the engine number is stamped into the crankcase flange for the generator support. The number can readily be seen by looking through the center of the fan belt.

On all Type 3 and 4 models, and on 1972–76 Type 2/1700, Type 2/1800, and Type 2/2000 models using the "suitcase" engine, the engine number is stamped into the crankcase along the crankcase joint near the oil breather.

TRANSMISSION IDENTIFICATION

Transmission identification marks are stamped either into the bellhousing or on the final drive housing.

Routine Maintenance

AIR CLEANER SERVICE

Oil Bath Type

This type cleaner should be cleaned at 6,000 mile intervals, or when the oil is changed.

TYPE 1 AND 2 (1970–73)

1. To clean the air cleaner, remove the hoses attached to the air cleaner.
CAUTION: *Be careful to note the places where the hoses are attached. Interchanging the hoses will affect the operation of the engine.*
2. Next, loosen the air cleaner support bracket screw and the air cleaner clamp screw.
3. On 1970 models, disconnect the

Chassis Number Chart

Model Year	Vehicle	Model No.	Chassis Number					
			From			To		
1970	Beetle	113	110	2000	001	110	3096	945
	Karmann Ghia	14	140	2000	001	140	3100	000
	Beetle Convertible	15	150	2000	001	150	3100	000
	Van	21	210	2000	001	210	2300	000
	Bus	22	220	2000	001	220	2300	000
	Camper, Kombi	23	230	2000	001	230	2300	000
	Type 3 Fastback	31	310	2000	001	310	2500	000
	Type 3 Squareback	36	360	2000	001	360	2500	000
1971	Beetle/Super Beetle	111/113	111	2000	001	111	3143	118
	Karmann Ghia	14	141	2000	001	141	3200	000
	Beetle Convertible	15	151	2000	001	151	3200	000
	Van	21	211	2000	001	211	2300	000
	Bus	22	221	2000	001	221	2300	000
	Camper, Kombi	23	231	2000	001	231	2300	000
	Type 3 Fastback	31	311	2000	001	311	2500	000
	Type 3 Squareback	36	361	2000	001	361	2500	000
	411 2 Door	41	411	2000	001	411	2100	000
	411 4 Door	42	421	2000	001	421	2100	000
	411 Wagon	46	461	2000	001	461	2100	000
1972	Beetle/Super Beetle	111/113	112	2000	001	112	2961	362
	Karmann Ghia	14	142	2000	001	142	3200	000
	Beetle Convertible	15	152	2000	001	152	3200	000
	Van	21	212	2000	001	212	2300	000
	Bus	22	222	2000	001	222	2300	000
	Camper, Kombi	23	232	2000	001	232	2300	000

Chassis Number Chart (cont.)

Model Year	Vehicle	Model No.	Chassis Number From			To		
1972	Type 3 Fastback	31	312	2000	001	312	2500	000
	Type 3 Squareback	36	362	2000	001	362	2500	000
	411 2 Door	41	412	2000	001	412	2100	000
	411 4 Door	42	422	2000	001	422	2100	000
	411 Wagon	46	462	2000	001	462	2100	000
1973	Beetle	111	113	2000	001	113	3021	954
	Super Beetle	113	133	2000	001	133	3021	860
	Karmann Ghia	14	143	2000	001	143	3200	000
	Beetle Convertible	15	153	2000	001	153	3200	000
	Van	21	213	2000	001	213	2300	000
	Bus	22	223	2000	001	223	2300	000
	Camper, Kombi	23	233	2000	001	233	2300	000
	Type 3 Fastback	31	313	2000	001	313	2500	000
	Type 3 Squareback	36	363	2000	001	363	2500	000
	412 2 Door	41	413	2000	001	413	2100	000
	412 4 Door	42	423	2000	001	423	2100	000
	412 Wagon	46	463	2000	001	463	2100	000
1974	Beetle	111	114	2000	001	114	2818	456
	Super Beetle	113	134	2000	001	134	2798	165
	Karmann Ghia	14	144	2000	001	144	3200	000
	Beetle Convertible	15	154	2000	001	154	3200	000
	Van	21	214	2000	001	214	2300	000
	Bus	22	224	2000	001	224	2300	000
	Camper, Kombi	23	234	2000	001	234	2300	000
	412 2 Door	41	414	2000	001	414	2100	000

Chassis Number Chart (cont.)

Model Year	Vehicle	Model No.	Chassis Number From			To		
1974	412 4 Door	42	424	2000	001	424	2100	000
	412 Wagon	46	464	2000	001	464	2100	000
1975	Beetle	111	115	2000	001	115	3200	000
	Super Beetle (La Grande Bug)	113	135	2000	001	135	3200	000
	Beetle Convertible	15	155	2000	001	155	3200	000
	Van	21	215	2000	001	215	2300	000
	Bus	22	225	2000	001	225	2300	000
	Camper, Kombi	23	235	2000	001	235	2300	000
1976	Beetle	111	116	2000	001	116	3200	000
	Beetle Convertible	15	156	2000	001	156	2000	001
	Bus	22	226	2000	001	226	2300	000
	Camper, Kombi	23	236	2000	001	236	2300	001
1977	Beetle	111	117	2000	001	——		
	Beetle Convertible	15	157	2000	001	——		
	Bus	22	227	2000	001	——		
	Camper, Kombi	23	237	2000	001	——		

Capacities Chart

Year	Type and Model	Engine Displacement (cc)	Engine Crankcase (qts) With Filter	Without	Transaxle (pts) Manual	Automatic Conv	Final Drive	Gasoline Tank (gals)
1970–77	1, 111, 114	1600	——	2.5	6.3	7.6	6.3①	10.6
1970–77	1,113,15	1600	——	2.5	6.3	7.6	6.3①	11.1
1970–71	2, All	1600	——	2.5	7.4	12.6②	3.0	15.8
1972–77	2, All	1700, 1800, 2000	3.7	3.2	7.4	12.6②	3.0	15.8
1970–73	3, All	1600	——	2.5	6.3	12.6②	2.1	10.6
1971–74	4, All	1700, 1800	3.7	3.2	5.3	12.6②	2.1	13.2

Conv—Torque Converter ① 5.3 when changed ② 6.3 when changed

Engine Identification Chart

Engine Code Letter	Type Vehicle	First Production Year	Last Production Year ①	Engine Type	Common Designation
B	1, 2	1967	1970	Upright Fan	1600
AE	1, 2	1971	1972	Upright Fan	1600
AH (Calif)	1	1972	1974	Upright Fan	1600
AK	1	1973	1974	Upright Fan	1600
AJ	1	1975	In Production	Upright Fan	1600
CB	2	1972	1973	Suitcase	1700
CD	2	1973	1973	Suitcase	1700
AW	2	1974	1974	Suitcase	1800
ED	2	1975	1975	Suitcase	1800
GD	2	1976	In Production	Suitcase	2000
U	3	1968	1973	Suitcase	1600
X	3	1972	1973	Suitcase	1600
W	4	1971	1971	Suitcase	1700
EA	4	1972	1974	Suitcase	1700
EB (Calif)	4	1973	1973	Suitcase	1700
EC	4	1974	1974	Suitcase	1800

① In production as of the publication of this book

warm air flap cable. Lift the air cleaner off the engine. Keep the carburetor hole down to prevent spilling the oil out of the air cleaner.

4. Loosen the spring clips which secure the top of the air cleaner to the bottom and then separate the halves. Do not invert the upper half.

5. Put the upper half of the air cleaner down with the filter element facing downward. Thoroughly clean the bottom half.

6. Fill the air cleaner with 0.9 pints of SAE 30 (SAE 10W in sub-freezing climates) oil or, if present, to the oil level mark stamped into the side of the air cleaner.

7. Reassemble the air cleaner and install it on the engine.

ALL TYPE 3, TYPE 4 (1971–72)

1. Disconnect the activated charcoal filter hose, the rubber elbow, and the crankcase ventilation hose. Remove the wing nut in the center of the air cleaner and lift the air cleaner assembly off of the engine.

2. Release the spring clips which keep the air cleaner halves together and take the cleaner apart. Do not invert the upper half 0.085 pints of SAE 30 (SAE 10W in sub-freezing climates).

3. Clean the lower half and refill it

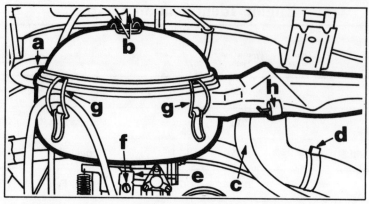

Oil bath air cleaner—1972–73 Type 1 Beetle, Super Beetle

A. Hose for evaporative control
B. Intake air preheating vacuum control hoses
C. PCV hose
D. Hose clamp

E. Air cleaner support bracket screw
F. Air cleaner support bracket screw
G. Retaining spring clips
H. Intake air preheating weighted flap

Oil bath air cleaner—1973–74 Type 1 Karmann Ghia

A. Hose clamp
B. Hose clamp
C. Hose
D. Hose
E. Intake air preheating vacuum control hoses
F. Mounting spring clips
G. Retaining spring clips
H. Intake air preheating weighted flap

with oil to the level mark. When reassembling the air cleaner, align the marks for the upper and lower halves.

Oil bath air cleaner—1972 Type 2

4. Reinstall the air cleaner on the engine. Make sure it is properly seated.

Paper Element Type

TYPE 1 (1973–77),
AND TYPE 4 (1973–74)

1. Label and disconnect the hoses from the air cleaner.
CAUTION: *Do not interchange the position of the hoses.*
2. Loosen the air cleaner clamp and remove the air cleaner from the engine. Release spring clamps which keep the halves of the cleaner together and separate the halves.
3. Clean the inside of the air cleaner housing.
4. The paper element should be replaced every 18,000 miles under normal service. It should be replaced more often under severe operating conditions. A

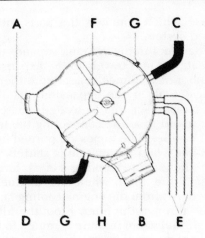

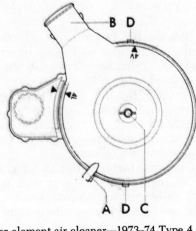

Oil bath air cleaner—1973 Type 3

A. Hose clamp
B. Retaining clip
C. Hose
D. Hose
E. Hoses
F. Wing nut
G. Retaining spring clips
H. Alignment marks for upper and lower halves

Paper element air cleaner—1973–74 Type 4

A. Hose to air intake pipe
B. Hose to intake air distributor
C. Wing nut
D. Retaining spring clips
4L. Alignment mark for 2 and 4-door sedans
      (match arrow on lower half)
4V. Alignment mark for station wagons
      (match arrow on lower half)

paper element may be cleaned by blowing through the element from the inside with compressed air. Never use a liquid solvent to clean a paper element.

5. Install the air cleaner element in the air cleaner housing and install the spring clips, making sure the halves are properly aligned. Install the cleaner on the engine.

TYPE 2/1700 ENGINE (1973), TYPE 2/1800 ENGINE (1974)

1. Label and disconnect the hoses from the air cleaner.

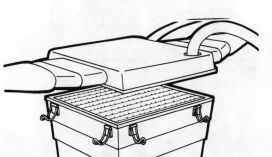

Paper element air cleaner—1973–74 Type 2

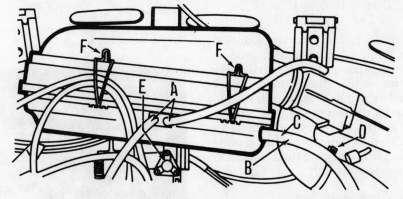

Paper element air cleaner—1973–74 Type 1 Beetle, Super Beetle

A. Intake air preheating vacuum control hoses
B. Hose for evaporative control
C. PCV hose
D. Hose Clamp
E. Air cleaner clamp screw
F. Retaining spring clips

CAUTION: *Do not interchange the position of the hoses.*

2. Release the two clamps which secure the air cleaner to the carburetors. Release the clips which secure the air ducts to each carburetor.

3. Remove the air ducts separately. Remove the air cleaner housing.

4. Release the four spring clips which secure the cleaner halves together and then separate the halves.

5. Clean the inside of the housing. The paper element should be replaced every 18,000 miles under normal service. It should be replaced more often under severe operating conditions. A paper element may be cleaned by blowing through the element from the inside with compressed air. Never use a liquid solvent.

6. Assemble the air cleaner halves, making sure that they are properly aligned. Install the air cleaner by reversing the above. Make sure that the rubber sleeves on the air ducts and the rubber seals on the carburetors are seated properly.

CRANKCASE VENTILATION SERVICE

TYPE 1/600, 2/1600, 2/1700, 2/1800 (CARBURETED)

The crankcase is vented by a hose running from the crankcase breather to the air cleaner. In some cases the hose is attached to the air inlet for the air cleaner. No PCV valve is used. No regular service is required.

TYPE 3/1600, 4/1700, 4/1800 (INJECTED)

Air is drawn in from the air cleaner to the cylinder head covers and pushrod tubes where it passes into the crankcase. Blow-by fumes then pass into the crankcase breather where they are drawn into the intake air distributor. A PCV valve is used to control the flow of crankcase fumes. These systems need no maintenance other than keeping the hoses clear, and all connections tight.

FUEL EVAPORATION CONTROL SYSTEM SERVICE

This system consists of an expansion chamber, an activated charcoal filter, and a hose which connects the parts into a closed system.

When fuel in the gas tank expands due to heat, the fuel travels to the expansion chamber. Any fumes generated either in the gas tank or the expansion chamber are trapped in the activated charcoal filter found in a line connecting the tank and chamber. The fumes are purged from the filter when the engine is started. Air from the engine cooling fan is forced through the filter when the engine is started. Air from the engine cooling fan is forced through the filter. From the filter, this air/fuel vapor mixture is routed to the inside of the air cleaner where it is sent to the engine to be burned.

The only maintenance required on the system is checking the tightness of all

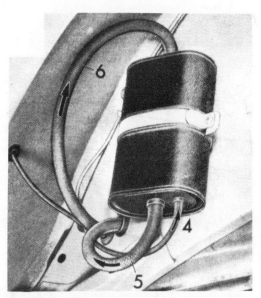

Evaporative control canister location—Type 1 Beetle; Super Beetle

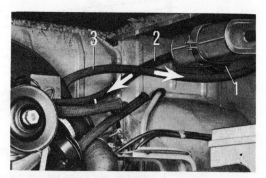

Evaporative control canister locations—1970–71 Type 2/1600

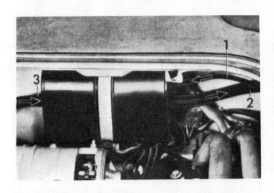

Evaporative control canister location—Type 3

Checking drive belt (V-belt) tension

a. ¼ to ½ in.

Evaporative control canister location—Type 4

hose connections, and replacement of the charcoal filter element at 48,000 miles or 2 year intervals (whichever occurs first).

The filter canister is located under the right rear fender on Beetles and Super Beetles, at the lower right hand side of the engine compartment on Karmann Ghias, at the upper right hand side of the engine compartment on Type 3 models, and beneath the floor near the forward end of the transaxle on Type 4 models.

V-BELTS

Generator/Alternator Drive Belt Adjustment

Improper fan belt adjustment can lead to either overheating of the engine or to loss in generating power, or both. In the Type 1, Type 2 or Type 4 a loose fan belt can cause both, while the slipping of the generator or alternator belt of the Type 3 engine will cause loss of generator ef-

ficiency only. In any case, it is important that the fan belt adjustment be checked and, if necessary, corrected at periodic intervals. When adjusted properly, the belt of any Volkswagen engine should deflect approximately ½ in. when pressed firmly in the center with the thumb. Check the tension at 6,000 mile intervals.

TYPE 1/1600, TYPE 2/1600

Adjustment of the Type 1/1600 and Type 2/1600 fan belt is made as follows: loosen the fan pulley by unscrewing the nut while at the same time holding the pulley from rotating by using a screwdriver inserted into the slot cut into the inner half of the generator pulley and

Use a screwdriver to keep generator/alternator from turning while loosening/tightening pulley nut—Type 1/1600, 2/1600 and 3/1600

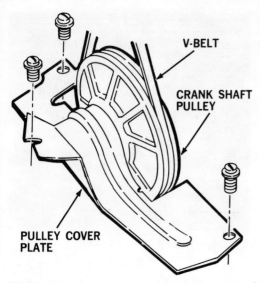

Remove this plate to replace the V-belt on Type 1 engines

supported against the upper generator bolt to cause a counter-torque. Remove the nut from the generator shaft pulley and remove the outer half of the pulley. The spacer washers must then be arranged so as to make the fan belt tension either greater or less. The greater the number of washers between the pulley halves, the smaller the effective diameter of the pulley, and the less the fan belt tension will be. Conversely, the subtraction of washers from between the pulley halves will lead to a larger effective diameter and to a greater degree of fan belt tension. If it is impossible to achieve proper adjustment with all the washers removed, then the fan belt is excessively stretched, and must be replaced. If it is impossible to adjust a new belt properly by using some combination of the available washers, the belt is the wrong size and must not be used. After the correct

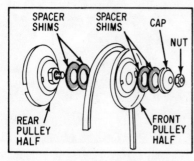

Type 1/1600, 2/1600, and 3/1600 generator/alternator belt adjustment showing arrangement of shims

number of washers has been applied between the pulley halves, install the outer pulley half and place all surplus washers between the outer pulley half and the pulley nut so that they will be available if needed in a subsequent adjustment. Tighten the pulley nut and recheck the adjustment. If incorrect, add or subtract washers between the pulley halves until the proper amount of deflection is achieved. If the belt is too tight, the generator bearings will be subjected to undue stress and to very early failure. On the other hand, if the belt is too loose, it will slip and cause overheating. Cracked or frayed belts should be replaced. There is no comparison between the cost of a fan belt and that of repairing a badly overheated engine. If it is necessary to replace the belt, remove the three sheet metal screws and the crankshaft pulley cover plate to gain access to the pulley.

TYPE 3/1600

Adjustment of the fan belt on the Type 3 engine is much the same as that of the smaller Volkswagen engines. On the Type 3 engine, the fan belt is subject to a great deal less stress because it has no fan to turn. Therefore, a loose adjustment is not quite so critical as on the beetle models. However, the ½ in. deflection should nevertheless be maintained, because a loose fan belt could possibly climb over the pulley and foul the fan. In addition, loose fan belts have a shorter service life. In adjusting the Type 3 fan belt, the first step is to remove the cover of the air intake housing. Next, hold the generator pulley with a suitable wrench, and unscrew the retaining nut. (Note: a 27 mm. and a 21 mm. wrench will come in handy here. Also, be careful that no adjusting washers fall off the shaft into the air intake housing, for they could be quite difficult to remove.) Loosen the generator strap and push the generator slightly forward. Remove the outer pulley half, sleeve and washers included. Arrange the spacer washers as was described in the Type 1/1600, 2/1600 belt adjustment; i.e., more washers between halves mean a looser belt, and fewer washers mean a tighter belt. Install outer half of pulley. Install unused washers on outside of outer pulley half so that the total number of washers on the shaft will remain the same. Fit the nut into place and tighten down the generator strap after pulling the generator back to the rear. Tighten the retaining nut and make sure that the generator belt is parallel to the air intake housing and at least 4 mm. away from it at all points. Install housing cover.

TYPE 2/1700, 2/1800, 2/2000 AND TYPE 4

To adjust the alternator/cooling belt tension on these models, first remove the plastic insert in the cover plate over the alternator. Then, loosen the 12 point allen head adjusting bolt and the hex-

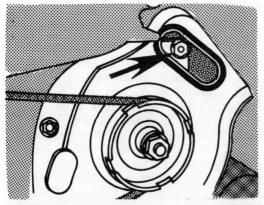

Type 2/1700, 2/1800, 2/2000 and Type 4 alternator adjusting nut (12 point allen head)

head mounting bolt. Adjust the tension so that light thumb pressure applied midway in the belts longest run causes a deflection of approximately ½ in. Tighten the bolts.

When installing a new belt, move the alternator fully to the left and slip off the old belt. Install a new belt and tighten by moving the alternator to the right.

Air Injection Air Pump Drive Belt Adjustment

1973–74 TYPE 2

To provide proper air pump output for the emission control system on 1973–74 Type 2 models, the belt tension must be checked at 6,000 mile intervals. Deflection is correct when light thumb pressure applied midway in the longest run of the belt deflects about ¼ in. To adjust, loosen the adjusting and mounting bolts (black arrows). Hold the air pump in position while tightening the bolts.

Type 2 air pump adjusting nut locations

FLUID LEVEL CHECKS

Engine Oil

To check the engine oil level, park the car on level ground and wait 5 minutes to allow all the oil in the engine to drain into the crankcase.

Check the oil level by withdrawing the dipstick and wiping it clean. Insert the dipstick into its hole and note the position of the oil level on the bottom of the stick. The level should be between the two marks on the bottom of the stick. The distance between the two marks represents one quart of oil.

On upright fan engines, the dipstick is located directly beneath the generator or alternator; oil is added at the cap on the passenger side of the generator (alternator). On Type 2 suitcase engines, the dipstick is located next to the alternator. On Type 3 vehicles, it is necessary to raise the back door or engine compartment lid and locate the dipstick in the lower door jamb. On Type 4 two door and four models, the dipstick is located at the center of the engine next to the oil filler cap; on wagon models, it is under the rear door jamb.

Transmission

MANUAL TRANSMISSION

The oil level is checked by removing the 17 mm socket head plug located on the driver's side of the transaxle. The oil level should be even with the hole. Check it with your finger.

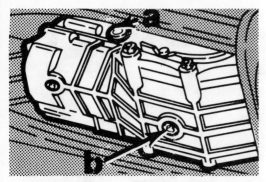

Typical transaxle drain and filler plug locations

A. Filler plug   B. Drain plug

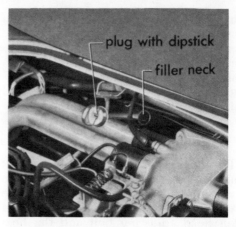

Type 3 and Type 4 Automatic transmission dipstick location; Type 2 dipstick similar

CAUTION: *Do not fill the transaxle too quickly because it may overflow from the filler hole and give the impression that the unit has been filled when it has n*

Top up as necessary with SAE 90 gear oil.

AUTOMATIC STICK SHIFT TRANSMISSION—TYPE 1

The automatic Stick Shift transmission is checked by means of a dipstick. The oil level should be between two marks at the bottom of the stick. The engine should be warm when the transmission oil level is checked. Top up as necessary with DEXRON®.

NOTE: *The engine must be turned off when checking the transmission oil level.*

AUTOMATIC TRANSMISSION— TYPES 2, 3, AND 4

Automatic transmissions are checked in the same manner as Automatic Stick Shift transmissions, except that the engine should be running at an idle, transmission in neutral, and parking brake firmly applied. Top up as necessary with DEXRON® through the transmission dipstick tube located above the distributor (Type 2) or above the air manifold pipes (Types 3 and 4). The difference between the two marks on the dipstick is less than one pint.

Brake Fluid Reservoir

The brake fluid reservoir is located under the driver's seat on 1973–77 Type 2 vehicles, behind the drivers seat on 1971–72 Type 2 models, and in the luggage compartment on all other vehi-

Type 1 Automatic stick shift dipstick location

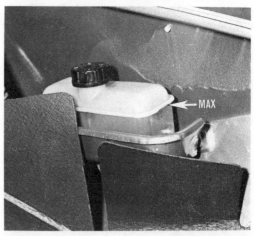

Luggage compartment-mounted master cylinder reservoir maximum fill (arrow)—Type 1, 3, and 4

1971–72 Type 2 master cylinder reservoir locations

1973–77 Type 2 master cylinder reservoir location showing minimum fill line visible through access window

cles. The fluid level in all vehicles should be above the upper seam of the reservoir. On 1973–77 Type 2 models, the fluid level is visible through a cutout beneath the seat. Fill the reservoir only with the new, clean heavy-duty brake fluid. If the vehicle is equipped with disc brakes make sure the fluid is marked for use with disc brakes. All fluid used should meet DOT 3, DOT 4, or SAE J1703 specifications.

Steering Gear (Except Rack and Pinion Type)

Types 1 and 3, except the Super Beetle and 1971–74 Beetle Convertible, are filled with 5.4 ozs of gear oil which is added to a plug at the top of the gearbox. The 1971–74 Super Beetle and 1971–74 Convertible hold 5.9 ozs of steering gear oil. The Type 2 holds 9.4 ozs of gear oil in the steering gear box. Type 4 holds 9 ozs.

Unless the steering gear box has been rebuilt or is leaking severely, there is no reason to add or change gear box oil.

Battery

The battery is located in the engine compartment on all Type 2 and Type 1 Karmann Ghia vehicles. On all Type 1 (except Karmann Ghia) and Type 3 vehicles, the battery is located under the back seat. On Type 4 vehicles, it is located under the driver's seat.

Make it a habit to check the electrolyte level frequently. Use only distilled water to top up the battery. Tap water contains minerals that will shorten battery lifetime. Keep the top of the battery clean and dry to prevent current leakage which can completely discharge the battery. Wire brush the battery posts and cable clamps occasionally and coat the posts (with the clamps installed) with grease.

To properly clean dirty battery posts, the clamp must be removed from the posts and the contacting surfaces cleaned to shiny metal.

TIRES AND WHEELS

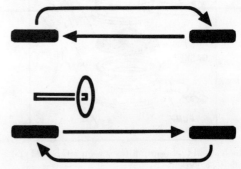

Tire rotation diagram for both bias-ply and radial ply tires

FUEL FILTER SERVICE

On carbureted models, the fuel filter is located in the mechanical fuel pump. There are three types of fuel pumps. Two types have a single screw holding a cover on the top of the pump. To remove the filter screen, undo the screw and carefully lift the cover off the pump. Remove the cover gasket and filter screen taking careful note of the position of the screen. Blow the screen out with air and replace the screen and cover using a new gasket if necessary.

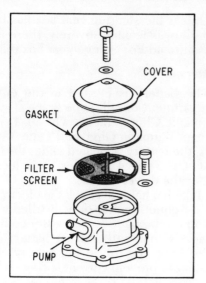

Mechanical fuel pump filter screen—1970 Type 2

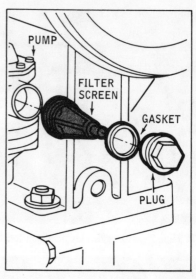

Mechanical fuel pump filter screen—1970 Type 1; 1973–74 Type 2 screen similar

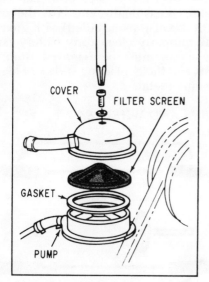

Mechanical fuel pump filter screen 1971–74 Type 1 and 1971 Type 2

Fuel filter location—Types 3 and 4

The third type of fuel pump has four screws securing the top cover to the pump. This type of pump has a large plug with a hexagonal head. Remove this plug and washer (gasket) to gain access to the cylindrical filter screen located beneath the plug. Blow the screen out with air and replace it in its bore with the open end facing into the pump. Install the washer and plug. Do not overtighten the plug.

Fuel injected engines have an electric fuel pump located near the front axle. This type of engine has an in-line fuel filter located atop the fuel pump in the

Fuel filter direction of flow—Types 3 and 4

suction line for the fuel pump. The suction line is the line running from the gas tank to the "S" connection at the fuel pump. To change the fuel filter, clamp the lines shut, then release the retaining pin and bracket, disconnect the gas lines from either end of the filter and insert a new filter. This type of filter cannot be cleaned. VW recommends replacement at 12,000 mile intervals. A small speck of dirt entering a fuel injector may completely block the flow of fuel, necessitating disassembly of the injection system.

Lubrication

OIL AND FUEL RECOMMENDATIONS

Only oils which are high detergent and are graded MS or SE should be used in the engine. Oils should be selected for the SAE viscosity which will perform satisfactorily in the temperatures expected before the next oil change.

Factory recommendations for fuel are regular gasoline with an octane rating of 91 RON or higher for Types 1, 2, 3, 1972–73 Type 4 and 1974 Type 4 equipped with automatic transmission. The 1971 Type 4 and 1974 Type 4 equipped with manual transmission require premium gasoline with an octane rating of 98 RON or better.

All 1975–77 models sold in California and in 1977 in the other 49 states, use catalytic converters to lower exhaust emissions, requiring the use of only lead-free regular (91 RON) fuel. Failure to do so will render the converter ineffective.

If the vehicle is used for towing, it may be necessary to buy a higher grade of gasoline. The extra load caused by the trailer may be sufficient to cause elevated engine knock or ping. This condition, when allowed to continue over a period of time, will cause extreme damage to the engine. Furthermore, ping or knock has several causes besides low octane. An engine in need of a tune-up will ping. If there is an excessive carbon build-up and lead deposits in the combustion chamber, ping will also result.

OIL CHANGES

Engine

The engine oil should be changed only after the engine has been warmed up to operating temperatures. In this way, the oil holds in suspension many of the contaminants that would otherwise remain in the engine. As the oil drains, it carries dirt and sludge from the engine. After the initial oil change at 600 miles the oil should be changed regularly at a period not to exceed 3,000 miles or three months. If the car is being operated mainly for short low speed trips, it may be advisable to change the oil at 2,000 mile intervals.

TYPES 1, 2/1600, 3/1600

When changing the oil in Type 1, 2/1600, and 3 vehicles, first unscrew the drain plug in the crankcase (1970–72 models) or strainer cover cap nuts (1973–77 models); and allow dirty oil to drain. The oil strainer should also be cleaned. This wire mesh strainer is held in place by six cap nuts, and should be cleaned thoroughly with solvent. The

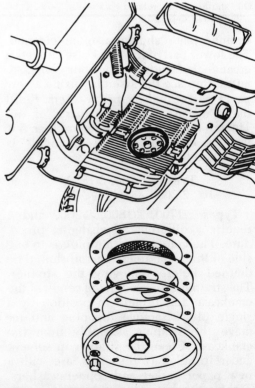

Oil strainer and related parts—1970–72 Type 1/1600, 1970–71 Type 2/1600, 1970–72 Type 3/1600

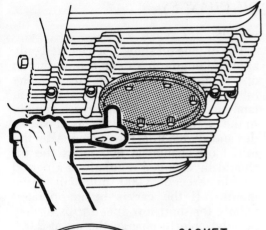

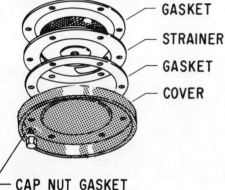

— GASKET
— STRAINER
— GASKET
— COVER

— CAP NUT GASKET

Oil strainer and related parts—1973–77 Type 1/1600, 1973 Type 3/1600

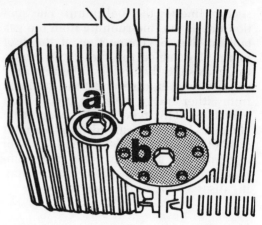

Oil strainer and related parts—1973–77 Type 1/1600, 1973 Type 3/1600

A. Drain plug   B. Strainer retaining nut

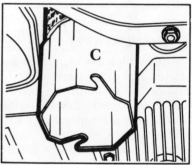

Using a special adapter (c) to remove oil filter on Type 2/1700, 2/1800, 2/2000 and Type 4 models

strainer plate should also be cleaned. The lower part of the crankcase collects a great deal of sludge in the course of 3,000 miles. Replace the assembly using a new paper gasket and copper washers. Refill the crankcase with 2.5 quarts of oil. Tighten the cap nuts to no more than 5 ft lbs. The drain plug (1970–72 models) is tightened to 9 ft lbs.

TYPES 2/1700, 2/1800, 2/2000 AND TYPE 4

Types 2/1700, 2/1800, 2/2000 and 4 require a different oil changing procedure. The crankcase drain plug is to one side of the oil strainer. The oil should be drained before removing the strainer. The strainer is located in the center of the crankcase and is held in position by a single plug. Remove the plug and remove the strainer assembly from the crankcase. Clean the strainer in solvent and reinstall it in the crankcase with a new paper gasket and copper washers. Tighten the drain plug and strainer nut to 9 ft lbs.

The Type 2/1700, 2/1800, 2/2000 and Type 4 also have a spin-on oil filter located near the engine cooling fan. This filter is removed by unscrewing it from its fitting using a special adaptor extension (C). When reinstalling the new filter, lubricate the filter gasket with oil. Refill the crankcase and start the engine. Run

Oil Selection Chart

SAE Viscosity	Outside Temperature
SAE 40	In warm seasons and all hot climates. Do not use when the average seasonal temperature is below 45°
SAE 30	Same as above. Temperature range is from 80° to 30°
SAE 20	In winter seasons. Temperature range is from 40° to 0°
SAE 10	In areas where the average temperature is below 0°; no long distance high speed driving, if temperature is above 10°

the engine until it picks up oil pressure and then stop the engine. Recheck the engine oil level.

Transmission

AUTOMATIC TRANSMISSION— TYPES 2, 3 AND 4

The automatic transmission fluid (ATF) should be changed every 30,000 miles, or every 18,000 miles under heavy duty operating conditions.

Drain the ATF by removing the drain plug (E) from the pan. Remove the pan and clean the ATF strainer. Install the pan using a new gasket and tighten the pan screws in a criss-cross pattern to 7 ft lbs. Retighten the screws two or three

Automatic transmission and final drive drain plug location—Types, 2, 3, and 4

A. Final drive filler plug
E. Automatic transmission drain plug
F. Automatic transmission fluid pan retaining bolts
G. Final drive drain plug

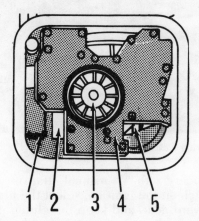

Automatic transmission strainer location—Types 2, 3, and 4

1. Manual valve
2. Kickdown solenoid
3. ATF strainer
4. Transfer plate
5. Valve body

times at five minute intervals to compensate for settling of the gasket. Refill the transmission with the proper type transmission fluid using a funnel with a 20 in. long neck. Use Type A or Dexron®.

MANUAL TRANSMISSION

The manual transmission is drained by removing the 17 mm plug in the bottom of the transmission case. It is refilled through another 17 mm plug in the side of the transmission case. The plug in the side of the case also functions as the fluid level hole.

NOTE: *When refilling the transmission, do not fill it too fast because it may overflow from the filler hole and give the impression that the unit has been filled when it has not.*

After the transmission oil is changed at 600 miles, it is generally not necessary to change the oil. However, the factory does recommend the fluid level be checked every 6,000 miles and topped up if necessary. Refill the transmission with SAE 90 hypoid gear oil.

AUTOMATIC STICK SHIFT—TYPE 1

The Automatic Stick Shift transmission uses hypoid gear oil in the rear section of the transmission and is drained and refilled using the same method as the manual transmission. The front section of the transmission uses ATF, however it does not have to be changed. The level should be checked every 6,000 miles.

NOTE: *The engine should be off when the level is checked.*
Use Type A or Dexron®.

CHASSIS GREASING

There are four grease fittings on Type 1 and 3 models. They are located at the end of each front torsion bar housing. There is a fifth fitting at the center of the front torsion bar housing for the steering linkage on Type 2 vehicles. Wipe off each fitting before greasing. Super Beetles, 1971–77 Super Beetle Convertibles, and Type 4 models require no greasing. The vehicle should be greased every 6,000 miles (1970–72 Types 1 and 3 and 1970 Type 2) or 18,000 miles (1973–77 Type 1, 1973 Type 3, 1971–77 Type 2).

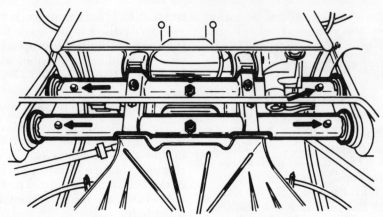

Type 1 front end grease fitting locations

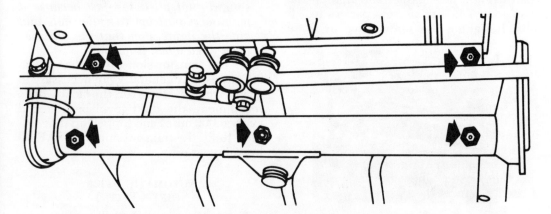

Type 2 front end grease fitting locations

Type 3 front end grease fitting locations

Pushing, Towing, and Jump Starting

A vehicle equipped with an automatic or Automatic Stick Shift cannot be pushed or tow started. To push start a vehicle with a manual transmission, switch on the ignition, select the highest forward gear, and keep the clutch pedal depressed until suitable speed has been provided by pushing the vehicle. When the vehicle is going about 15 mph, slowly release the clutch to start the engine.

There are two towing eyes on all mod-

Rear

Front

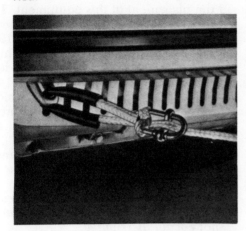 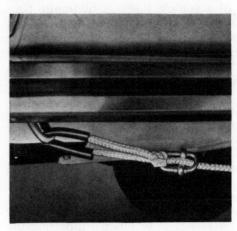

Typical towing sling location—1971–72 Type 4 shown

els except the 1973–74 Type 4. The front eye is located on the lower right front and the rear eye is located under the right rear bumper bracket. Tow the vehicle with the transmission in Neutral and the brakes off. Tow the 1973–74 Type 4 by its bumper bracket.

When jump starting the car, be sure that the booster cables are properly connected. Connect the positive pole of the jumper battery to the positive pole of the car battery. Be careful to avoid causing sparks.

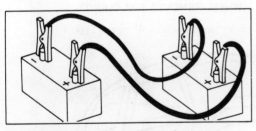

Typical jumper cable installation diagram

Jacking and Hoisting

Jacking points are provided at the sides of all models for the standard equipment jack. The jack supplied with the car should never be used for any service operation other than tire changing. NEVER get under the car while it is supported by just a jack. If the jack should slip or tip over, as jacks often do, it would be exceedingly difficult to raise the car

again while pinned underneath. Always block the wheels when changing tires.

The service operations in this book often require that one end or the other, or both, of the car be raised and supported

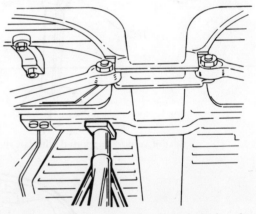

Front of vehicle supported with jackstand under crossmember—Type 1 Super Beetle and Type 4

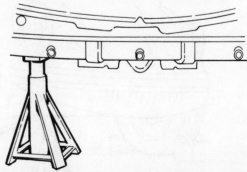

Front of vehicle supported with jackstand under front axle—Type 1 Beetle, Karmann Ghia, all Type 2 and Type 3

safely. The best arrangement is a grease pit or a vehicle hoist. A hydraulic floor jack is also referred to. It is realized that these items are not often found in the home garage, but there are reasonable and safe substitutes. Small hydraulic, screw, or scissors jacks are satisfactory for raising the car. Heavy wooden blocks or adjustable jackstands should be used to support the car while it is being worked on.

Drive-on trestles, or ramps, are a handy and safe way to raise the car. These can be bought or constructed from suitable heavy boards or steel.

When raising the car with a floor, screw or scissors jack, or when supporting the car with jack stands, care should be taken in the placement of this equipment. The front of the car may be supported beneath the axle tube on Type 1 Beetles, 1970 Beetle convertibles, all Karmann Ghias, all Type 2 models, and all Type 3 models. The front of all Super Beetles, 1971–77 Beetle convertibles, and all Type 4 models may be supported at the reinforced member to the rear of the lower control arms.

In any case, it is always best to spend a little extra time to make sure that the car is lifted and supported safely.

NOTE: *Concrete blocks are not recommended. They may break if the load is not evenly distributed.*

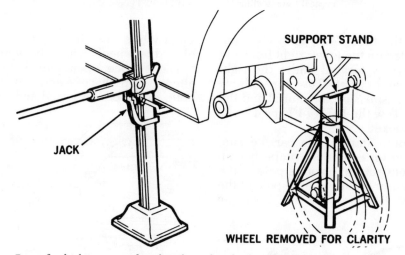

Rear of vehicle supported with jackstand under box member—all except Type 4

One side of car raised (as in rotating radials) with supports front and rear and opposite wheels blocked

Chapter Two

Tune-Up and Troubleshooting

Tune-Up Procedures

The tune-up is a routine maintenance operation which is essential for the efficient and economical operation, as well as the long life of your car's engine. The interval between tune-ups is a variable factor which depends upon the way you drive your car, the conditions under which you drive it (weather, road type, etc.), and the type of engine installed in your car. It is generally correct to say that no car should be driven more than 12,000 miles between tune-ups, especially in this age of emission controls and fuel shortages. If you plan to drive your car extremely hard or under severe weather conditions, the tune-ups should be performed at closer intervals. High-performance engines require more frequent tuning than other engines, regardless of weather or driving conditions.

The replaceable parts involved in a tune-up include the spark plugs, breaker points, condenser, distributor cap, rotor, spark plug wires and the ignition coil high-tension (secondary) wire. In addition to these parts and the adjustments involved in properly adapting them to your engine, there are several adjustments of other parts involved in completing the job. These include carburetor idle speed and air/fuel mixture, ignition timing, and dwell angle.

This section gives specific procedures on how to tune-up your Volkswagen and is intended to be as complete and basic as possible. Later in this book, there is another, more generalized section for tune-ups that includes troubleshooting diagnosis for the more experienced weekend mechanic.

CAUTION: *When working with a running engine, make sure that there is proper ventilation. Also make sure that the transmission is in Neutral (unless otherwise specified) and the parking brake is fully applied. Always keep hands, long hair, clothing, neckties and tools well clear of the engine. On a warm engine, keep clear of the hot exhaust manifold(s) and exhaust pipe. When the ignition is turned on and the engine running, do not grasp the ignition wires, distributor cap, or coil wire, as a shock in excess of 20,000 volts may result. Whenever working around the distributor, even if the engine is not running, make sure that the ignition is switched off.*

SPARK PLUGS

Before attempting any work on the cylinder head, it is very important to note that the cylinder head is cast aluminum alloy. This means that it is extremely easy

Tune-Up Specifications

Engine Code	Type	Common Designation	Factory Recommended Spark Plugs Type	Gap (in.)	Distributor Point Dwell (deg)	Point Gap (in.)	Ignition Timing (deg) MT	AT	Fuel Pump Pressure (psi) @ 4000 rpm	Compression Pressure (psi)	Idle Speed (rpm) MT	AT	Valve Clearance (in.) Cold In	Ex
1970														
B	1, 2	1600	Bosch W145T1 Champion L88A	.024	44–50	.016	TDC②	TDC②	3.5	114–142	800–900	900–1000	.006	.006
U	3	1600	Bosch W145T1 Champion L88A	.024	44–50	.016	TDC②	TDC②	28	114–142	800–900	900–1000	.006	.006
1971														
AE	1, 2	1600	Bosch W145T1 Champion L88A	.024	44–50	.016	5ATDC①	5ATDC①	3.5	114–142	800–900	900–1000	.006	.006
U	3	1600	Bosch W145T1 Champion L88A	.024	44–50	.016	TDC②	TDC②	28	114–142	800–900	900–1000	.006	.006
W	4	1700	Bosch W175T2	.024	44–50	.016	27BTDC③	27BTDC③	28	128–156	800–900	900–1000	.006	.006
1972														
AE	1	1600	Bosch W145T1 Champion L88A	.024	44–50	.016	5ATDC①	5ATDC①	3.5	107–135	800–900	900–1000	.006	.006
AH (Calif only)	1	1600	Bosch W145T1 Champion L88A	.024	44–50	.016	5ATDC①	5ATDC①	3.5	107–135	800–900	900–1000	.006	.006
CB	2	1700	Bosch W145T2 Champion N88	.024	44–50	.016	5ATDC①	—	5.0	100–135	800–900	—	.006	.006
U, X	3	1600	Bosch W145T1 Champion L88A	.024	44–50	.016	5BTDC②	5BTDC②	28	107–135	800–900	900–1000	.006	.006
EA	4	1700	Bosch W175T2	.024	44–50	.016	27BTDC③	27BTDC③	28	128–156	800–900	900–1000	.006	.006

Year	Code	No.	Engine	Spark Plugs		Gap	Gap	Timing	Timing		Comp.	Idle	Idle	Gap	Gap
1973	AK	1	1600	Bosch W145T1	Champion L88A	.024	44–50	.016	5ATDC①④	5ATDC①④	3.5	107–135	800–900	900–1000	.006	.006
	AH (Calif only)	1	1600	Bosch W145T1	Champion L88A	.024	44–50	.016	5ATDC①	5ATDC①	3.5	107–135	800–900	900–1000	.006	.006
	CB	2	1700	Bosch W145T2	Champion N88	.024	44–50	.016	10ATDC①	—	5.0	100–135	800–900	—	.006	.008
	CD	2	1700	Bosch W145T2	Champion N88	.024	44–50	.016	—	5ATDC①	5.0	100–135	—	900–1000	.006	.008
	U, X	3	1600	Bosch W145T1	Champion L88A	.024	44–50	.016	5BTDC②	5BTDC②	28	107–135	800–900	900–1000	.006	.006
	EA	4	1700	Bosch W175T2	Champion N88	.024	44–50	.016	27BTDC③	27BTDC③	28	128–156	800–900	900–1000	.006	.006
	EB (Calif only)	4	1700	Bosch W175T2	Champion N88	.024	44–50	.016	27BTDC③	27BTDC③	28	107–135	800–900	900–1000	.006	.006
1974	AK	1	1600	Bosch W145T1	Champion L88A	.024	44–50	.016	7½BTDC②	7½BTDC②	3.5	107–135	800–900	900–1000	.006	.006
	AH (Calif only)	1	1600	Bosch W145T1	Champion L88A	.024	44–50	.016	5ATDC①	5ATDC①	3.5	107–135	800–900	900–1000	.006	.006
	AW	2	1800	Bosch W175T2	Champion N88	.024	44–50	.016	10ATDC①	5ATDC①	5.0	85–135	800–900	900–1000	.006	.008
	EA	4	1700	Bosch W175T2	Champion N88	.024	44–50	.016	27BTDC③	—	28	128–156	800–900	—	.006	.006
	EC	4	1800	Bosch W175T2	Champion N88	.024	44–50	.016	—	7½BTDC②	28	85–135	—	900–1000	.006	.006

Tune-Up Specifications (cont.)

Engine Code	Type	Common Designation	Factory Recommended Spark Plugs Type	Gap (in.)	Distributor Point Dwell (deg)	Point Gap (in.)	Ignition Timing (deg) MT	AT	Fuel Pump Pressure (psi) @ 4000 rpm	Compression Pressure (psi)	Idle Speed (rpm) MT	AT	Valve Clearance (in.) Cold In	Ex
1975														
AJ	1	1600	Bosch W145M1 Champion L288	.024	44–50	.016	5ATDC⑤	TDC⑤	28	85–135	875	875	.006	.006
ED	2	1800	Bosch W145M2 Champion N288	.024	44–50	.016	5ATDC⑤	5ATDC⑤	28	85–135	900	900	.006	.006
1976 –77														
AJ	1	1600	Bosch W145M1 Champion L288	.024⑥	44–50	.016	5ATDC⑤	TDC⑤	28	85–135	875	925	.006	.006
GD	2	2000	Bosch W145M2 Champion N288	.028	44–50	.016	7½BTDC⑤	7½BTDC⑤	28	85–135	900	950	.006	.006

① At idle, throttle valve closed (Types 1 & 2), vacuum hose(s) on
② At idle, throttle valve closed (Types 1 & 2), vacuum hose(s) off
③ At 3,500 rpm, vacuum hose(s) off
④ From March 1973, vehicles with single diaphragm distributor (one vacuum hose); adjust timing to 7½° BTDC with hose disconnected and plugged. The starting serial numbers for those type 1 vehicles using the single diaphragm distributors are #113 2674 897 (manual trans) and 113 2690 032 (auto stick shift)

⑤ Carbon canister hose at air cleaner disconnected; at idle; vacuum hose(s) on
MT Manual Transmission
AT Automatic Transmission
BTDC Before Top Dead Center
ATDC After Top Dead Center
⑥ 1977—.028

to damage threads in the cylinder head. Care must be taken not to cross-thread the spark plugs or any bolts or studs. Never overtighten the spark plugs, bolts, or studs.

CAUTION: *To prevent seizure, always lubricate the spark plug threads with liquid silicon or Never-Seez®.*

To avoid cross-threading the spark plugs, always start the plugs in their threads with your fingers. Never force the plugs into the cylinder head. Do not use a wrench until you are certain that the plug is correctly threaded.

Set spark plug gap (a) to 0.024 in. for longer service

VW spark plugs should be cleaned and regapped every 6,000 miles and replaced every 12,000 miles.

Removal and Installation

To install the spark plugs, remove the spark plug wire from the plug. Grasp the plug connector and, while removing, do not pull on the wire. Using a 13/16 in. spark plug socket, remove the old spark plugs. Examine the threads of the old plugs; if one or more of the plugs have aluminum clogged threads, it will be necessary to rethread the spark plug hole. See the following section for the necessary information.

Obtain the proper heat range and type of new plug. Set the gap by bending the side electrode only. Do not bend the center electrode to adjust the gap. The proper gap is listed in the "Tune-Up

Specifications" chart. Lubricate the plug threads.

Start each new plug in its hole using your fingers. Tighten the plug several turns by hand to assure that the plug is not cross-threaded. Using a wrench, tighten the plug just enough to compress the gasket. Do not overtighten the plug. Consult the torque specifications chart.

Rethreading Spark Plug Hole

It is possible to repair light damage to spark plug hole threads by using a spark plug hole tap of the proper diameter and thread. Plenty of grease should be used on the tap to catch any metal chips. Exercise caution when using the tap as it is possible to cut a second set of threads instead of straightening the old ones.

If the old threads are beyond repair, then the hole must be drilled and tapped to accept a steel bushing or Heli-Coil®. It is not always necessary to remove the cylinder head to rethread the spark plug holes. Bushing kits, Heli-Coil® kits, and spark plug hole taps are available at most auto parts stores. Heli-Coil® information is contained in the "Engine Rebuilding" section of this book.

BREAKER POINTS AND CONDENSER

Removal and Installation

1. Release the spring clips which secure the distributor cap and lift the cap

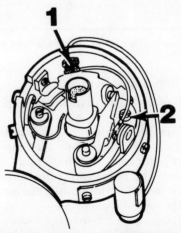

Breaker point removal is accomplished by disconnecting snap connection (1) and removing attaching screw

from the distributor. Pull the rotor from the distributor shaft.

2. Disconnect the points wire from the condenser snap connection (1) inside the distributor.

3. Remove the locking screw (2) from the stationary breaker point.

4. To remove the condenser which is located on the outside of the distributor, remove the screw which secures the condenser bracket and condenser connection to the distributor.

5. Disconnect the condenser wire from the coil.

6. With a clean rag, wipe the excess oil from the breaker plate.

NOTE: *Make sure that the new point contacts are clean and oil free.*

7. Installation of the point set and condenser is the reverse of the above; however, it will be necessary to adjust the point gap, also known as the dwell, and check the timing. Lubricate the point cam with a small amount of lithium or white grease. Set the dwell, or gap, before the ignition timing.

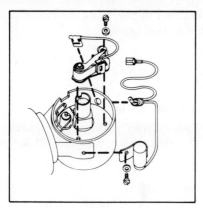

Location of breaker points and condenser on distributor

Point Gap Adjustment

1. Remove the distributor cap and rotor.

2. Turn the engine by hand until the fiber rubbing block on the movable breaker point rests on a high point of the cam lobe. The point gap is the maximum distance between the points and must be set at the top of a cam lobe.

3. Using a screwdriver, loosen the locking screw of the stationary breaker point.

4. Move the stationary point plate so

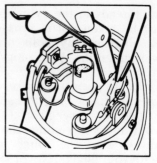

Checking point gap with feeler gauge

that the gap is set as specified and then tighten the screw. Make sure that the feeler gauge is clean. After tightening the screw, recheck the gap.

5. It is important to set the point gap before setting the timing.

DWELL ANGLE

Setting the dwell angle with a dwell meter achieves the same effect as setting the point gap but offers better accuracy.

NOTE: *The dwell must be set before setting the timing. Setting the dwell will alter the timing, but when the timing is set, the dwell will not change.*

Attach the positive lead of the dwell meter to that coil terminal which has a wire leading to the distributor. The negative lead should be attached to a good ground.

Remove the distributor cap and rotor. Turn the ignition ON and turn the engine over using the starter or a remote starter switch. Read the dwell from the meter and open or close the points to adjust the dwell.

NOTE: *Increasing the gap decreases the dwell and decreasing the gap increases the dwell.*

Dwell specifications are listed in the "Tune-Up Specifications" chart.

Reinstall the cap and rotor and start the engine. Check the dwell and reset it if necessary.

IGNITION TIMING

Dwell or point gap must be set before the timing is set. Also, the idle speed must be set to specifications.

NOTE: *The engine must be warmed up before the timing is set (oil temperature of 122° F–158° F).*

1. Remove the No. 1 spark plug wire from the distributor cap and attach the

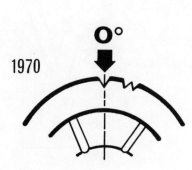

Type 1—1970 engines.

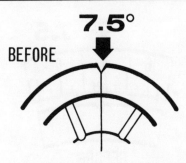

Type 1—carbureted cars with a single vacuum hose to the distributor, starting spring 1973

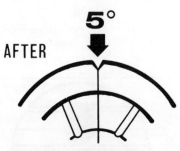

Type 1—carburetor cars from August 1970 to spring 1973 and fuel injected cars with manual transmissions.

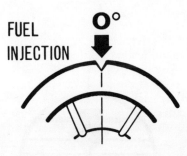

Type 1—fuel injected cars equipped with the Automatic Stick Shift.

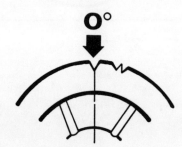

Type 2—1970 engines.

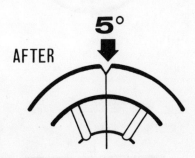

Type 2—1971 engines.

Type 2—1972 all engines, 1972–74 models equipped with automatic transmission, and 1975 all models.

Type 2—1973–74 carbureted models with manual transmissions.

Type 2—1976–77 fuel injected models.

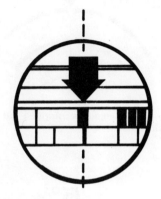

Type 3—1970–71 engines.

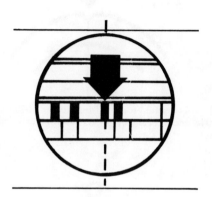

Type 3—1972–73 engines.

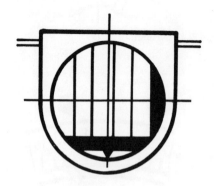

Type 4—1971–74 engines.

timing light lead. Disconnect the vacuum hose if so advised by the "Tune-Up Specifications" chart (and re-adjust the idle speed if necessary).

2. Start the engine and run it at the specified rpm. Aim the timing light at the crankshaft pulley on upright fan engines and at the engine cooling fan on the suitcase engines. The rubber plug in the fan housing will have to be removed before the timing marks on Type 3 and Type 4 engines can be seen.

3. Read the timing and rotate the distributor accordingly.

NOTE: *Rotate the distributor in the opposite direction of normal rotor rotation to advance the timing. Retard the timing by turning the distributor in the normal direction of rotor rotation.*

4. It is necessary to loosen the clamp at the base of the distributor before the distributor can be rotated. It may also be necessary to put a small amount of white paint or chalk on the timing marks to make them more visible.

VALVE LASH ADJUSTMENT

Preference should be given to the valve clearance specified on the engine fan housing sticker, if they differ from those in the "Tune-Up Specifications" chart.

Valve clearance sticker location on engine shroud—Type 4

NOTE: *The engine must be as cool as possible before adjusting the valves.*
NOTE: *If the spark plugs are removed, rotating the crankshaft from position to position will be much easier. The*

crankshaft may be rotated on manual shift models by placing the car in fourth gear and pushing it.
Adjust the valves as follows:

1. Remove the distributor cap and turn the engine until the rotor points to the No. one spark plug wire post in the distributor cap. To bring the piston to exactly top dead center (TDC) on the compression stroke, align the crankshaft timing marks on TDC.

No. 1 piston at Top Dead Center—Types 1, 2/1600

No. 1 piston at Top Dead Center—Type 3

2. Remove the rocker arm covers. At TDC, the pushrods should be down and there should be clearance between the rocker arms and valve stems of both valves of the subject cylinder.

3. With the proper feeler gauge, check the clearance between the adjusting screw and the valve stem of both valves for the No. 1 cylinder (see cylinder numbering diagram). If the feeler gauge

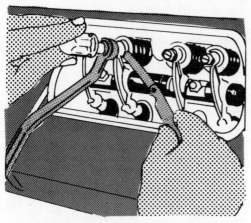

Checking valve clearance with feeler gauge

slides in snugly without being forced, the clearance is correct. It is better that the clearance is a little loose than a little tight, as a tight adjustment may result in burned exhaust valves.

4. If the clearance is incorrect, the locknut must be loosened and the adjusting screw turned until the proper clearance is obtained. After tightening down the locknut, it is then advisable to recheck the clearance. It is possible to alter the adjustment when tightening the locknut.

5. The valves are adjusted in a 1–2–3–4 (exact opposite of firing [1–4–3–2] order) sequence. To adjust cylinders 2 through 4, the distributor rotor must be pointed at the appropriate distributor cap post 90° apart from each other. In addition, the crankshaft must be rotated counterclockwise (opposite normal rotation) in 180° degree increments to adjust valves 2, 3 and 4.

NOTE: *There should be a red paint mark on the crankshaft 180° opposite of the TDC mark for adjusting valves 2 and 4.*

NOTE: *Always use new valve cover gaskets.*

FUEL SYSTEM ADJUSTMENTS

Carburetor Idle Speed and Mixture

A carburetor adjustment should be performed only after all other variables in a tune-up have been checked and adjusted. This includes checking valve clearance, spark plug gap, breaker point gap and/or dwell angle, and ignition timing. Prior to making any carburetor adjustments, the engine should be brought to operating temperature (122–158° F oil temperature) and you should make sure that the automatic choke is fully open and off of the fast idle cam. Once you have performed all of the preliminary steps, shut off the engine and hook up a tachometer. Connect the hot lead to the distributor side of the ignition coil and the ground wire to an engine bolt or other good metal to metal connection. Keep the wire clear of the fan.

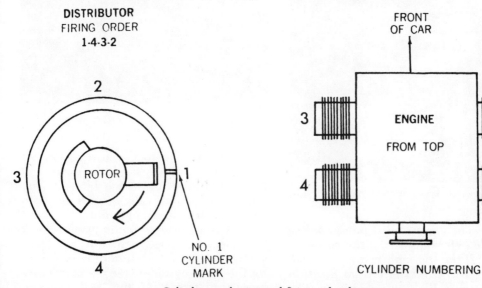

Cylinder numbering and firing order diagram

NOTE: *An improper carburetor adjustment may have an adverse effect on exhaust emission levels. If any doubt exists, check your state laws regarding the adjusting of emission control equipment.*

SOLEX 30 PICT-3
(1970 TYPE 1 AND
TYPE 2 MODELS)

1. Start the engine and bring it to operating temperature. Make sure the car is in neutral.

2. Using the idle speed (bypass) screw, adjust the idle speed to that specified in the "Tune-Up Specifications" chart.

NOTE: *The bypass screw adjustment is the only adjustment that should be made to the 30 PICT-3 carburetor. Do not attempt to adjust the mixture or idle speed by turning the throttle valve adjustment screw, as increased exhaust emissions or poor driveability would result. The bypass screw is the larger adjustment screw.*

SOLEX 34 PICT-3
(1971–74 TYPE 1 MODELS,
1971 TYPE 2 MODELS) AND
SOLEX 34 PICT-4 (1973–74 TYPE 1
CALIFORNIA MODELS)

1. Start the engine and bring it to operating temperature. Make sure the car is in neutral.

2. Shut off the engine. On 1971 models, turn out the throttle valve adjustment screw until it clears the fast idle cam. Then turn in the screw until it makes contact with the fast idle cam. Finally, turn the throttle valve adjusting screw in another one-quarter turn.

3. Slowly turn in the idle mixture (volume control) screw until it bottoms. Then, carefully counting the complete revolutions of the screwdriver, turn it out 2½ to 3 turns.

4. With a tachometer connected to the engine as previously described, start the engine.

5. Using the idle speed (bypass) screw, adjust the idle speed to specifications. Then, using the idle mixture (volume control) screw, adjust until the fastest idle is obtained. Observing the tachometer, turn the volume control screw until the engine speed drops by 20–30 rpm.

6. Finally, using the bypass screw, adjust the idle to specifications.

SOLEX 34 PDSIT-2/3 TWIN CARB
(1972–74 TYPE 2 MODELS)

Periodic Adjustment

1. Start the engine and bring it to operating temperature (122–158° F oil temperature). Make sure the car is in

Solex 34 PICT-3 and 34 PICT-4 idle adjustments (30 PICT-3 similar)

1. Throttle valve adjustment
2. Volume control (mixture) screw
3. By-pass (idle speed) screw

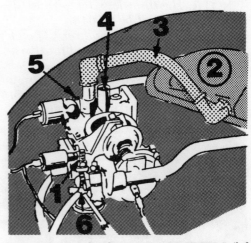

Type 2 twin carb adjustments—34 PDSIT-2 (left carburetor shown)

1. Synchronizing screw
2. Central idling system left end piece
3. Central idling system left end connecting hose
4. Central idling (idle speed) adjusting screw
5. Central mixture control screw
6. Volume control screw

neutral and the parking brake firmly applied.

2. Using the central idle speed adjusting screw (4) on the left carburetor, adjust the idle speed to that listed in the "Tune-Up Specifications" chart.

3a. If a CO meter/exhaust analyzer is available, adjust the carbon monoxide (CO) level to 1–3% CO using the central mixture control screw (5) also on the left carburetor.

3b. If a CO meter is not available, the following procedure is used: First, slowly turn the central mixture control screw (5) in (clockwise) until the engine speed drops noticeably, then turn the screw out (counterclockwise) until maximum idle speed is attained. Next, turn the screw in once again until rpm drops by 20–50 rpm. Finally, turn the screw out ¼ turn.

4. Recheck the idle speed, and adjust as necessary using the central idle speed adjusting screw (4) on the left carburetor.

5. If a satisfactory idle cannot be obtained using this procedure, proceed to "Basic Adjustment."

Basic Adjustment

Whenever a carburetor has been removed for service, or if a new or rebuilt carburetor has been installed, a basic carburetor adjustment should be performed.

NOTE: *The throttle valve setting (distance "a") must be 0.004 in.*

NOTE: *An exhaust analyzer/CO meter and tachometer is required for this adjustment.*

1. Check the synchronization of the carburetors as outlined under "Balancing Multiple Carburetor Installations."

34 PDSIT-2/3 carburetors, the throttle valve closing gap (distance "a") must be 0.004 in.

2. Disconnect the throttle linkage rod from the right carburetor.

3. Disconnect the vacuum retard hose from the distributor.

4. Disconnect the cut-off valve wire at the central idling system. Disconnect and plug the left side air pump hose (1973–74 models).

Terminal connection for central idling system electromagnetic cut-off valve—34 PDSIT-2

Arrow indicates volume control screw in throttle bodies of 34 PDSIT-2 (left), 34 PDSIT-3 (right) carburetors

5. Turn the idle volume control screws (6) in on both carburetors until they contact their seats.

CAUTION: *Do not force the screws or the tips may become distorted.*

Then, turn both screws out exactly 2½ turns.

6. Start the engine and bring it to operating temperature (122–158° F oil temperature). Set the idle speed to 500–700 rpm by equally adjusting both volume control screws (6).

7. Disconnect the wire from the electromagnetic idling cut-off valve (smaller

Terminal connection for idling cut-off valve of both left and right carburetors

of the two valves) at the left carburetor and note the decrease in idle speed. Then, repeat this operation for the right carburetor. The idle speed drop should be equal for both sides. If not, readjust the volume control screws accordingly.

8. Connect the wire for the cut-off valve at the central idling system. Unplug, and connect the left air pump hose. Connect the vacuum retard hose.

9. Take the engine through the upper rpm range for a few quick bursts. Then, adjust the idle speed to specifications as outlined under steps 2–5 of "Periodic Adjustment."

Balancing Multiple Carburetor Installations

SYNCHRONIZING 1972–74 TYPE 2 TWIN CARB

If a carburetor has been removed or disassembled, or if any part of the linkage has been repaired, the carburetors must be synchronized prior to performing any idle adjustments. To synchronize the carburetors, a special instrument is used to measure air flow, such as the UniSyn® or Auto-Syn®. This commonly available device measures the vacuum created inside the carburetors and provides an index for adjusting the carburetors equally. In order to use the air flow gauge on the 34 PDSIT carburetors, a special diameter adaptor (or a small frozen juice can with both ends removed) must be used.

1. Disconnect the linkage connecting rod from the lower socket of the right carburetor. Without moving the throttle valve from its closed position, check the ball and socket alignment of the linkage for the right carburetor. If the ball and socket at the *right* carburetor do not align *perfectly*, adjust, as necessary, using the synchronizing screw (1) at the *left* carburetor. Connect the linkage. Hook up a tachometer.

2. Remove the air cleaner ducts from the tops of both carburetors, taking care to leave the central idle system connecting hose (3) and left end piece (2) connected.

3. Start the engine and bring it to operating temperature (122–158° F oil temperature). Make sure the choke flaps are fully open. Using the air flow meter, balance the carburetors using the synchronizing screw (1) on the left carburetor, at 2,000 to 3,000 rpm. After balancing, install the air cleaners.

4. Adjust the idle speed to specifications.

Airflow meter installed on left carburetor

Fuel injection idle speed adjustment—Type 3

a. Slower
b. Faster
c. Tighten locknut

FUEL INJECTION IDLE SPEED

All Type 3 and Type 4,
1975–76 Type 1 and Type 2

The idle speed is adjusted by a screw located on the left side of the intake air distributor. To adjust the idle speed, loosen the lock nut (Type 3 only) and turn the screw with a screwdriver until the idle speed is adjusted to specification.

On Type 4 and 1975–76 Type 2 models equipped with automatic transmission, the idling speed regulator dashpot must also be adjusted. With the car idling in neutral at 900 rpm, firmly apply the parking brake, bock the front wheels, and place the transmission in drive. Under this load, the car should idle at 600–700 rpm. Check that clearance "a" between the end of the dashpot plunger and the bracket is 0.002–0.004 in. Adjust as necessary with the M5 bolt indicated by the arrow (see illustration).

NOTE: *Disregard sections 11.2–11.7 in the following "Troubleshooting" section.*

Fuel injection idle speed adjustment—Type 4

Fuel injection idle speed adjustment (by-pass screw)—1975–77 Type 2

Fuel injection idle speed (by-pass screw) adjustment—1975–77 Type 1

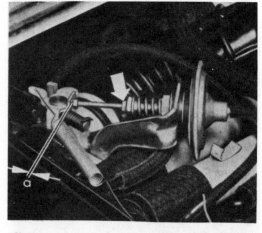

Idling speed regulator dashpot adjustment—Type 4 and 1975–77 Type 2 automatic (distance "a" is 0.002-0.004 in.)

Engine Tune-Up

Engine tune-up is a procedure performed to restore engine performance, deteriorated due to normal wear and loss of adjustment. The three major areas considered in a routine tune-up are compression, ignition, and carburetion, although valve adjustment may be included.

A tune-up is performed in three steps: *analysis*, in which it is determined whether normal wear is responsible for performance loss, and which parts require replacement or service; *parts replacement or service*; and *adjustment*, in which engine adjustments are returned to original specifications. Since the advent of emission control equipment, precision adjustment has become increasingly critical, in order to maintain pollutant emission levels.

Analysis

The procedures below are used to indicate where adjustments, parts service or replacement are necessary within the realm of a normal tune-up. If, following these tests, all systems appear to be functioning properly, proceed to the Troubleshooting Section for further diagnosis.

—Remove all spark plugs, noting the cylinder in which they were installed. Remove the air cleaner, and position the throttle and choke in the full open position. Disconnect the coil high tension lead from the coil and the distributor cap. Insert a compression gauge into the spark plug port of each cylinder, in succession, and crank the engine with

Maxi. Press. Lbs. Sq. In.	Min. Press. Lbs. Sq. In.	Max. Press. Lbs. Sq. In.	Min. Press. Lbs. Sq. In.
134	101	188	141
136	102	190	142
138	104	192	144
140	105	194	145
142	107	196	147
146	110	198	148
148	111	200	150
150	113	202	151
152	114	204	153
154	115	206	154
156	117	208	156
158	118	210	157
160	120	212	158
162	121	214	160
164	123	216	162
166	124	218	163
168	126	220	165
170	127	222	166
172	129	224	168
174	131	226	169
176	132	228	171
178	133	230	172
180	135	232	174
182	136	234	175
184	138	236	177
186	140	238	178

Compression pressure limits
© Buick Div. G.M. Corp.)

the starter to obtain the highest possible reading. Record the readings, and compare the highest to the lowest on the compression pressure limit chart. If the difference exceeds the limits on the chart, or if all readings are excessively low, proceed to a wet compression check (see Troubleshooting Section).

—Evaluate the spark plugs according to the spark plug chart in the Troubleshooting Section, and proceed as indicated in the chart.

—Remove the distributor cap, and inspect it inside and out for cracks and/or carbon tracks, and inside for excessive wear or burning of the rotor contacts. If any of these faults are evident, the cap must be replaced.

—Check the breaker points for burning, pitting or wear, and the contact heel resting on the distributor cam for excessive wear. If defects are noted, replace the entire breaker point set.

—Remove and inspect the rotor. If the contacts are burned or worn, or if the rotor is excessively loose on the distributor shaft (where applicable), the rotor must be replaced.

—Inspect the spark plug leads and the coil high tension lead for cracks or brittleness. If any of the wires appear defective, the entire set should be replaced.

—Check the air filter to ensure that it is functioning properly.

Parts Replacement and Service

The determination of whether to replace or service parts is at the mechanic's discretion; however, it is suggested that any parts in questionable condition be replaced rather than reused.

—Clean and regap, or replace, the spark plugs as needed. Lightly coat the threads with engine oil and install the plugs. CAUTION: *Do not over-torque taper-seat spark plugs, or plugs being installed in aluminum cylinder heads.*

43

—If the distributor cap is to be reused, clean the inside with a dry rag, and remove corrosion from the rotor contact points with fine emery cloth. Remove the spark plug wires one by one, and clean the wire ends and the inside of the towers. If the boots are loose, they should be replaced.

If the cap is to be replaced, transfer the wires one by one, cleaning the wire ends and replacing the boots if necessary.

—If the original points are to remain in service, clean them lightly with emery cloth, lubricate the contact heel with grease specifically designed for this purpose. Rotate the crankshaft until the heel rests on a high point of the distributor cam, and adjust the point gap to specifications.

When replacing the points, remove the original points and condenser, and wipe out the inside of the distributor housing with a clean, dry rag. Lightly lubricate the contact heel and pivot point, and install the points and condenser. Rotate the crankshaft until the heel rests on a high point of the distributor cam, and adjust the point gap to specifications. NOTE: *Always replace the condenser when changing the points.*

—If the rotor is to be reused, clean the contacts with solvent. Do not alter the spring tension of the rotor center contact. Install the rotor and the distributor cap.

—Replace the coil high tension lead and/or the spark plug leads as necessary.

—Clean the carburetor using a spray solvent (e.g., Gumout Spray). Remove the varnish from the throttle bores, and clean the linkage. Disconnect and plug the fuel line, and run the engine

until it runs out of fuel. Partially fill the float chamber with solvent, and reconnect the fuel line. In extreme cases, the jets can be pressure flushed by inserting a rubber plug into the float vent, running the spray nozzle through it, and spraying the solvent until it squirts out of the venturi fuel dump.

—Clean and tighten all wiring connections in the primary electrical circuit.

Additional Services

The following services *should* be performed in conjunction with a routine tune-up to ensure efficient performance.

—Inspect the battery and fill to the proper level with distilled water. Remove the cable clamps, clean clamps and posts thoroughly, coat the posts lightly with petroleum jelly, reinstall and tighten.

—Inspect all belts, replace and/or adjust as necessary.

—Test the PCV valve (if so equipped), and clean or replace as indicated. Clean all crankcase ventilation hoses, or replace if cracked or hardened.

—Adjust the valves (if necessary) to manufacturer's specifications.

Adjustments

—Connect a dwell-tachometer between the distributor primary lead and ground. Remove the distributor cap and rotor (unless equipped with Delco externally adjustable distributor). With the ignition off, crank the engine with a remote starter switch and measure the point dwell angle. Adjust the dwell angle to specifications. NOTE: *Increasing the gap decreases the dwell angle and*

vice-versa. Install the rotor and distributor cap.

—Connect a timing light according to the manufacturer's specifications. Identify the proper timing marks with chalk or paint. NOTE: *Luminescent (day-glo) paint is excellent for this purpose.* Start the engine, and run it until it reaches operating temperature. Disconnect and plug any distributor vacuum lines, and adjust idle to the speed required to adjust timing, according to specifications. Loosen the distributor clamp and adjust timing to specifications by rotating the distributor in the engine. NOTE: *To advance timing, rotate distributor opposite normal direction of rotor rotation, and vice-versa.*

—Synchronize the throttles and mixture of multiple carburetors (if so equipped) according to procedures given in the individual car sections.

—Adjust the idle speed, mixture, and idle quality, as specified in the car sections. Final idle adjustments should be made with the air cleaner installed. CAUTION: *Due to strict emission control requirements on 1969 and later models, special test equipment (CO meter, SUN Tester) may be necessary to properly adjust idle mixture to specifications.*

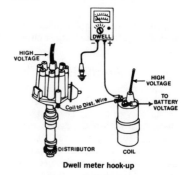

Dwell meter hook-up

Trouble-shooting

The following section is designed to aid in the rapid diagnosis of engine problems. The systematic format is used to diagnose problems ranging from engine starting difficulties to the need for engine overhaul. It is assumed that the user is equipped with basic hand tools and test equipment (tach-dwell meter, timing light, voltmeter, and ohm-meter).

Troubleshooting is divided into two sections. The first, *General Diagnosis*, is used to locate the problem area. In the second, *Specific Diagnosis*, the problem is systematically evaluated.

General Diagnosis

PROBLEM: Symptom	Begin diagnosis at Section Two, Number ———
Engine won't start:	
Starter doesn't turn	1.1, 2.1
Starter turns, engine doesn't	2.1
Starter turns engine very slowly	1.1, 2.4
Starter turns engine normally	3.1, 4.1
Starter turns engine very quickly	6.1
Engine fires intermittently	4.1
Engine fires consistently	5.1, 6.1
Engine runs poorly:	
Hard starting	3.1, 4.1, 5.1, 8.1
Rough idle	4.1, 5.1, 8.1
Stalling	3.1, 4.1, 5.1, 8.1
Engine dies at high speeds	4.1, 5.1
Hesitation (on acceleration from standing stop)	5.1, 8.1
Poor pickup	4.1, 5.1, 8.1
Lack of power	3.1, 4.1, 5.1, 8.1
Backfire through the carburetor	4.1, 8.1, 9.1
Backfire through the exhaust	4.1, 8.1, 9.1
Blue exhaust gases	6.1, 7.1
Black exhaust gases	5.1
Running on (after the ignition is shut off)	3.1, 8.1
Susceptible to moisture	4.1
Engine misfires under load	4.1, 7.1, 8.4, 9.1
Engine misfires at speed	4.1, 8.4
Engine misfires at idle	3.1, 4.1, 5.1, 7.1, 8.4

PROBLEM: Symptom	Probable Cause
Engine noises: ①	
Metallic grind while starting	Starter drive not engaging completely
Constant grind or rumble	*Starter drive not releasing, worn main bearings
Constant knock	Worn connecting rod bearings
Knock under load	Fuel octane too low, worn connecting rod bearings
Double knock	Loose piston pin
Metallic tap	*Collapsed or sticky valve lifter, excessive valve clearance, excessive end play in a rotating shaft
Scrape	*Fan belt contacting a stationary surface
Tick while starting	S.U. electric fuel pump (normal), starter brushes
Constant tick	*Generator brushes, shreaded fan belt
Squeal	*Improperly tensioned fan belt
Hiss or roar	*Steam escaping through a leak in the cooling system or the radiator overflow vent
Whistle	*Vacuum leak
Wheeze	Loose or cracked spark plug

①—It is extremely difficult to evaluate vehicle noises. While the above are general definitions of engine noises, those starred (*) should be considered as possibly originating elsewhere in the car. To aid diagnosis, the following list considers other potential sources of these sounds.

Metallic grind:
Throwout bearing; transmission gears, bearings, or synchronizers; differential bearings, gears; something metallic in contact with brake drum or disc.

Metallic tap:
U-joints; fan-to-radiator (or shroud) contact.

Scrape:
Brake shoe or pad dragging; tire to body contact; suspension contacting undercarriage or exhaust; something non-metallic contacting brake shoe or drum.

Tick:
Transmission gears; differential gears; lack of radio suppression; resonant vibration of body panels; windshield wiper motor or transmission; heater motor and blower.

Squeal:
Brake shoe or pad not fully releasing; tires (excessive wear, uneven wear, improper inflation); front or rear wheel alignment (most commonly due to improper toe-in).

Hiss or whistle:
Wind leaks (body or window); heater motor and blower fan.

Roar:
Wheel bearings; wind leaks (body and window).

Specific Diagnosis

This section is arranged so that following each test, instructions are given to proceed to another, until a problem is diagnosed.

INDEX

Group		Topic
1	*	Battery
2	*	Cranking system
3	*	Primary electrical system
4	*	Secondary electrical system
5	*	Fuel system
6	*	Engine compression
7	**	Engine vacuum
8	**	Secondary electrical system
9	**	Valve train
10	**	Exhaust system
11	**	Cooling system
12	**	Engine lubrication

*—The engine need not be running.
**—The engine must be running.

SAMPLE SECTION

Test and Procedure	Results and Indications	Proceed to
4.1—Check for spark: Hold each spark plug wire approximately ¼" from ground with gloves or a heavy, dry rag. Crank the engine and observe the spark.	→ If no spark is evident:	→ 4.2
	→ If spark is good in some cases:	→ 4.3
	→ If spark is good in all cases:	→ 4.6

DIAGNOSIS

1.1—Inspect the battery visually for case condition (corrosion, cracks) and water level.	If case is cracked, replace battery:	1.4
	If the case is intact, remove corrosion with a solution of baking soda and water (CAUTION: *do not get the solution into the battery*), and fill with water:	1.2
1.2—Check the battery cable connections: Insert a screwdriver between the battery post and the cable clamp. Turn the headlights on high beam, and observe them as the screwdriver is gently twisted to ensure good metal to metal contact. **Testing battery cable connections using a screwdriver**	If the lights brighten, remove and clean the clamp and post; coat the post with petroleum jelly, install and tighten the clamp:	1.4
	If no improvement is noted:	1.3
1.3—Test the state of charge of the battery using an individual cell tester or hydrometer.	If indicated, charge the battery. NOTE: *If no obvious reason exists for the low state of charge (i.e., battery age, prolonged storage), the charging system should be tested:*	1.4

Spec. Grav. Reading	Charged Condition
1.260-1.280	Fully Charged
1.230-1.250	Three Quarter Charged
1.200-1.220	One Half Charged
1.170-1.190	One Quarter Charged
1.140-1.160	Just About Flat
1.110-1.130	All The Way Down

State of battery charge

Electrolyte temperature (°F)	Specific gravity correction
+120	+.016
+100	+.012 / +.008 / +.004 ADD to reading
+80	no correction
+60	−.004 / −.008
+40	−.012 / −.016
+20	−.020 / −.024 SUBTRACT from reading
0	−.028 / −.032
−20	−.036 / −.040

The effect of temperature on the specific gravity of battery electrolyte

Test and Procedure	Results and Indications	Proceed to
1.4—Visually inspect battery cables for cracking, bad connection to ground, or bad connection to starter.	If necessary, tighten connections or replace the cables:	2.1

Tests in Group 2 are performed with coil high tension lead disconnected to prevent accidental starting.

Test and Procedure	Results and Indications	Proceed to
2.1—Test the starter motor and solenoid: Connect a jumper from the battery post of the solenoid (or relay) to the starter post of the solenoid (or relay).	If starter turns the engine normally:	2.2
	If the starter buzzes, or turns the engine very slowly:	2.4
	If no response, replace the solenoid (or relay).	3.1
	If the starter turns, but the engine doesn't, ensure that the flywheel ring gear is intact. If the gear is undamaged, replace the starter drive.	3.1
2.2—Determine whether ignition override switches are functioning properly (clutch start switch, neutral safety switch), by connecting a jumper across the switch(es), and turning the ignition switch to "start".	If starter operates, adjust or replace switch:	3.1
	If the starter doesn't operate:	2.3
2.3—Check the ignition switch "start" position: Connect a 12V test lamp between the starter post of the solenoid (or relay) and ground. Turn the ignition switch to the "start" position, and jiggle the key.	If the lamp doesn't light when the switch is turned, check the ignition switch for loose connections, cracked insulation, or broken wires. Repair or replace as necessary:	3.1
	If the lamp flickers when the key is jiggled, replace the ignition switch.	3.3

Checking the ignition switch "start" position

Test and Procedure	Results and Indications	Proceed to
2.4—Remove and bench test the starter, according to specifications in the car section.	If the starter does not meet specifications, repair or replace as needed:	3.1
	If the starter is operating properly:	2.5
2.5—Determine whether the engine can turn freely: Remove the spark plugs, and check for water in the cylinders. Check for water on the dipstick, or oil in the radiator. Attempt to turn the engine using an 18″ flex drive and socket on the crankshaft pulley nut or bolt.	If the engine will turn freely only with the spark plugs out, and hydrostatic lock (water in the cylinders) is ruled out, check valve timing:	9.2
	If engine will not turn freely, and it is known that the clutch and transmission are free, the engine must be disassembled for further evaluation:	Next Chapter

Tests and Procedures	Results and Indications	Proceed to
3.1—Check the ignition switch "on" position: Connect a jumper wire between the distributor side of the coil and ground, and a 12V test lamp between the switch side of the coil and ground. Remove the high tension lead from the coil. Turn the ignition switch on and jiggle the key.	If the lamp lights:	3.2
	If the lamp flickers when the key is jiggled, replace the ignition switch:	3.3
	If the lamp doesn't light, check for loose or open connections. If none are found, remove the ignition switch and check for continuity. If the switch is faulty, replace it:	3.3

Checking the ignition switch "on" position

3.2—Check the ballast resistor or resistance wire for an open circuit, using an ohmmeter.	Replace the resistor or the resistance wire if the resistance is zero.	3.3
3.3—Visually inspect the breaker points for burning, pitting, or excessive wear. Gray coloring of the point contact surfaces is normal. Rotate the crankshaft until the contact heel rests on a high point of the distributor cam, and adjust the point gap to specifications.	If the breaker points are intact, clean the contact surfaces with fine emery cloth, and adjust the point gap to specifications. If pitted or worn, replace the points and condenser, and adjust the gap to specifications: NOTE: *Always lubricate the distributor cam according to manufacturer's recommendations when servicing the breaker points.*	3.4
3.4—Connect a dwell meter between the distributor primary lead and ground. Crank the engine and observe the point dwell angle.	If necessary, adjust the point dwell angle: NOTE: *Increasing the point gap decreases the dwell angle, and vice-versa.*	3.6
	If dwell meter shows little or no reading:	3.5

Dwell meter hook-up

Dwell angle

3.5—Check the condenser for short: Connect an ohmmeter across the condenser body and the pigtail lead.	If any reading other than infinite resistance is noted, replace the condenser:	3.6

Checking the condenser for short

Test and Procedure	Results and Indications	Proceed to
3.6—Test the coil primary resistance: Connect an ohmmeter across the coil primary terminals, and read the resistance on the low scale. Note whether an external ballast resistor or resistance wire is utilized.	Coils utilizing ballast resistors or resistance wires should have approximately 1.0Ω resistance; coils with internal resistors should have approximately 4.0Ω resistance. If values far from the above are noted, replace the coil:	4.1

Testing the coil primary resistance

Test and Procedure	Results and Indications	Proceed to
4.1—Check for spark: Hold each spark plug wire approximately $\frac{1}{4}''$ from ground with gloves or a heavy, dry rag. Crank the engine, and observe the spark.	If no spark is evident:	4.2
	If spark is good in some cylinders:	4.3
	If spark is good in all cylinders:	4.6
4.2—Check for spark at the coil high tension lead: Remove the coil high tension lead from the distributor and position it approximately $\frac{1}{4}''$ from ground. Crank the engine and observe spark. CAUTION: *This test should not be performed on cars equipped with transistorized ignition.*	If the spark is good and consistent:	4.3
	If the spark is good but intermittent, test the primary electrical system starting at 3.3:	3.3
	If the spark is weak or non-existent, replace the coil high tension lead, clean and tighten all connections and retest. If no improvement is noted:	4.4
4.3—Visually inspect the distributor cap and rotor for burned or corroded contacts, cracks, carbon tracks, or moisture. Also check the fit of the rotor on the distributor shaft (where applicable).	If moisture is present, dry thoroughly, and retest per 4.1:	4.1
	If burned or excessively corroded contacts, cracks, or carbon tracks are noted, replace the defective part(s) and retest per 4.1:	4.1
	If the rotor and cap appear intact, or are only slightly corroded, clean the contacts thoroughly (including the cap towers and spark plug wire ends) and retest per 4.1:	
	If the spark is good in all cases:	4.6
	If the spark is poor in all cases:	4.5
4.4—Check the coil secondary resistance: Connect an ohmmeter across the distributor side of the coil and the coil tower. Read the resistance on the high scale of the ohmmeter.	The resistance of a satisfactory coil should be between $4K\Omega$ and $10K\Omega$. If the resistance is considerably higher (i.e., $40K\Omega$) replace the coil, and retest per 4.1: NOTE: *This does not apply to high performance coils.*	4.1

Testing the coil secondary resistance

Test and Procedure	Results and Indications	Proceed to
4.5—Visually inspect the spark plug wires for cracking or brittleness. Ensure that no two wires are positioned so as to cause induction firing (adjacent and parallel). Remove each wire, one by one, and check resistance with an ohmmeter.	Replace any cracked or brittle wires. If any of the wires are defective, replace the entire set. Replace any wires with excessive resistance (over 8000Ω per foot for suppression wire), and separate any wires that might cause induction firing.	4.6
4.6—Remove the spark plugs, noting the cylinders from which they were removed, and evaluate according to the chart below.	See below.	See below.

	Condition	Cause	Remedy	Proceed to
	Electrodes eroded, light brown deposits.	Normal wear. Normal wear is indicated by approximately .001" wear per 1000 miles.	Clean and regap the spark plug if wear is not excessive: Replace the spark plug if excessively worn:	4.7
	Carbon fouling (black, dry, fluffy deposits).	If present on one or two plugs: Faulty high tension lead(s).	Test the high tension leads:	4.5
		Burnt or sticking valve(s).	Check the valve train: (Clean and regap the plugs in either case.)	9.1
		If present on most or all plugs: Overly rich fuel mixture, due to restricted air filter, improper carburetor adjustment, improper choke or heat riser adjustment or operation.	Check the fuel system:	5.1
	Oil fouling (wet black deposits)	Worn engine components. NOTE: *Oil fouling may occur in new or recently rebuilt engines until broken in.*	Check engine vacuum and compression: Replace with new spark plug	6.1
	Lead fouling (gray, black, tan, or yellow deposits, which appear glazed or cinderlike).	Combustion by-products.	Clean and regap the plugs: (Use plugs of a different heat range if the problem recurs.)	4.7

	Condition	Cause	Remedy	Proceed to
	Gap bridging (deposits lodged between the electrodes).	Incomplete combustion, or transfer of deposits from the combustion chamber.	Replace the spark plugs:	4.7
	Overheating (burnt electrodes, and extremely white insulator with small black spots).	Ignition timing advanced too far.	Adjust timing to specifications:	8.2
		Overly lean fuel mixture.	Check the fuel system:	5.1
		Spark plugs not seated properly.	Clean spark plug seat and install a new gasket washer: (Replace the spark plugs in all cases.)	4.7
	Fused spot deposits on the insulator.	Combustion chamber blow-by.	Clean and regap the spark plugs:	4.7
	Pre-ignition (melted or severely burned electrodes, blistered or cracked insulators, or metallic deposits on the insulator).	Incorrect spark plug heat range.	Replace with plugs of the proper heat range:	4.7
		Ignition timing advanced too far.	Adjust timing to specifications:	8.2
		Spark plugs not being cooled efficiently.	Clean the spark plug seat, and check the cooling system:	11.1
		Fuel mixture too lean.	Check the fuel system:	5.1
		Poor compression.	Check compression:	6.1
		Fuel grade too low.	Use higher octane fuel:	4.7

Test and Procedure	Results and Indications	Proceed to
4.7—Determine the static ignition timing: Using the flywheel or crankshaft pulley timing marks as a guide, locate top dead center on the *compression* stroke of the No. 1 cylinder. Remove the distributor cap.	Adjust the distributor so that the rotor points toward the No. 1 tower in the distributor cap, and the points are just opening:	4.8
4.8—Check coil polarity: Connect a voltmeter negative lead to the coil high tension lead, and the positive lead to ground (NOTE: *reverse the hook-up for positive ground cars*). Crank the engine momentarily. **Checking coil polarity**	If the voltmeter reads up-scale, the polarity is correct:	5.1
	If the voltmeter reads down-scale, reverse the coil polarity (switch the primary leads):	5.1

Test and Procedure	Results and Indications	Proceed to
5.1—Determine that the air filter is functioning efficiently: Hold paper elements up to a strong light, and attempt to see light through the filter.	Clean permanent air filters in gasoline (or manufacturer's recommendation), and allow to dry. Replace paper elements through which light cannot be seen:	5.2
5.2—Determine whether a flooding condition exists: Flooding is identified by a strong gasoline odor, and excessive gasoline present in the throttle bore(s) of the carburetor.	If flooding is not evident:	5.3
	If flooding is evident, permit the gasoline to dry for a few moments and restart.	
	If flooding doesn't recur:	5.6
	If flooding is persistant:	5.5
5.3—Check that fuel is reaching the carburetor: Detach the fuel line at the carburetor inlet. Hold the end of the line in a cup (not styrofoam), and crank the engine.	If fuel flows smoothly:	5.6
	If fuel doesn't flow (NOTE: *Make sure that there is fuel in the tank*), or flows erratically:	5.4
5.4—Test the fuel pump: Disconnect all fuel lines from the fuel pump. Hold a finger over the input fitting, crank the engine (with electric pump, turn the ignition or pump on); and feel for suction.	If suction is evident, blow out the fuel line to the tank with low pressure compressed air until bubbling is heard from the fuel filler neck. Also blow out the carburetor fuel line (both ends disconnected):	5.6
	If no suction is evident, replace or repair the fuel pump:	5.6
	NOTE: *Repeated oil fouling of the spark plugs, or a no-start condition, could be the result of a ruptured vacuum booster pump diaphragm, through which oil or gasoline is being drawn into the intake manifold (where applicable).*	
5.5—Check the needle and seat: Tap the carburetor in the area of the needle and seat.	If flooding stops, a gasoline additive (e.g., Gumout) will often cure the problem:	5.6
	If flooding continues, check the fuel pump for excessive pressure at the carburetor (according to specifications). If the pressure is normal, the needle and seat must be removed and checked, and/or the float level adjusted:	5.6
5.6—Test the accelerator pump by looking into the throttle bores while operating the throttle.	If the accelerator pump appears to be operating normally:	5.7
	If the accelerator pump is not operating, the pump must be reconditioned. Where possible, service the pump with the carburetor(s) installed on the engine. If necessary, remove the carburetor. Prior to removal:	5.7
5.7—Determine whether the carburetor main fuel system is functioning: Spray a commercial starting fluid into the carburetor while attempting to start the engine.	If the engine starts, runs for a few seconds, and dies:	5.8
	If the engine doesn't start:	6.1

Test and Procedures	*Results and Indications*	*Proceed to*
5.8—Uncommon fuel system malfunctions: See below:	If the problem is solved:	6.1
	If the problem remains, remove and recondition the carburetor.	

Condition	*Indication*	*Test*	*Usual Weather Conditions*	*Remedy*
Vapor lock	Car will not restart shortly after running.	Cool the components of the fuel system until the engine starts.	Hot to very hot	Ensure that the exhaust manifold heat control valve is operating. Check with the vehicle manufacturer for the recommended solution to vapor lock on the model in question.
Carburetor icing	Car will not idle, stalls at low speeds.	Visually inspect the throttle plate area of the throttle bores for frost.	High humidity, 32-40° F.	Ensure that the exhaust manifold heat control valve is operating, and that the intake manifold heat riser is not blocked.
Water in the fuel	Engine sputters and stalls; may not start.	Pump a small amount of fuel into a glass jar. Allow to stand, and inspect for droplets or a layer of water.	High humidity, extreme temperature changes.	For droplets, use one or two cans of commercial gas dryer (Dry Gas) For a layer of water, the tank must be drained, and the fuel lines blown out with compressed air.

Test and Procedure	*Results and Indications*	*Proceed to*
6.1—Test engine compression: Remove all spark plugs. Insert a compression gauge into a spark plug port, crank the engine to obtain the maximum reading, and record.	If compression is within limits on all cylinders:	7.1
	If gauge reading is extremely low on all cylinders:	6.2
	If gauge reading is low on one or two cylinders:	6.2
	(If gauge readings are identical and low on two or more adjacent cylinders, the head gasket must be replaced.)	

Testing compression
(© Chevrolet Div. G.M. Corp.)

Compression pressure limits
(© Buick Div. G.M. Corp.)

Maxi. Press. Lbs. Sq. In.	Min. Press. Lbs. Sq. In.	Maxi. Press. Lbs. Sq. In.	Min. Press. Lbs. Sq. In.	Max. Press. Lbs. Sq. In.	Min. Press. Lbs. Sq. In.	Max. Press. Lbs. Sq. In.	Min. Press. Lbs. Sq. In.
134	101	162	121	188	141	214	160
136	102	164	123	190	142	216	162
138	104	166	124	192	144	218	163
140	105	168	126	194	145	220	165
142	107	170	127	196	147	222	166
146	110	172	129	198	148	224	168
148	111	174	131	200	150	226	169
150	113	176	132	202	151	228	171
152	114	178	133	204	153	230	172
154	115	180	135	206	154	232	174
156	117	182	136	208	156	234	175
158	118	184	138	210	157	236	177
160	120	186	140	212	158	238	178

Test and Procedure	*Results and Indications*	*Proceed to*
6.2—Test engine compression (wet): Squirt approximately 30 cc. of engine oil into each cylinder, and retest per 6.1.	If the readings improve, worn or cracked rings or broken pistons are indicated:	Next Chapter
	If the readings do not improve, burned or excessively carboned valves or a jumped timing chain are indicated:	7.1
	NOTE: *A jumped timing chain is often indicated by difficult cranking.*	
7.1—Perform a vacuum check of the engine: Attach a vacuum gauge to the intake manifold beyond the throttle plate. Start the engine, and observe the action of the needle over the range of engine speeds.	See below.	See below

Reading	*Indications*	*Proceed to*
Steady, from 17-22 in. Hg.	Normal.	8.1
Low and steady.	Late ignition or valve timing, or low compression:	6.1
Very low	Vacuum leak:	7.2
Needle fluctuates as engine speed increases.	Ignition miss, blown cylinder head gasket, leaking valve or weak valve spring:	6.1, 8.3
Gradual drop in reading at idle.	Excessive back pressure in the exhaust system:	10.1
Intermittent fluctuation at idle.	Ignition miss, sticking valve:	8.3, 9.1
Drifting needle.	Improper idle mixture adjustment, carburetors not synchronized (where applicable), or minor intake leak. Synchronize the carburetors, adjust the idle, and retest. If the condition persists:	7.2
High and steady.	Early ignition timing:	8.2

Test and Procedure	Results and Indications	Proceed to
7.2—Attach a vacuum gauge per 7.1, and test for an intake manifold leak. Squirt a small amount of oil around the intake manifold gaskets, carburetor gaskets, plugs and fittings. Observe the action of the vacuum gauge.	If the reading improves, replace the indicated gasket, or seal the indicated fitting or plug: If the reading remains low:	8.1 7.3
7.3—Test all vacuum hoses and accessories for leaks as described in 7.2. Also check the carburetor body (dashpots, automatic choke mechanism, throttle shafts) for leaks in the same manner.	If the reading improves, service or replace the offending part(s): If the reading remains low:	8.1 6.1
8.1—Check the point dwell angle: Connect a dwell meter between the distributor primary wire and ground. Start the engine, and observe the dwell angle from idle to 3000 rpm.	If necessary, adjust the dwell angle. NOTE: *Increasing the point gap reduces the dwell angle and vice-versa.* If the dwell angle moves outside specifications as engine speed increases, the distributor should be removed and checked for cam accuracy, shaft endplay and concentricity, bushing wear, and adequate point arm tension (NOTE: *Most of these items may be checked with the distributor installed in the engine, using an oscilloscope*):	8.2
8.2—Connect a timing light (per manufacturer's recommendation) and check the dynamic ignition timing. Disconnect and plug the vacuum hose(s) to the distributor if specified, start the engine, and observe the timing marks at the specified engine speed.	If the timing is not correct, adjust to specifications by rotating the distributor in the engine: (Advance timing by rotating distributor opposite normal direction of rotor rotation, retard timing by rotating distributor in same direction as rotor rotation.)	8.3
8.3—Check the operation of the distributor advance mechanism(s): To test the mechanical advance, disconnect all but the mechanical advance, and observe the timing marks with a timing light as the engine speed is increased from idle. If the mark moves smoothly, without hesitation, it may be assumed that the mechanical advance is functioning properly. To test vacuum advance and/or retard systems, alternately crimp and release the vacuum line, and observe the timing mark for movement. If movement is noted, the system is operating.	If the systems are functioning: If the systems are not functioning, remove the distributor, and test on a distributor tester:	8.4 8.4
8.4—Locate an ignition miss: With the engine running, remove each spark plug wire, one by one, until one is found that doesn't cause the engine to roughen and slow down.	When the missing cylinder is identified:	4.1

Test and Procedure	Results and Indications	Proceed to
9.1—Evaluate the valve train: Remove the valve cover, and ensure that the valves are adjusted to specifications. A mechanic's stethoscope may be used to aid in the diagnosis of the valve train. By pushing the probe on or near push rods or rockers, valve noise often can be isolated. A timing light also may be used to diagnose valve problems. Connect the light according to manufacturer's recommendations, and start the engine. Vary the firing moment of the light by increasing the engine speed (and therefore the ignition advance), and moving the trigger from cylinder to cylinder. Observe the movement of each valve.	See below	See below

Observation	Probable Cause	Remedy	Proceed to
Metallic tap heard through the stethoscope.	Sticking hydraulic lifter or excessive valve clearance.	Adjust valve. If tap persists, remove and replace the lifter:	10.1
Metallic tap through the stethoscope, able to push the rocker arm (lifter side) down by hand.	Collapsed valve lifter.	Remove and replace the lifter:	10.1
Erratic, irregular motion of the valve stem.*	Sticking valve, burned valve.	Recondition the valve and/or valve guide:	Next Chapter
Eccentric motion of the pushrod at the rocker arm.*	Bent pushrod.	Replace the pushrod:	10.1
Valve retainer bounces as the valve closes.*	Weak valve spring or damper.	Remove and test the spring and damper. Replace if necessary:	10.1

*—When observed with a timing light.

Test and Procedure	Results and Indications	Proceed to
9.2—Check the valve timing: Locate top dead center of the No. 1 piston, and install a degree wheel or tape on the crankshaft pulley or damper with zero corresponding to an index mark on the engine. Rotate the crankshaft in its direction of rotation, and observe the opening of the No. 1 cylinder intake valve. The opening should correspond with the correct mark on the degree wheel according to specifications.	If the timing is not correct, the timing cover must be removed for further investigation:	

Test and Procedure	Results and Indications	Proceed to
10.1—Determine whether the exhaust manifold heat control valve is operating: Operate the valve by hand to determine whether it is free to move. If the valve is free, run the engine to operating temperature and observe the action of the valve, to ensure that it is opening.	If the valve sticks, spray it with a suitable solvent, open and close the valve to free it, and retest.	
	If the valve functions properly:	10.2
	If the valve does not free, or does not operate, replace the valve:	10.2
10.2—Ensure that there are no exhaust restrictions: Visually inspect the exhaust system for kinks, dents, or crushing. Also note that gasses are flowing freely from the tailpipe at all engine speeds, indicating no restriction in the muffler or resonator.	Replace any damaged portion of the system:	11.1
11.1—Visually inspect the fan belt for glazing, cracks, and fraying, and replace if necessary. Tighten the belt so that the longest span has approximately ½″ play at its midpoint under thumb pressure.	Replace or tighten the fan belt as necessary:	

Checking the fan belt tension
(© Nissan Motor Co. Ltd.)

Test and Procedure	Results and Indications	Proceed to
12.1—Check the oil pressure gauge or warning light: If the gauge shows low pressure, or the light is on, for no obvious reason, remove the oil pressure sender. Install an accurate oil pressure gauge and run the engine momentarily.	If oil pressure builds normally, run engine for a few moments to determine that it is functioning normally, and replace the sender.	—
	If the pressure remains low:	12.2
	If the pressure surges:	12.3
	If the oil pressure is zero:	12.3
12.2—Visually inspect the oil: If the oil is watery or very thin, milky, or foamy, replace the oil and oil filter.	If the oil is normal:	12.3
	If after replacing oil the pressure remains low:	12.3
	If after replacing oil the pressure becomes normal:	—
12.3—Inspect the oil pressure relief valve and spring, to ensure that it is not sticking or stuck. Remove and thoroughly clean the valve, spring, and the valve body.	If the oil pressure improves:	—
	If no improvement is noted:	12.4

Oil pressure relief valve
(© British Leyland Motors)

Test and Procedure	*Results and Indication*	*Proceed to*
12.4—Check to ensure that the oil pump is not cavitating (sucking air instead of oil): See that the crankcase is neither over nor underfull, and that the pickup in the sump is in the proper position and free from sludge.	Fill or drain the crankcase to the proper capacity, and clean the pickup screen in solvent if necessary. If no improvement is noted:	12.5
12.5—Inspect the oil pump drive and the oil pump:	If the pump drive or the oil pump appear to be defective, service as necessary and retest per 12.1:	12.1
	If the pump drive and pump appear to be operating normally, the engine should be disassembled to determine where blockage exists:	Next Chapter
12.6—Purge the engine of ethylene glycol coolant: Completely drain the crankcase and the oil filter. Obtain a commercial butyl cellosolve base solvent, designated for this purpose, and follow the instructions precisely. Following this, install a new oil filter and refill the crankcase with the proper weight oil. The next oil and filter change should follow shortly thereafter (1000 miles).		

Chapter Three

Engine and Engine Rebuilding

Engine Electrical

DISTRIBUTOR

Removal and Installation

1. Take off the vacuum hoses at the distributor.

2. Disconnect the coil wire and remove the distributor cap.

3. Disconnect the condenser wire.

4. Bring No. 1 cylinder to top dead center (TDC) on the compression stroke by rotating the engine so that the rotor points to the No. 1 spark plug wire tower on the distributor cap and the timing marks are aligned at 0°. Mark the rotor-to-distributor relationship. Also match mark the distributor housing-to-crankcase relationship.

5. Unscrew the distributor retaining screw on the crankcase and lift the distributor out.

6. If the engine has been rotated since the distributor was removed, bring the No. 1 cylinder to TDC on the compression stroke and align the timing marks on 0°. Align the match marks and insert the distributor into the crankcase. If the match marks are gone, have the rotor pointing to the No. 1 spark plug wire tower upon insertion.

7. Replace the distributor retaining

Type 4 timing mark and distributor rotor alignment

screw and reconnect the condenser and coil wires. Reinstall the distributor cap.

8. Retime the engine.

Firing Order

A general firing order diagram is shown (on page 38) because distributor positioning varies from model to model. All VW distributors have a scribed notch on the housing which locates the No. 1 rotor position.

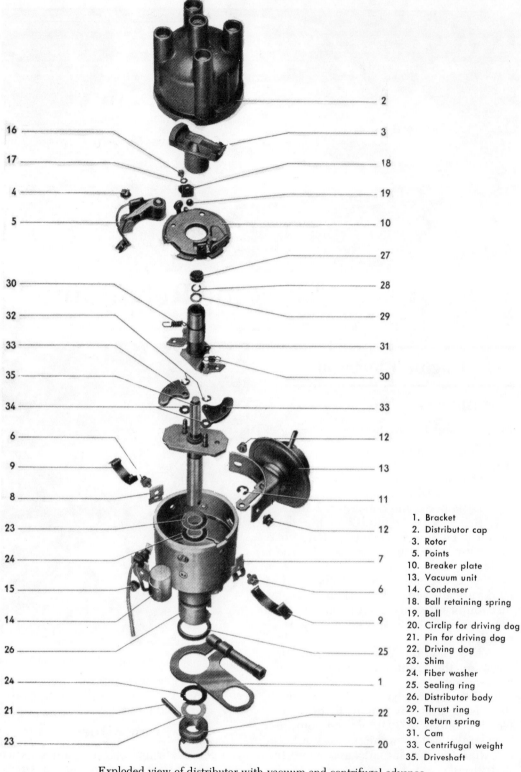

1. Bracket
2. Distributor cap
3. Rotor
5. Points
10. Breaker plate
13. Vacuum unit
14. Condenser
18. Ball retaining spring
19. Ball
20. Circlip for driving dog
21. Pin for driving dog
22. Driving dog
23. Shim
24. Fiber washer
25. Sealing ring
26. Distributor body
29. Thrust ring
30. Return spring
31. Cam
33. Centrifugal weight
35. Driveshaft

Exploded view of distributor with vacuum and centrifugal advance

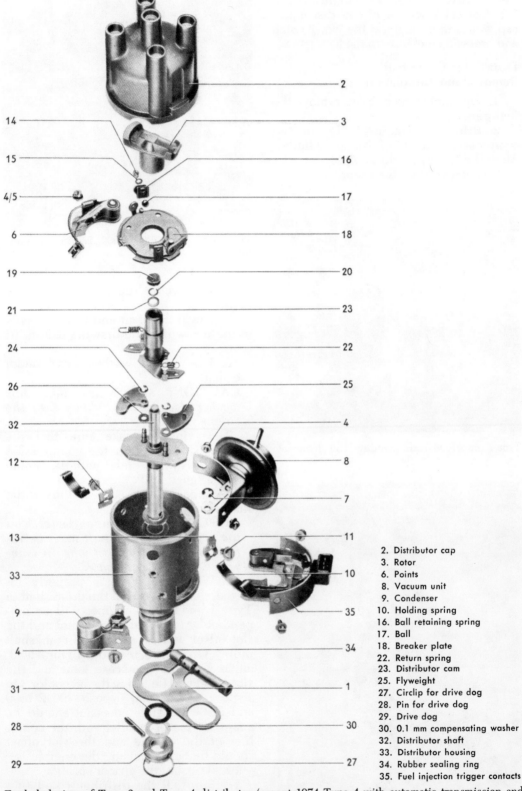

2. Distributor cap
3. Rotor
6. Points
8. Vacuum unit
9. Condenser
10. Holding spring
16. Ball retaining spring
17. Ball
18. Breaker plate
22. Return spring
23. Distributor cam
25. Flyweight
27. Circlip for drive dog
28. Pin for drive dog
29. Drive dog
30. 0.1 mm compensating washer
32. Distributor shaft
33. Distributor housing
34. Rubber sealing ring
35. Fuel injection trigger contacts

Exploded view of Type 3 and Type 4 distributor (except 1974 Type 4 with automatic transmission and airflow controlled fuel injection

The firing order of all VW engines is 1-4-3-2. Correct rewiring of the distributor cap would then begin at the No. 1 notch and proceed clockwise in the firing order.

Distributor Driveshaft
Removal and Installation

1. On carbureted engines remove the fuel pump.

2. Bring the engine to TDC on the compression stroke of No. 1 cylinder. Align the timing marks at 0°.

3. Remove the distributor.

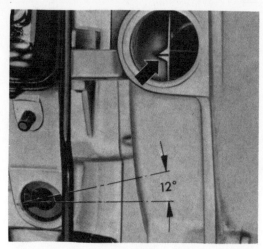

Type 4, Type 2/1700, 2/1800, 2/2000 distributor driveshaft alignment

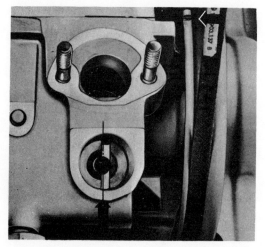

Type 1 and 2/1600 distributor driveshaft alignment

Type 3 distributor driveshaft alignment

4. Remove the spacer spring from the driveshaft.

5. Grasp the shaft and turn it slowly to the left while withdrawing it from its bore.

6. Remove the washer found under the shaft.

CAUTION: *Make sure that this washer does not fall down into the engine.*

7. To install, make sure that the engine is at TDC on the compression stroke for No. 1 cylinder with the timing marks aligned at 0°.

8. Replace the washer and insert the shaft into its bore.

NOTE: *Due to the slant of the teeth on the drive gears, the shaft must be rotated slightly to the left when it is inserted into the crankcase.*

9. When the shaft is properly inserted, the offset slot in the drive shaft of Type 1 and 2/1600 engines will be perpendicular to the crankcase joint and the slot offset will be facing the crankshaft pulley. On Type 3, the slot will form a 60° angle with the crankcase joint and the slot offset will be facing the oil cooler. On Type 4 engines, and Type 2/1700, 2/1800 and 2/2000 engines, the slot should be about 12° out of parallel with the center line of the engine and the slot offset should be facing outside the engine.

10. Reinstall the spacer spring.

11. Reinstall the distributor and fuel pump, if removed.

12. Retime the engine.

GENERATOR AND ALTERNATOR

Alternator Precautions

1. Battery polarity should be checked before any connections, such as jumper cables or battery charger leads, are made. Reversing the battery connections will damage the diodes in the alternator. It is recommended that the battery cables be disconnected before connecting a battery charger.

2. The battery must never be disconnected while the alternator is running.

3. Always disconnect the battery ground lead before working on the charging system, especially when replacing an alternator.

4. Do not short across or ground any alternator or regulator terminals.

5. If electric arc welding has to be done to the car, first disconnect the battery and alternator cables. Never start the car with the welding unit attached.

Belts (See Chapter One)

Generator/Alternator
Removal and Installation

TYPES 1 AND 2/1600

1. Disconnect the battery.

2. Disconnect the leads from the generator (alternator), noting their position on the generator (alternator).

3. Remove the air cleaner and the carburetor.

4. Separate the generator (alternator) pulley halves, noting the number and position of the pulley shims, and remove the belt from the pulley.

5. Remove the retaining strap from the generator (alternator).

6. Remove the cooling air thermostat.

7. Remove the hot air hoses from the fan housing, take out the fan housing screws, and lift off the housing.

8. The generator (alternator) fan, and

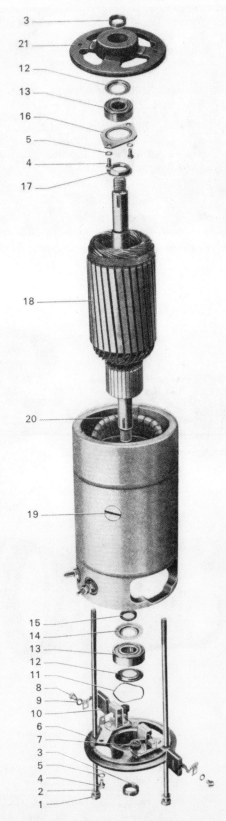

1. Through-bolt	12. Dished washer
2. Lockwasher	13. Ball bearing
3. Spacer ring	14. Splash shield
4. Fillister head screw	15. Thrust washer
5. Lockwasher	16. Retaining plate
6. Commutator end plate	17. Splash shield
7. Brush spring	18. Armature
8. Fillister head screw	19. Pole shoe screw
9. Lockwasher	20. Field coil
10. Carbon brush	21. Fan end plate
11. Lockwasher	

Exploded view of Type 1 and 2/1600 generator

Removing generator with fan cover—Type 1, 2/1600

fan cover may be removed as an assembly.

9. Remove the fan from the generator (alternator) by unscrewing the special nut and pulling the fan off the keyed generator (alternator) shaft. Note the position of any shims found on Type 2 generators, from chassis number 219000001, as these shims are used to maintain a gap of 0.047 in. between the fan and the fan cover. The Type 1 gap is 0.08 in.

10. Reverse the above steps to install. When reinstalling the generator (alternator) the cooling air intake slot in the fan cover must face downward and the generator (alternator) pulley must align with the crankshaft pulley.

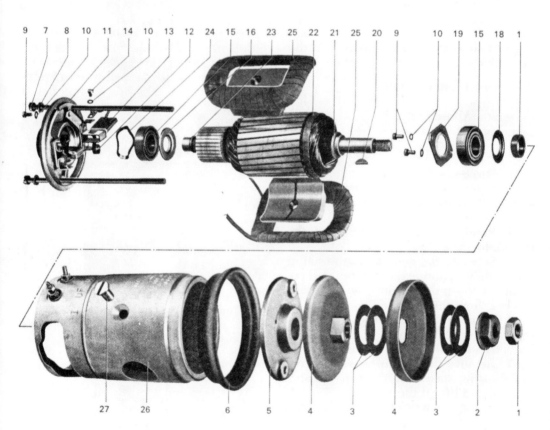

Exploded view of Type 3 generator

1. Nut for pulley	10. Washer	20. Woodruff key
2. Special washer	11. End plate with carbon brushes	21. Splash shield
3. Shim	12. Spring	22. Armature
4. Pulley	13. Carbon brushes	23. Armature flange
5. End plate	14. Screw	24. Gasket
6. End ring	15. Ball bearing	25. Field coil
7. Through-bolt	16. Splash shield	26. Housing
8. Washer	18. Splash shield	27. Field screw
9. Screw	19. Retaining plate	

Type 2/1800, 2/2000
(Fuel Injected)

1. Disconnect the negative battery cable.

2. Disconnect the alternator wiring harness at the voltage regulator and starter.

3. Pull out the dipstick and remove the oil filler neck.

4. Loosen the alternator adjusting bolt and remove the drive belt.

5. Remove the right rear engine cover plate and the alternator cover plate.

6. Disconnect the warm air duct at the right side, and remove the heat exchanger bracket and connecting pipe from the blower.

7. Disconnect the cool air intake elbow at the alternator. Remove the attaching bolt and lift out the alternator from above.

8. Reverse the above procedure to install, taking care to ensure that the rubber grommet on the intake cover for the wiring harness is installed correctly. After installation, adjust the drive belt so that the moderate thumb pressure midway on the belt depresses the belt about ½ in.

Type 3

1. Remove the cooling air intake cover and disconnect the battery.

2. Loosen the fan belt adjustment and remove the fan belt. Removal of the belt is accomplished by removing the nut in the center of the generator pulley and removing the outer pulley half.

3. Remove the two nuts which hold the generator securing strap in place and then remove the strap.

Type 3 generator alignment

4. Disconnect the generator wiring.

5. Remove the generator.

6. Installation is the reverse of the above. Install the generator so that the mark on the generator housing is in line with the notch on the clamping strap. The generator pulley must be aligned with the crankshaft pulley. Make sure that the boot which seals the generator to the air intake housing is properly placed.

Type 4, Type 2/1700, 2/1800, 2/2000

The factory procedure recommends removing the engine to remove the alternator. However, it is possible to reach the alternator by first removing the right heater box which will provide access to the alternator.

1. Disconnect the battery.

2. The following is the alternator removal and installation procedure after removing the engine; however, all bolts and connections listed below must be removed, except the engine cooling fan, if the right heater box is removed to gain access to the alternator.

3. Remove the engine.

4. Remove the dipstick, if necessary, and the rear engine cover plate.

5. Remove the fan belt.

6. Remove the lower alternator bolt and the alternator cover plate.

7. Disconnect the wiring harness from the alternator.

8. Remove the allen head screws which attach the engine cooling fan, then remove the fan.

9. Remove the rubber elbow from the fan housing.

NOTE: *This elbow must be in position upon installation because it provides cooling air for the alternator.*

10. Remove the alternator adjusting bracket.

11. Remove the alternator.

12. Installation is the reverse of the above. Make sure that the belt is properly adjusted.

VOLTAGE REGULATOR
Removal and Installation

Type 1 and 3

The regulator is located under the rear seat on the left side. It is secured to the

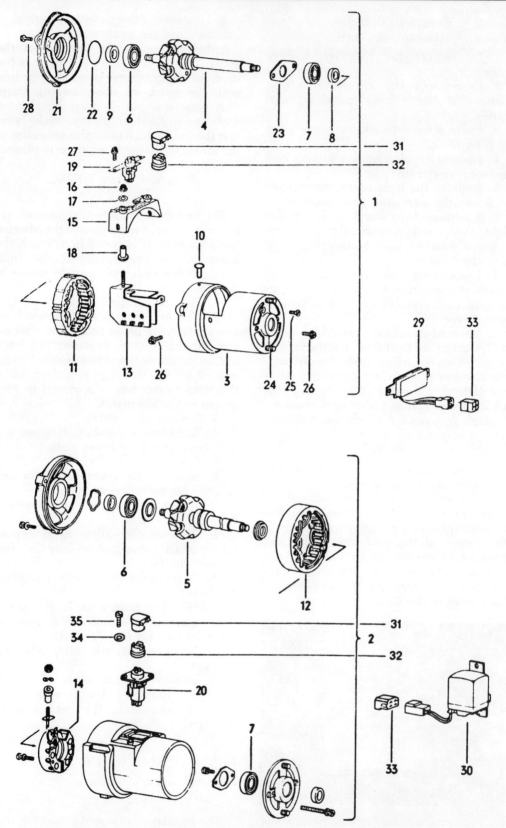

Exploded view of 50 amp alternator used in 1973–77 Type 1/1600 models

frame by two screws. Take careful note of the wiring connections before removing the wiring from the regulator. Disconnect the battery before removing the regulator.

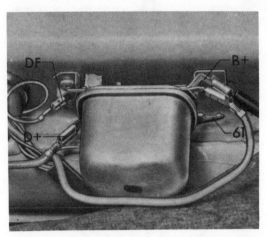

Voltage regulator details—Type 1 Beetle, Super Beetle, Type 3 similar

D+ to generator D+
DF to generator DF (protected by cap on 1972 and later models)
B+/51 to negative battery terminal and terminal 30 of electrical system
61 to generator charging warning light

CAUTION: *Interchanging the connections on the regulator will destroy the regulator and generator.*

TYPE 2 AND MODEL 14 (KARMANN GHIA)

Disconnect the battery. The regulator is located in the engine compartment and is secured in place by two screws. Take careful note of the wiring connections before removing the wiring from the regulator.

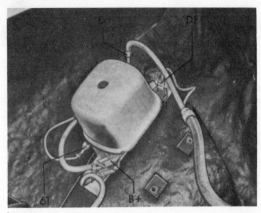

Voltage regulator details—Type 1 Karmann Ghia; Type 2 and Type 4 similar

TYPE 4

Disconnect the battery and do not disconnect any other wiring until the engine is turned off. Make careful note of the wiring connections. The regulator is located near the air cleaner and is mounted either on the air cleaner or on the firewall. It is secured by two screws.

Voltage Adjustment

Volkswagen voltage regulators are sealed and cannot be adjusted. A malfunctioning regulator must be replaced as a unit.

STARTER

The starter motor of the Volkswagen is of the sliding gear type and is rated at about 0.6 or 0.7 horsepower. The motor used in the starter is a series wound type

1. Motorola alternator
2. Bosch alternator
3. Housing
4. Claw-pole rotor
5. Claw-pole rotor
6. End plate ball bearing
7. Ball bearing
8. Fan end spacer ring
9. Drive end spacer ring
10. Rotor locating plate
11. Stator winding
12. Stator winding
13. Diode carrier
14. Diode carrier
15. Diode carrier retainer
16. B+ terminal nut
17. B+ terminal insulating washer
18. B+ terminal insulating bushing

19. Brush holder
20. Carbon brush holder plate
21. End plate
22. O-ring
23. Retaining plate
24. Fan cover bolt
25. Diode carrier screw
26. Retaining plate screw
27. Brush holder cover screw
28. End plate screw
29. Voltage regulator
30. Voltage regulator
31. Boot
32. Terminal sleeve housing
33. Terminal pin housing
34. Spring washer
35. Screw

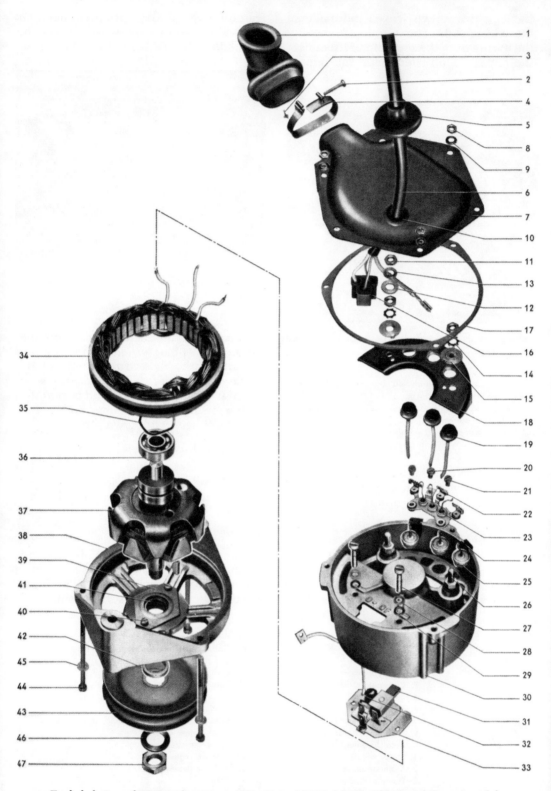

Exploded view of 55 amp alternator used in Type 2/1700, 2/1800, 2/2000, and Type 4 models

Alternator, Generator, and Regulator Specifications

		Generator		Alternator			Regulator	
Year	Type	Maximum Output (Amps)	Maximum Output (Amps)	Stator Winding Resistance (Ohms)	Exciter Winding Resistance (Ohms)	Load Current (Amps)	Regulating Voltage Under Load (Volts)
1970–73	1	30	—	—	—	25①	12.5–14.5
1973–77	1	—	50	0.13 ± 0.013	4.0 ± 0.4	25–30	13.8–14.9②
1970–71	2/1600	38	—	—	—	25①	12.5–14.5
1972–73	2/1700	—	55	0.13 ± 0.013	4.0 ± 0.4	25–30	13.8–14.9②
1974–77	2/1800, 2/2000	—	55	0.13 ± 0.013	4.0 ± 0.4	25–30	13.8–14.9②
1970–73	3	30	—	—	—	25①	12.5–14.5
1971–74	4	—	55	0.13 ± 0.013	4.0 ± 0.4	25–30	13.8–14.9②

① @ 2000–2500 generator rpm   ② @ 2000 engine rpm   — Not Applicable

and draws a heavy current in order to provide the high torque needed to crank the engine during starting. The starter cannot be switched on accidently while the engine is still running—the device responsible for this safeguard is a non-repeat switch in the ignition switch. If the engine should stall for any reason, the ignition key must be turned to the "off" position before it is possible to re-start the engine.

The starter is flange-mounted on the right-hand side of the transmission housing. Attached to the starter motor housing is a solenoid which engages the pinion and connects the starting motor to the battery when the ignition key is turned

on. When the engine starts, and the key is released from the start position, the solenoid circuit is opened and the pinion is returned to its original position by the return spring. However, if for any reason the starter is not switched off immediately after the engine starts, a pinion free-wheeling device stops the armature from being driven so that the starter will not be damaged.

Starter/Seat Belt Interlock

All 1974 and some 1975 models are equipped with a seat belt/starter interlock system. This system prevents operation of the starter motor until both

1. Elbow
2. Screw for hose clip
3. Threaded portion for hose clip
4. Cable hose clamp
5. Rubber grommet
6. Alternator wiring harness
7. Intake cover for alternator
8. Hex nut
9. Lockwasher
10. Rubber grommet for intake cover
11. B+ connection hex nut
12. Washer
13. Washer
14. Star washer
15. Contact disc
16. Three pin plug
17. Intake cover gasket
18. Positive diode carrier
19. Positive diodes
20. Screw
21. Stator winding connection screw
22. Exciter diode carrier
23. Exciter diodes
24. Seal
25. Negative diodes
26. Positive diode carrier pin
27. Brush holder screw
28. Washer
29. Spring washer
30. Alternator housing
31. Carbon brush
32. Brush retaining spring
33. Brush holder
34. Stator
35. Spring washer
36. Slip ring ball bearings
37. Claw pole rotor
38. End plate
39. Bearing end plate
40. Screw
41. Drive end ball bearing
42. Intermediate ring
43. Pulley
44. Housing bolt
45. Washer
46. Washer
47. Nut

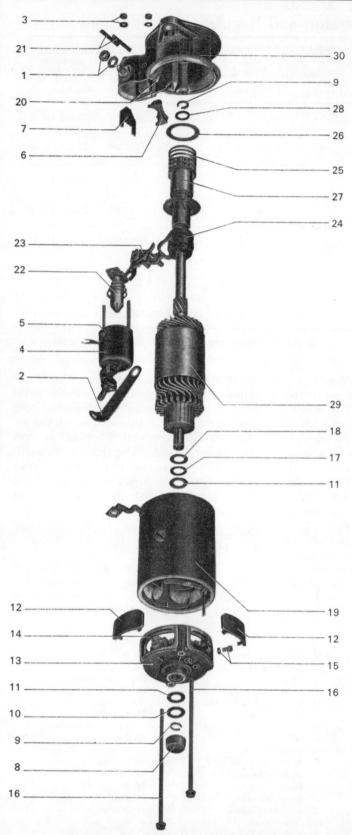

1. Nut and lockwasher
2. Connecting strip
3. Nut and lockwasher
4. Solenoid
5. Insulating disc
6. Seal
7. Insulating plate
8. Cap
9. Circlip
10. Steel washer
11. Bronze washer
12. Brush inspection cover
13. Commutator end plate
14. Brush holder
15. Screw and lockwasher
16. Housing screws
17. Dished washer
18. Steel washer
19. Housing and field windings
20. Spring clip
21. Pin
22. Solenoid core
23. Linkage
24. Bushing
25. Spring
26. Washer
27. Drive pinion
28. Dished washer
29. Armature
30. Mounting bracket

Exploded view of VW No. 111 911 023A starter

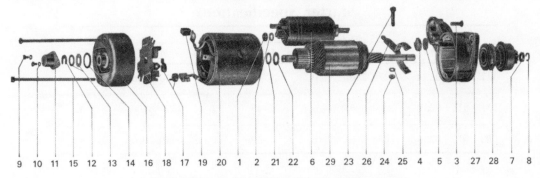

9 10 11 15 12 13 14 16 18 17 19 20 1 2 21 22 6 29 23 26 24 25 4 5 3 27 28 7 8

Exploded view of Bosch No. 311 911 023B starter

1. Nut	11. End cap	21. Insulating washer
2. Lockwasher	12. C-washer	22. Thrust washer
3. Screw	13. Shim	23. Pin
4. Rubber seal	14. Sealing ring	24. Nut
5. Disc	15. Housing screw	25. Lockwasher
6. Solenoid switch	16. End plate	26. Operating lever
7. Stop-ring	17. Spring	27. Drive end plate
8. Circlip	18. Brush holder	28. Drive pinion
9. Screw	19. Rubber grommet	29. Armature
10. Washer	20. Housing	

front seat occupants buckle up their seat belts. For details, see Chapter 5.

Starter Removal and Installation

1. Disconnect the battery.

2. Disconnect the wiring from the starter.

3. The starter is held in place by two bolts. Remove the upper bolt through the engine compartment. Remove the lower bolt from underneath the car.

4. Remove the starter from the car.

5. Before installing the starter, lubricate the outboard bushing with grease. Apply sealing compound to the mating surfaces between the starter and the transmission.

6. Place the long starter bolt in its hole in the starter and locate the starter on the transmission housing. Install the other bolt.

7. Connect the starter wiring and battery cables.

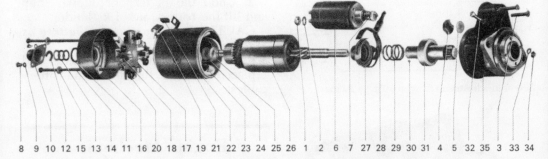

8 9 10 12 15 13 14 11 16 20 18 17 19 21 22 23 24 25 26 1 2 6 7 27 28 29 30 31 4 5 32 35 3 33 34

Exploded view of Bosch No. 003 911 023A starter

1. Nut	13. Shim	25. Thrust washer
2. Lockwasher	14. Screws	26. Armature
3. Screw	15. Washer	27. Operating sleeve
4. Molded rubber	16. End plate	28. Engaging lever
5. Disc	17. Brush holder	29. Engaging spring
6. Solenoid	18. Negative brush	30. Detent balls
7. Spring	19. Positive brush	31. Drive pinion
8. Screw	20. Retaining spring	32. Pin
9. Washer	21. Rubber grommet	33. Lockwasher
10. End cap	22. Housing	34. Nut
11. Seal	23. Field winding	35. Drive end plate
12. C-ring	24. Insulating washer	

Starter Specifications

Starter Number	Lock Test		No-Load Test			Brush Spring Tension (oz)
	Amps	Volts	Amps	Volts	rpm	
111 911 023A	270–290	6	25–40	12	6700–7800	42
311 911 023B	250–300	6	35–45	12	7400–8100	42
003 911 023A	250–300	6	35–50	12	6400–7900	42

Solenoid Replacement

1. Remove the starter.
2. Remove the nut which secures the connector strip at the end of the solenoid.
3. Take out the two retaining screws on the mounting bracket and withdraw the solenoid after it has been unhooked from its actuating lever.
4. When replacing a defective solenoid with a new one, care should be taken to see that the distance (a) in the accompanying diagram is 19 mm when the magnet is drawn inside the solenoid.
5. Installation is the reverse of removal. In order to facilitate engagement of the actuating rod, the pinion should be pulled out as far as possible when inserting the solenoid.

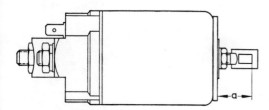

Solenoid adjustment (distance "a" is 19 mm)

When installing the solenoid make sure that the eye hooks on the actuating lever

BATTERY

The electrical system of the Volkswagen is a negative grounded type. All models except the 1975–77 Type 2 use a 45 amp battery. The 1975–77 Type 2 uses a 54 amp battery. On most VW models, the battery is located under the right-hand side of the rear seat. On Karmann Ghia, and Type 2 models, it is located in the engine compartment. On Type 4 models, the battery lives beneath the drivers seat. On Type 2 Campmobiles equipped with a refrigerator, an additional 45 amp battery is available.

Removal and Installation

1. Disconnect the battery cables. Note the position of the battery cables for installation. The small diameter battery post is the negative terminal. The negative battery cable is usually black.
2. Undo the battery holddown strap and lift the battery out of its holder.
CAUTION: *Do not tilt the battery as acid will spill out.*
3. Install the battery in its holder and replace the clamp. Reconnect the battery cables.

Engine Mechanical

The Volkswagen engine is a flat four cylinder design. This four cycle, overhead valve engine has two pairs of horizontally opposed cylinders. All rear engined VW models engines are air cooled.

The Type 1 and 2/1600 engine is known as an upright fan engine, that is, the engine cooling fan is mounted vertically on top of the engine and is driven by the generator shaft. The Type 2/1700, Type 2/1800, Type 2/2000, Type 3 and 4 engine, although of the same basic design, i.e. flat four, has the cooling fan driven by the crankshaft and is therefore mounted on the front of the engine. This type of engine is known as the suitcase engine.

Because it is air cooled, the VW engine is slightly noisier than a water cooled engine. This is due to the lack of water jacketing around the cylinders which provides sound deadening on water cooled engines. In addition, air cooled engines tend to run at somewhat higher temperatures, necessitating larger operating clearances to allow more room for the expansion of the parts. These larger operating clearances cause an increase in noise level over a water cooled engine.

The crankshaft of all Volkswagen engines is mounted in a two piece crankcase. The halves are machined to very close tolerances and line bored as a pair and, therefore, should always be replaced in pairs. When fitting them, it is necessary to coat only the mating surfaces with sealing compound and tighten

General Engine Specifications

Year	Engine Code	Displacement (cc)	Horsepower @ rpm	Torque @ rpm (ft lbs)	Bore x Stroke (in.)	Ratio Compression	Oil Pressure @ rpm (psi)
1970	B	1584	57/4400	82/3000	3.37 x 2.72	7.5 : 1②	42
1971–72	AE	1584	46/4000	72/2000	3.37 x 2.72	7.3 : 1	42
1971–74	AK	1584	46/4000	72/2000	3.37 x 2.72	7.3 : 1	42
1972–74	AH①, AM	1584	46/4000	72/2000	3.37 x 2.72	7.5 : 1	42
1972–73	CB	1679	63/4800	81/3200	3.54 x 2.60	7.3 : 1	42
1973	CD	1679	59/4200	82/3200	3.54 x 2.60	7.3 : 1	42
1970–73	U	1584	65/4600	87/2800	3.37 x 2.72	7.7 : 1	42
1972–73	X	1584	52/4000	77/2200	3.37 x 2.72	7.3 : 1	42
1971	W	1679	85/5000	99.5/3500	3.54 x 2.60	8.2 : 1	42
1972–74	EA	1679	76/4900	95/2700	3.54 x 2.60	8.2 : 1	42
1973	EB①	1679	69/5000	87/2700	3.54 x 2.60	7.3 : 1	42
1974	EC	1795	72/4800	91/3400	3.66 x 2.60	7.3 : 1	42
1974	AW	1795	65/4200	92/3000	3.66 x 2.60	7.3 : 1	42
1975–77	AJ	1584	48/4200	73.1/2800	3.37 x 2.72	7.3 : 1	42
1975	ED	1795	67/4400	90/2400	3.66 x 2.60	7.3 : 1	42
1976–77	GD	1970	67/4200	101/3000	3.70 x 2.80	7.3 : 1	42

① California only
② Type 2—7.7 : 1

Valve Specifications

Year	Vehicle Type Displacement	Seat Angle (deg) Intake	Seat Angle (deg) Exhaust	Face Angle (deg) Intake	Face Angle (deg) Exhaust	Valve Seat Width (in.) Intake	Valve Seat Width (in.) Exhaust	Spring Test Pressure (lbs @ in.)	Valve Guide Inside Dia (in.) Intake	Valve Guide Inside Dia (in.) Exhaust	Stem to Guide Clearance (in.) Intake	Stem to Guide Clearance (in.) Exhaust	Stem Diameter (in.) Intake	Stem Diameter (in.) Exhaust
1970–77	1, 2, 3 1600	45	45	44	45	0.05–0.10	0.05–0.10	117.7–134.8 @ 1.22	0.3150–0.3157	0.3150–② 0.3157	0.009–0.010	0.009–0.010	0.3125–0.3129	0.3113–① 0.3117
1971–77	2, 4 1700, 1800, 2000	30	45	30	45	0.07–0.08	0.078–0.098	168–186 @ 1.14	0.3150–0.3157	0.3534–0.3538	0.018	0.014	0.3125–0.3129	0.3507–0.3511

① On 1975 Type 1 models, exhaust valve stem diameter is 0.350–0.351 in.
② On 1975 Type 1 models, exhaust valve guide inside diameter is 0.353–0.354 in.

Crankshaft and Connecting Rod Specifications

(All measurements are given in inches)

Year	Type Engine	Crankshaft Main Bearing Journal Dia No. 1, 2, 3	Main Bearing Journal Dia No. 4	Main Bearing Oil Clearance No. 1, 3	Oil Clearance No. 2	Oil Clearance No. 4	Crankshaft End-Play	Thrust on No.	Connecting Rods Journal Dia	Oil Clearance	End-Play
1970–77	1, 2, 3 1600	2.1640–2.1648	1.5379–1.5748	0.0016–0.004	0.001–0.003	0.002–0.004	0.0027–0.005	1 at flywheel	2.1644–2.1653	0.0008–0.0027	0.004–0.016
1971–77	2, 4 1700, 1800, 2000	2.3609–2.3617	1.5739–1.5748	0.002–0.004	0.0012–0.0035	0.002–0.004	0.0027–0.005	1 at flywheel	2.1644–① 2.1653	0.0008–0.0027	0.004–0.016

① On 1976 Type 2/2000 models, connecting rod journal diameter is 1.968 in. (50 mm)

Piston and Ring Specifications
(All measurements in inches)

Year	Type, Engine Displacement	Piston Clearance	Ring Gap			Ring Side Clearance		
			Top Compression	Bottom Compression	Oil Control	Top Compression	Bottom Compression	Oil Control
1970–77	1, 2, 3 1600	0.0016–0.0023	0.012–0.018	0.012–0.018	0.010–0.016	0.0027–0.0039	0.002–0.0027	0.0011–0.0019
1971–77	2, 4 1700, 1800, 2000	0.0016–0.0023	0.014–0.021	0.012–0.022	0.010–0.016	0.0023–0.0035	0.0016–0.0027	0.0008–0.0019

Torque Specifications
(All readings in ft lbs)

Year	Type Vehicle	Cylinder Head Nuts	Rod Bearing Bolts	Generator Pulley	Crankshaft Pulley Bolt	Flywheel to Crankshaft Bolts	Fan to Hub	Hub to Crankshaft	Crankcase Half Nuts		Drive Plate to Crankshaft	Spark Plugs	Oil Strainer Cover
									Sealing Nuts	Non-Sealing Nuts			
1970–77	1	23	22–25	40–47	29–36	253	—	—	18	14	—	25	5
1970–71	2/1600	23	22–25	40–47	29–36	253	—	—	18	14	—	25	5
1972–77	2/1700, 1800, 2000	23	24	—	—	80	14	23	23	14	61	22	7–9
1970–73	3	23	22–25	40–47	94–108	253	—	—	18	14	—	25	5
1971–74	4	23	24	—	—	80	14	23	23	14	61	22	7–9

them down to the correct torque. No gasket is used.

The pistons and cylinders are identical on any particular engine. However, it is not possible to interchange pistons and cylinders between engines. The four pistons each have three rings, two compression rings and one oil scraper. Each piston is attached to its connecting rod with a fully floating piston pin.

Each pair of cylinders shares a detachable cylinder head made of light aluminum alloy casting. The cylinder head contains the valves for both cylinders. Shrunk-in valve guides and valve seats are used.

ENGINE REMOVAL AND INSTALLATION

TYPE 1, 2, AND 3

The Volkswagen engine is mounted on the transmission, which in turn is attached to the frame. In the Type 1 and 2 models, there are two bolts and two studs attaching the engine to the transmission. Type 3 engines have an extra mounting at the rear of the engine. Type 3 engines with automatic transmissions have front and rear engine and transmission mounts. At the front, the gearbox is supported by the rear tubular crossmember; at the rear, a crossmember is bolted to the crankcase and mounted to the body at ei-ther end.

When removing the engine from the car, it is recommended that the rear of the car be about 3 ft off the ground. Remove the engine by bringing it out from underneath the car. Proceed with the following steps to remove the engine.

1. Disconnect the battery ground cable.

2. Disconnect the generator wiring.

3. Remove the air cleaner. On Type 1 engines, remove the rear engine cover plate. On Type 2/1600 cc engines, remove the rear crossmember.

4. Disconnect the throttle cable and remove the electrical connections to the automatic choke, coil, electromagnetic cut-off jet, and the oil pressure sending unit.

5. Disconnect the fuel hose at the front engine cover plate and seal it to prevent leakage.

6. On Type 3 models, remove the oil dipstick and the rubber boot between the oil filter and the body.

7. Remove the cooling air intake bellows on Type 3 engines after loosening the clip that secures the unit.

8. On Type 3 models, remove the warm air hose.

9. On Type 3 fuel injected engines, remove and plug the pressure line to the left fuel distributor pipe and to the return line on the pressure regulator. Disconnect the fuel injection wiring harness.

10. Raise the car and support it with jackstands.

11. Remove the flexible air hoses between the engine and heat exchangers, disconnect the heater flap cables, unscrew the two lower engine mounting nuts, and slide a jack under the engine. On Type 2 engines, remove the two bolts from the rubber engine mounts located next to the muffler.

12. On Type 1 Automatic Stick Shift models, disconnect the control valve cable and the manifold vacuum hoses.

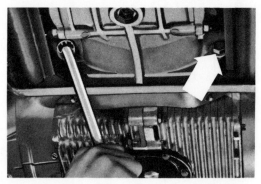

Removing lower engine mounting nuts

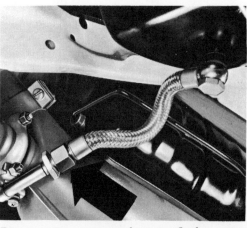

Disconnecting union nut between fluid reservoir and oil pump on Type 1 automatic stick shift models

Disconnect the ATF suction line and plug it. On Type 3 fully automatic transmission models, disconnect the vacuum hose and the kick-down cable.

13. On all Automatic Stick Shift and fully automatic models, remove the four bolts from the converter drive plate through the holes in the transmission case. After the engine is removed, hold the torque converter on the transmission input shaft by using a strap bolted to the bellhousing.

14. Raise the jack until it just contacts the engine and have an assistant hold the two upper mounting bolts so that the nuts can be removed from the bottom.

15. When the engine mounts are disconnected and there are no remaining cables or wires left to be disconnected, move the engine toward the back of the car so that the clutch or converter plate disengages from the transmission.

16. Lower the engine out of the car.

17. Installation is the reverse of the

Retaining torque converter with strap

Type 3 engine mounts

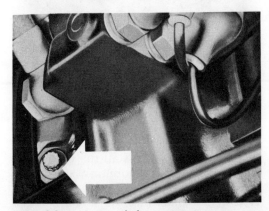
One of four 12 point bolts retaining torque converter to drive plate on Type 1 automatic stick shift models

Supporting transmission during engine installation

above. When the engine is lifted into position, it should be rotated using the generator pulley so that the clutch plate hub will engage the transmission shaft splines. Tighten the upper mounting

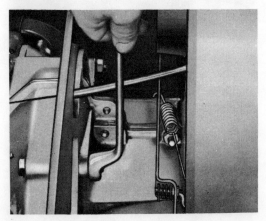
Removing upper engine mounting nuts

bolts first. Check the clutch, pressure plate, throwout bearing, and pilot bearing for wear.

On Type 3, synthetic washers are used to raise the engine about 3 mm when the rear engine mounting is attached and tightened. Use only enough washers in the rear mount so that the engine is lifted no more than 3 mm. Care should be used when installing the rear intake housing bellows of the Type 3 engine.

TYPE 4

1. Disconnect the battery.
2. Remove the cooling air bellows, warm air hoses, cooling air intake duct, and air cleaner. On sedans, remove the cooling air fan. On station wagons, remove the dipstick tube rubber boot and the dipstick.
3. Disconnect the fuel injection wiring.
4. Disconnect the coil wires and remove the coil and its bracket.
5. Disconnect the oil pressure switch and the alternator wiring.
6. Disconnect the vacuum hose for the intake air distributor.
7. Disconnect the accelerator cable.
8. Working through the access hole at the upper right corner of the flywheel housing, remove the three screws which secure the torque converter to the drive plate. Remove the ATF oil dipstick and the rubber boot.
9. Remove the two upper engine mounting bolts.
10. Jack up the car and, working beneath the car, remove the muffler shield and the heat exchanger.

11. Disconnect the starter wiring.
12. Remove the heater booster exhaust pipe.
13. Remove the two lower engine mounting nuts.
14. Jack up the engine slightly and remove the four engine carrier screws.

Engine carrier bolt location upon installation of engine—Type 4

NOTE: *Do not loosen the mountings on the body or the engine-transmission assembly will have to be recentralized in the chassis.*

15. Remove the engine from the car.
16. Reverse the removal procedures to install the engine. Install the engine on the lower engine mounting studs and then locate the engine in the engine carrier. When installing the engine in the

Access hole for torque converter bolts—Type 4

Checking that engine carrier is vertical and parallel to fan housing—Type 4

carrier, lift the engine up so that the four screws are at the top of the elongated holes and tighten them in this position. If it is necessary to raise or lower the engine for adjustment purposes, use the threaded shaft. After the engine is installed, make sure that the rubber buffer is centered in the rear axle carrier. Make sure that the engine carrier is vertical and parallel to the engine fan housing. Readjust it if necessary by moving the brackets on the side members.

CYLINDER HEAD

Removal and Installation

In order to remove the cylinder head from either pair of cylinders, it is necessary to lower the engine.

1. Remove the valve cover and gasket. Remove the rocker arm assembly. Unbolt the intake manifold from the cylinder head. The cylinder head is held in place by eight studs. Since the cylinder head also holds the cylinders in place in the

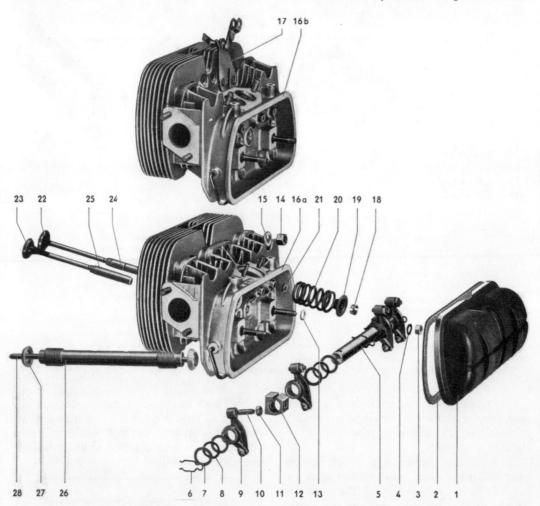

Cylinder head details—Types 1/1600, 2/1600, 3/1600

1. Cylinder head cover	11. Nut	20. Valve spring
2. Gasket	12. Support	21. Oil deflector ring
3. Nut	13. Stud seal	22. Intake valve
4. Spring washer	14. Nut	23. Exhaust valve
5. Rocker shaft	15. Washer	24. Intake valve guide
6. Clip	16a. Type 1, Type 2/1600 cylinder head	25. Exhaust valve guide
7. Thrust washer	16b. Type 3 cylinder head	26. Pushrod tube
8. Spring washer	17. Thermostat link	27. Sealing ring
9. Rocker arm	18. Valve cotter	28. Pushrod
10. Adjusting screw	19. Spring cap	

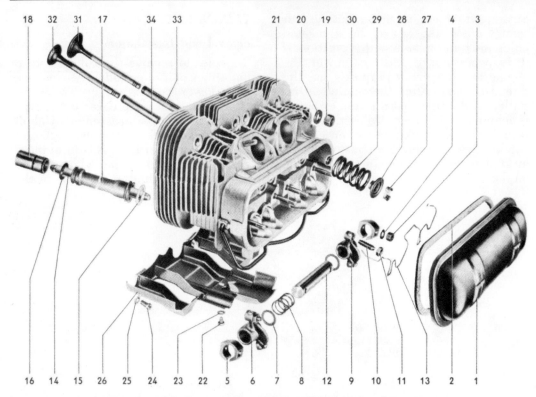

Cylinder head details—Types 2/1700, 2/1800, 2/2000 and Type 4

1. Cylinder head cover	13. Pushrod tube retaining wire	25. Washer
2. Cover gasket	14. Pushrods	26. Deflector plate
3. Nut	15. White sealing ring	27. Valve cotter
4. Lockwasher	16. Black sealing ring	28. Spring cap
5. Support	17. Pushrod tube	29. Valve spring
6. Exhaust rocker arm	18. Cam follower	30. Oil deflector ring
7. Thrust washer	19. Nut	31. Intake valve
8. Spring	20. Washer	32. Exhaust valve
9. Intake rocker arm	21. Cylinder head	33. Intake valve guide
10. Adjusting screw	22. Cheese head screw	34. Exhaust valve guide
11. Nut	23. Washer	
12. Rocker shaft	24. Cheese head screw	

VW engine, and the cylinders are not going to be removed, it will be necessary to hold the cylinders in place after the head is removed.

2. After the rocker arm cover, rocker arm retaining nuts, and rocker arm assembly have been removed, the cylinder head nuts can be removed and the cylinder head lifted off.

3. When reinstalling the cylinder head, the head should be checked for cracks both in the combustion chamber and in the intake and exhaust ports. Cracked heads must be replaced.

4. Spark plug threads should be checked. New seals should be used on the pushrod tube ends and they should be checked for proper seating.

5. The pushrod tubes should be turned so that the seam faces upward. In order to ensure perfect sealing, used tubes should be stretched slightly before they are reinstalled.

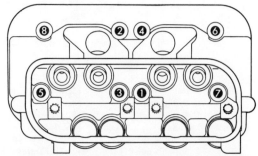

Cylinder head torque sequence—1700 cc, 1800 cc, 2000 cc

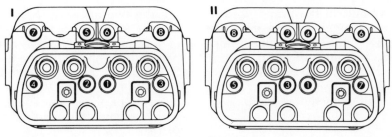

For 1600 cc engines, the cylinder head nuts should initially be tightened to 7 ft lbs in order I, then tightened to the recommended torque in order II

6. Install the cylinder head. Using new rocker shaft stud seals, install the pushrods and rocker shaft assembly.

NOTE: *Pay careful attention to the orientation of the shaft as described in the "Rocker Shaft" section.*

7. Torque the cylinder head in three stages. Adjust the valve clearance. Using a new gasket, install the rocker cover. It may be necessary to readjust the valves after the engine has been run a few minutes and allowed to cool.

Valve Seats

On all air-cooled VW engines, the valve seats are shrunk-fit into the cylinder head. This usually involves freezing the seat with liquid nitrogen or some other refrigerant to about 200° F below zero, and heating up the cylinder head to approximately 400° F. Due to the extreme temperatures required to shrink-fit these items, and because of the extra care needed when working with metals at these extreme temperatures, it is advised that this operation be referred to an experienced repair shop.

Cylinder Head Overhaul and Valve Guide Replacement

See the "Engine Rebuilding" section at the end of this chapter.

ROCKER SHAFTS

Rocker Shaft Removal and Installation

Before the valve rocker assembly can be reached, it is necessary to lever off the clip that retains the valve cover and then remove the valve cover. Remove the rocker arm retaining nuts, the rocker arm shaft, and the rocker arms. Remove the stud seals.

On Types 1, 2/1600, and 3, install the rocker shaft with the chamfer out and the slots up

On Types 2/1700, 2/1800, 2/2000, and 4, install the rocker shaft with the chamfer out and the slots down

Before installing the rocker arm mechanism, be sure that the parts are as clean as possible. Install new stud seals. On Type 1, 2/1600, and 3, install the rocker shaft assembly with the chamfered edges of the rocker shaft supports pointing outward and the slots pointing upward. On Type 4 and Type 2/1700, 2/1800 and 2/2000 models, the chamfered edges must point outward and the slots must face downward. The pushrod tube retaining wire must engage the slots in the rocker arm shaft supports as well as the grooves in the pushrod tubes. Tighten the retaining nuts to the proper torque. Use only the copper colored nuts that were supplied with the engine. Make sure that the ball ends of the push rods are centered in the sockets of the rocker arms. Adjust the valve clearance. Install the valve cover using a new gasket.

INTAKE MANIFOLD

Intake Manifold Removal and Installation

SINGLE CARBURETOR ENGINES

1. Disconnect the battery.
2. Disconnect the generator wiring.
3. Remove the generator. It will be necessary to loosen the fan housing and tilt it back to gain clearance to remove the generator.
4. Disconnect the choke and the accelerator cable.
5. On some models it will be necessary to remove the carburetor from the manifold.
6. Unbolt the manifold from the cylinder head and remove the manifold from the engine.
7. Reverse the above to install. Always use new gaskets.

TWIN CARBURETOR ENGINES

1. Remove the carburetors as outlined in Chapter four.
2. Disconnect the tubes from the central idling system mixture distributor.
3. Disconnect all vacuum lines. Label them for purposes of installation.
4. Remove the nuts and bolts retaining the manifolds to the cylinder heads. Carefully lift off each manifold.
5. Reverse the above procedure to install, taking care to carefully clean all mating surfaces to the carburetors and cylinder heads. Always use new gaskets.

Inlet Manifold Removal and Installation

FUEL INJECTION ENGINES

1. Remove the air cleaner.
2. Remove the pressure switch which is mounted under the right pair of intake manifold pipes. Disconnect the injector wiring.
3. Remove the fuel injectors by remov-

ing the two nuts which secure them in place. On Type 3, do not separate the pair of injectors; they can be removed as a pair and must be left in the injector plate. See Step 7 for proper injector installation.

4. After removing the intake manifold outer cover plate, remove the two screws which secure the manifold inner cover plate.
5. The manifold may be removed by removing the two nuts and washers which hold the manifold flange to the cylinder head.
6. Installation is the reverse of the above. The inner manifold cover should be installed first, but leave the cover loose until the outer cover and manifold are in place. Always use new gaskets. See the following step for proper injector installation.
7. Connect the fuel hoses to the injectors, if removed, after assembling the injectors with the injector retainer plate in place. Make sure that the sleeves are in place on the injector securing studs. Carefully slip the injectors into the manifold and install the securing nuts. Never force the injectors in or out of the manifold. Reconnect the injector wiring.

INTAKE AIR DISTRIBUTOR

Intake Air Distributor Removal and Installation

FUEL INJECTED ENGINES

The intake air distributor is located at the center of the engine at the junction of the intake manifold pipes.

NOTE: *It is not necessary to remove the distributor if only the manifold pipes are to be removed.*

1. Remove the air cleaner and pressure switch which are located under the right pair of manifold pipes.
2. Push the four rubber hoses onto the intake manifold pipes.
3. Remove the accelerator cable and the thottle valve switch.
4. Disconnect the accelerator cable.
5. Disconnect the vacuum hoses leading to the ignition distributor and the pressure sensor and disconnect the hose running to the auxiliary air regulator.
6. Remove those bolts under the air distributor which secure the air distributor to the crankcase and remove the air distributor.

7. Installation is the reverse of removal.

MUFFLERS, TAILPIPES, HEAT EXCHANGERS

Removal and Installation

MUFFLER, TYPE 1 AND 2/1600

1. Working under the hood, disconnect the pre-heater hoses.

2. Remove the pre-heater pipe protection plate on each side of the engine. The plates are secured by three screws.

3. Remove the crankshaft pulley cover plate.

4. Remove the rear engine cover plate from the engine compartment. It is held in place by screws at the center, right, and left sides.

5. Remove the four intake manifold

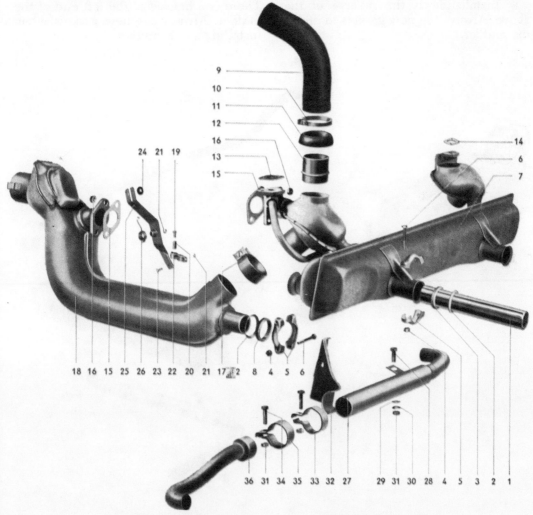

Exploded view of exhaust system—1970–74 Type 1, 1970–71 2/1600

1. Tail pipe	13. Gasket	25. Heater flap lever
2. Retaining ring	14. Gasket	26. Return spring
3. Seal	15. Gasket	27. Damper pipe
4. Nut	16. Self-locking nut	28. Bolt
5. Clamp	17. Clamp	29. Washer
6. Bolt	18. Heat exchanger	30. Lockwasher
7. Muffler	19. Bolt	31. Bolt
8. Seal	20. Pin	32. Damper pipe bracket
9. Heater hose	21. Circlip	33. Bracket clamp
10. Hose clamp	22. Link	34. Bolt
11. Rubber grommet	23. Pin	35. Clamp
12. Connecting pipe	24. Pin	36. Tailpipe

preheat pipe bolts. There are two bolts on each side of the engine.

6. Disconnect the warm air channel clamps at the left and right side of the engine.

7. Disconnect the heat exchanger clamps at the left and right side of the engine.

8. Remove the muffler from the engine.

9. Installation is the reverse of the above. Always use new gaskets to install the muffler.

MUFFLER, TYPE 3

The muffler is secured to the heat exchangers with clamps and, on some models, to the body with bolts at the top and at the ends.

MUFFLER, TYPE 4, 2/1700, 2/1800, 2/2000

The muffler is secured to the left and right heat exchangers by three bolts. There is a bracket at the left end of the muffler. Always use new gaskets when installing a new muffler.

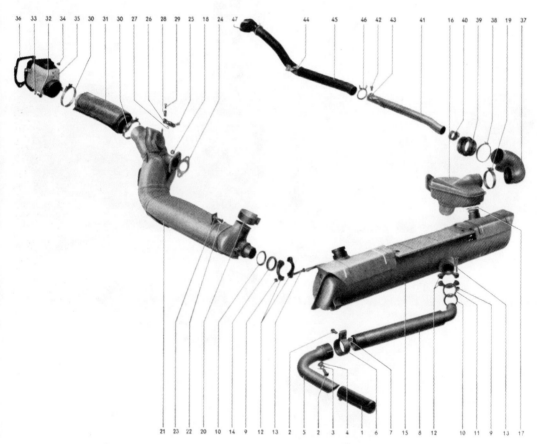

Exploded view of exhaust system—Type 3

1. Tail pipe trim	13. Hex bolt	25. Link pin	37. Elbow
2. Hex bolt	14. Seal	26. Link	38. Clip
3. Lockwasher	15. Muffler	27. C-washer	39. Connecting hose
4. Washer	16. Heat exchanger, rear	28. Pin	40. Clip
5. Tail pipe	17. Seal	29. Hex bolt	41. Fresh air pipe
6. Clamp	18. Nut, self-locking	30. Clip	42. Screw
7. Hex nut	19. Clamp	31. Metal hose	43. Washer
8. Damper pipe	20. Clip	32. Hex bolt	44. Hose support
9. Nut, self-locking	21. Heat exchanger	33. Lockwasher	45. Fresh air hose
10. Retaining ring	22. Hex bolt	34. Screw	46. Clip
11. Seal	23. Washer	35. Warm air mixer housing	47. Fresh air duct elbow
12. Clamp	24. Flange gasket	36. Seal	

HEAT EXCHANGERS, TYPE 1, 2/1600, AND 3

1. Disconnect the air tube at the outlet end of the exchanger.
2. Remove the clamp which secures the muffler to the exchanger.
3. Loosen the clamp which secures the exchanger to the heater hose connection at the muffler.
4. Remove the two nuts which secure the exchanger to the forward end of the cylinder head.
5. Remove the heater flap control wire.
6. Reverse the above to install. Always use new gaskets.

HEAT EXCHANGERS, TYPE 4, 2/1700, 2/1800, 2/2000

1. Disconnect the air hose at the outlet of each exchanger.
2. Disconnect the warm air tube at the outside end of the exchanger.
3. Disconnect the three bolts which secure each exchanger to the muffler.
4. Remove the four nuts, two at each exhaust port, which secure the exchanger to the cylinder head.
5. Installation is the reverse of the above. Always use new gaskets.

TAILPIPES, TYPE 1 AND 2/1600

Loosen the clamps on the tailpipes and apply penetrating oil. Work the pipe side-to-side while trying to pull the tailpipe out of the muffler.

NOTE: *Is it often difficult to remove the tailpipes without damaging them.*

TAILPIPE AND RESONATOR, TYPE 3

Loosen the clamp at the resonator-to-muffler connection. Remove the bolt at the bend of the tailpipie and remove the resonator and tailpipe assembly. To remove the tailpipe from the resonator, loosen the clamp which secures the tailpipe to the resonator and work them apart.

TAILPIPE, TYPE 4, 2/1700, 2/1800, 2/2000

Remove the bolt which secures the pipe to the muffler. Remove the bolt which secures the pipe to the body and remove the pipe.

PISTONS AND CYLINDERS

Pistons and cylinders are matched according to their size. When replacing pistons and cylinders, make sure that they are properly sized.

NOTE: *See the "Engine Rebuilding" section for cylinder refinishing.*

Cylinder Removal and Installation

1. Remove the engine. Remove the cylinder head, pushrod tubes, and the deflector plate.
2. Slide the cylinder out of its groove in the crankcase and off of the piston. Matchmark the cylinders for reassembly. The cylinders must be returned to their original bore in the crankcase. If a cylinder is to be replaced, it must be replaced with a matching piston.

Matchmarking pistons

3. Cylinders should be checked for wear and, if necessary, replaced with another matched cylinder and piston assembly of the same size.
4. Check the cylinder seating surface on the crankcase, cylinder shoulder, and gasket, for cleanliness and deep scores. When reinstalling the cylinders, a new gasket, if required, should be used between each cylinder and the crankcase.
5. The piston, as well as the piston rings and pin must be oiled before reassembly.
6. Be sure that the ring gaps are of the correct dimension. Stagger the ring gaps around the piston, but make sure that the oil ring gap is positioned up when the pistons are in position on the connecting rods.

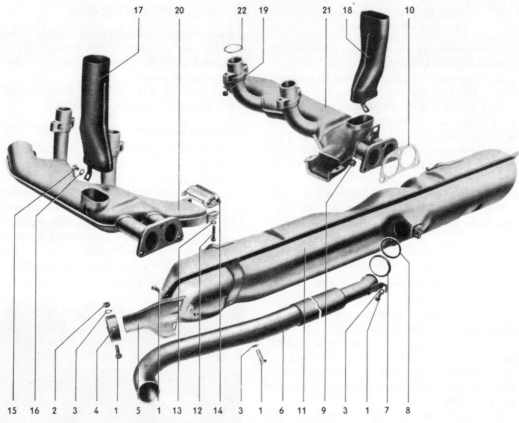

Exploded view of exhaust system—Type 2/1700, Type 2/1800, Type 2/2000, and Type 4

1. Screw
2. Nut
3. Spring washer
4. Clip
5. Bracket for tailpipe
6. Damper pipe
7. Seal
8. Sealing ring
9. Locknut
10. Gasket
11. Muffler
12. Screw
13. Spring washer
14. Heat exchanger cover
15. Screw
16. Spring washer
17. Warm air fan left connection
18. Warm air fan right connection
19. Locknut
20. Left heat exchanger
21. Right heat exchanger
22. Sealing rings

Installing a cylinder

7. Compress the rings with a ring compressor, oil the cylinder wall, and slide the cylinder onto the piston. Make sure that the cylinder base gasket is in place.

8. Install the deflector plates.

9. Install the pushrod tubes using new gaskets. Install the pushrods. Make sure that the seam in the pushrod tube is facing upward.

10. Install the cylinder head.

Piston Removal and Installation

NOTE: *See the "Engine Rebuilding" section for piston ring procedures.*

1. Remove the engine. Remove the cylinder head and, after matchmarking the cylinders, remove the cylinders.

2. Matchmark the pistons to indicate the cylinder number and which side points toward the clutch.

3. Remove the circlips which retain the piston pin.

4. Heat the piston to 176 F. To heat the piston, boil a clean rag in water and wrap it around the piston. Remove the piston pin after the piston has been heated.

5. Remove the piston from the connecting rod.

6. Before installing the pistons, they should first be cleaned and checked for wear. Remove the old rings. Clean the ring grooves using a groove cleaner or a broken piece of ring. Clean the piston with solvent but do not use a wire brush or sand paper. Check for any cracks or scuff marks. Check the piston diameter with a micrometer and compare the readings to the specifications. If the running clearance between the piston and cylinder wall is 0.008 in. (0.2 mm) or greater, the cylinder and piston should be replaced by a set of the same size grading. If the cylinder shows no sign of excessive wear or damage, it is permissible to install a new piston and rings of the appropriate size.

7. Place each ring in turn in its cylinder bore and check the piston ring end-gap. If the gap is too large, replace the ring. If the gap is too narrow, file the end of the ring until the proper gap is obtained.

8. Insert the rings on the piston and check the ring side clearance. If the clearance is too large, replace the piston. Install the rings with the marking "Oben" or "Top" pointing upward.

Checking piston ring side clearance

9. If new rings are installed in a used piston, the ring ridge at the top of the cylinder bore must be removed with a ridge reamer.

10. Install the piston and piston pin on the connecting rod from which it originally came. Make sure that the piston is facing the proper direction.

11. Install the cylinders and the cylinder heads.

CRANKCASE

Disassembly and Assembly

1. Remove the engine.

2. Remove the cylinder heads, cylinders, and pistons.

3. Remove the oil strainer, oil pressure switch, and the crankcase nuts. Remove the flywheel and oil pump. The flywheel is held in place by the bolt, (Type 4 and 1972–77 Type 2 have five bolts), at the center of the flywheel. Matchmark the flywheel so that it can be replaced in the same position.

4. Keep the cam followers in the right crankcase half in position by using a retaining spring.

Checking piston ring end-gap

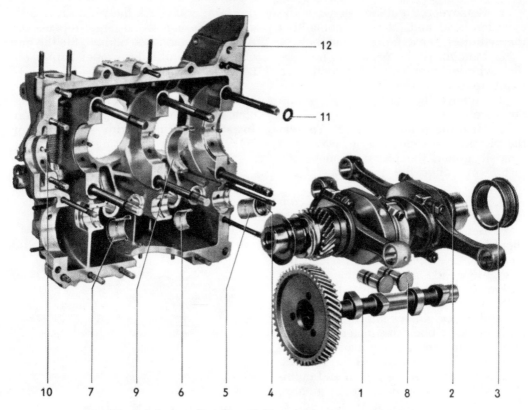

Exploded view of crankcase half assembly—Type 1, 2/1600, 3

1. Camshaft
2. Crankshaft and connecting rods
3. Main bearing No. 1
4. Camshaft bore end cap
5 Camshaft No. 1 bearing shell
6. Camshaft No. 2 bearing shell
7. Left shell for camshaft No. 3 bearing (with thrust shoulder)

8 Cam follower
9. Crankshaft No. 2 bearing shell
10. Crankshaft bearing dowel pin
11. Crankcase joint seal
12. Left crankcase half

5. Clean the sludge off of the crankcase and locate *all* of the crankcase retaining nuts. Do not try to separate the halves until you are sure you have removed *all* of the nuts. Use a rubber hammer to break the seal between the crankcase halves.

CAUTION: *Never insert sharp metal tools, wedges, or any prying device between the crankcase halves. This will ruin the gasket surface and cause serious oil leakage.*

6. After the seal between the crankcase halves is broken, remove the right hand crankcase half, the crankshaft oil seal and the camshaft end plug. The camshaft and crankshaft can now be lifted out of the crankcase half.

7. Remove the cam followers, bearing shells, and the oil pressure relief valve.

8. Before starting reassembly, check the crankcase for any damage or cracks.

9. Flush and blow out all ducts and oil passages. Check the studs for tightness. If the tapped holes are worn install a Heli-Coil®.

10. Install the crankshaft bearing dowel pins and bearing shells for the crankshaft and camshaft. Make sure that the bearing shells with thrust flanges are installed in the proper journal.

11. Install the crankshaft and camshaft after the bearings have been well lubricated. When installing the camshaft and crankshaft, make sure that the timing marks on the timing gears are aligned.

12. Install the oil pressure relief valve.

Exploded view of crankcase half assembly—Type 2/1700, 2/1800, 2/2000, and Type 4

1. Camshaft
2. Crankshaft and connecting rod assembly
3. Main bearing No. 1
4. Main bearing No. 4
5. End cap for camshaft bore
6. Camshaft No. 1 bearing shell
7. No. 2 camshaft bearing
8. No. 3 camshaft bearing with shoulder for thrust
9. Crankshaft bearing dowel pin
10. No. 2 crankshaft bearing half
11. Left crankcase half

13. Oil and install the cam followers. NOTE: *To keep them from falling out during assembly, liberally coat them with white grease.*

14. Install the camshaft end plug using sealing compound.

15. Install the thrust washers and crankshaft oil seal. The oil seal must rest squarely on the bottom of its recess in the crankcase. The thrust washers at the flywheel end of the crankshaft are shims used to set the crankshaft end-play.

16. Spread a thin film of sealing compound on the crankcase joining faces and place the two halves together. Torque the nuts in several stages. Tighten the 8 mm nut located next to the 12 mm stud of the No. 1 crankshaft bearing first. As the

Check dowel pins for tightness

Tighten this nut first on Type 1, 2/1600, and 3 models

crankcase halves are being torqued, continually check the crankshaft for ease of rotation.

17. Crankshaft end-play is checked when the flywheel is installed. It is adjusted by varying the number of thickness of the shims located behind the flywheel. Measure the end-play with a dial indicator mounted against the flywheel, and attached firmly to the crankcase.

CAMSHAFT AND TIMING GEARS

Removal and installation

Removal of the camshaft requires splitting the crankcases. The camshaft and its bearing shells are then removed from the crankcase halves. Before rein-

stalling the camshaft, it should be checked for wear on the lobe surfaces and on the bearing surfaces. In addition, the riveted joint between the camshaft timing gear and the camshaft should be checked for tightness. The camshaft should be checked for a maximum runout of 0.0008 in. The timing gear should be checked for the correct tooth contact and for wear. If the camshaft bearing shells are worn or damaged, new shells should be fitted. The camshaft bearing shells should be installed with the tabs engaging the notches in the crankcase. It is usually a good idea to replace the bearing shells under any circumstances. Before installing the camshaft, the bearing journals and cam lobes should be generously coated with oil. When the camshaft is installed, care should be taken to ensure that the timing gear tooth marked (O) is located between the two teeth of the crankshaft timing gear marked with a center punch. The camshaft end-play is measured at the No. 3 bearing. End-play is 0.0015–0.005 in. (0.04–0.12 mm) and the wear limit is 0.006 in. (0.16 mm).

Aligning marks on timing gears

CRANKSHAFT

Crankshaft Pulley Removal and Installation

On the Type 1 and 2/1600, the crankshaft pulley can be removed while the engine is still in the car. However, in this instance it is necessary for the rear cover plate of the engine to be removed. Remove the cover plate after taking out the screws in the cover plate below the crankshaft pulley. Remove the fan belt and the crankshaft pulley securing screw. Using a puller, remove the crankshaft pulley. The crankshaft pulley should be checked for proper seating and belt contact. The oil return thread should be cleaned and lubricated with oil. The crankshaft pulley should be installed in the reverse sequence. Check for oil leaks after installing the pulley.

On the Type 3, the crankshaft pulley can be removed only when the engine is out of the car and the muffler, generator, and cooling air intake housing are removed. After these parts have been removed, take out the plastic cap in the pulley. Remove the crankshaft pulley retaining bolt and remove the pulley.

Type 4 and Type 2/1700, 2/1800 and 2/2000, removal is the same as the Type 3. However, the pulley is secured by three socket head screws and a self locking nut.

Installation for Type 2/1700, 2/1800, 2/2000, 3 and 4 engines is the reverse of removal. When installing, use a new paper gasket between the fan and the crankshaft pulley. If shims are used, do not forget them. Don't use more than two shims. When inserting the pulley, make sure that the pin engages the hole in the fan. Ensure that the clearance between the generator belt and the intake housing is at least 4 mm and that the belt is parallel to the housing.

Type 2/1700, 2/1800, 2/2000, and Type 4 engine fan bolts

Flywheel Removal and Installation

NOTE: *In order to remove the flywheel, the crankshaft will have to be prevented from turning. This may be accomplished on Type 1, 2/1600 and*

Type 3 models by using a 3 or 4 foot length of angle iron or thick stock sheet steel, such as an old fence post. Drill out two holes in the metal bar that correspond to two of the pressure plate retaining bolt holes. The metal bar is installed as per the accompanying illustration.

TYPE 1, 2/1600, AND 3

The flywheel is attached to the crankshaft with a gland nut and is located by four dowel pins. An oil seal is recessed in the crankcase casting at No. 1 main bearing. A needle bearing, which supports the main driveshaft, is located in the gland nut. Prior to removing the flywheel, it is necessary to remove the clutch pressure plate and the clutch disc. Loosen the gland nut and remove it, using a 36 mm special wrench. Before removing the flywheel, matchmark the flywheel and the crankshaft.

Installation is the reverse of removal. Before installing the flywheel, check the flywheel teeth for any wear or damage. Check the dowel pins for correct fit in the crankshaft and in the flywheel. Adjust the crankshaft end-play and check the needle bearing in the gland nut for wear.

TYPE 2/1700, 2/1800, 2/2000 AND 4

Removal and installation is similar to the Type 1, 2/1600, and 3 except that the flywheel is secured to the crankshaft by five socket head screws.

Crankshaft Oil Seal (Flywheel End) Replacement

This seal is removed after removing the flywheel. After the flywheel is removed, inspect the surface on the flywheel joining flange where the seal makes contact. If there is a deep groove or any other damage, the flywheel must be replaced. Remove the oil seal by prying it out of its bore. Before installing a new seal, clean the crankcase oil seal recess and coat it thinly with a sealing compound. Be sure that the seal rests squarely on the bottom of its recess. Make sure that the correct side of the seal is facing outward, that is, the lip of the seal should be facing the inside of the crankcase. Reinstall the flywheel after

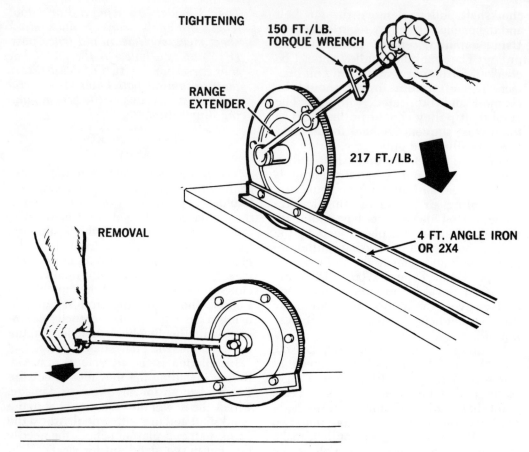

Removing/installing 1600 cc engine flywheel using special bar

coating the oil seal contact surface with oil.

NOTE: *Be careful not to damage the seal when sliding the flywheel into place.*

Removing burrs from rear oil seal housing in crankcase to ensure leak-free fit of oil seal

Crankshaft Removal and Installation

NOTE: *See the "Engine Rebuilding" section for crankshaft refinishing procedures.*

Removal of the crankshaft requires splitting the crankcase. After the crankcase is opened, the crankshaft can then be lifted out.

The crankshaft bearings are held in place by dowel pins. These pins must be checked for tightness.

When installing the bearings, make sure that the oil holes in the shells are properly aligned. Be sure that the bearing shells are seated properly on their dowel pins. Bearing shells are available in three undersizes. Measure the crankshaft bearing journals to determine the proper bearing size. Place one half of the No. 2 crankshaft bearing in the crankcase. Slide the No. 1 bearing on the crankshaft so that the dowel pin hole is toward the flywheel and the oil groove faces toward the fan. The No. 3 bearing is installed with the dowel pin hole facing toward the crankshaft web.

To remove the No. 3 main bearing, remove the distributor gear circlip and the distributor drive gear. Mild heat (176° F) must be applied to remove the gear. Next slide the spacer off of the crankshaft. The crankshaft timing gear should now be pressed off the crankshaft after mild heating. When the timing gear is reinstalled, the chamfer must face towards the No. 3 bearing. The No. 3 bearing can then be replaced. When removing and installing the gears on the crankshaft, be careful not to damage the No. 4 bearing journal.

When all of the crankshaft bearings are in place, lift the crankshaft and the connecting rod assembly into the crankcase and align the valve timing marks.

Install the crankcase half and reassemble the engine.

CONNECTING RODS

Connecting Rod Removal and Installation

NOTE: *See the "Engine Rebuilding" section for additional information.*

After splitting the crankcase, remove the crankshaft and the connecting rod assembly. Remove the connecting rods, clamping bolts, and the connecting rod caps. Inspect the piston pin bushing. With a new bushing, the correct clearance is indicated by a light finger push fit

Staking the connecting rod bolt

of the pin at room temperature. Reinsert the new connecting rod bearings after all parts have been thoroughly cleaned. Assemble the connecting rods on the crankshaft, making sure that the rods are oriented properly on the crankshaft. The identification numbers stamped on the connecting rods and connecting rod caps must be on the same side. Note that the marks on the connecting rods are pointing upward, while the rods are pointing toward their respective cylinders. Lubricate the bearing shells before installing them.

Tapping the connecting rod cap to relieve pretension

Forge marks on connecting rods must face up

Measuring the connecting rod side clearance

Tighten the connecting rod bolts to the specified torque. A slight pre-tension between the bearing halves, which is likely to occur when tightening the connecting rod bolts, can be eliminated by gently striking the side of the bearing cap with a hammer. Do not install the connecting rod in the engine unless it swings freely on its journal. Using a peening chisel, secure the connecting rod bolts in place.

Failure to swing freely on the journal may be caused by improper side clearance, improper bearing clearance or failure to lubricate the rod before assembly.

Engine Lubrication

Oil Strainer Removal and Installation

The oil strainer can be easily removed by removing the retaining nuts, washers, oil strainer plate, strainer, and gaskets. The Type 2/1700, 2/1800, 2/2000 and Type 4 strainer is secured by a single bolt at the center of the strainer. Once taken out, the strainer must be thoroughly cleaned and all traces of old gaskets removed prior to fitting new ones. The suc-

tion pipe should be checked for tightness and proper position. When the strainer is installed, be sure that the suction pipe is correctly seated in the strainer. If necessary, the strainer may be bent slightly. The measurement from the strainer flange to the tip of the suction pipe should be 10 mm. The measurement from the flange to the bottom of the strainer should be 6 mm. The cap nuts on Types 1, 2/1600, and 3 must not be overtightened. The Type 4 and Type 2/1700, 2/1800, 2/2000 have a spin-off replaceable oil filter as well as the strainer in the crankcase. The oil filter is located at the left rear corner of the engine.

Oil Cooler Removal and Installation

The Type 1 and 2/1600 oil cooler is located under the engine cooling fan housing at the left side of the engine. The Type 3 cooler is located at the same position but is mounted horizontally. The Type 4 and Type 2/1700, 2/1800, 2/2000 coolers are mounted near the oil filter, at the left corner of the engine.

The oil cooler may be removed without taking the engine out of the car. On Types 1 and 2/1600, the engine fan housing must be removed. On the Type 3, the cooler is accessible through the left-hand cylinder cover plate. The Type 4 and Type 2/1700, 2/1800, 2/2000 cooler is accessible through the left side engine cowling, working either in the engine compartment or from underneath the car.

The oil cooler can be removed after the

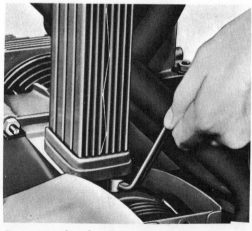

Removing oil cooler mounting using ring wrench—Type 1, 2/1600

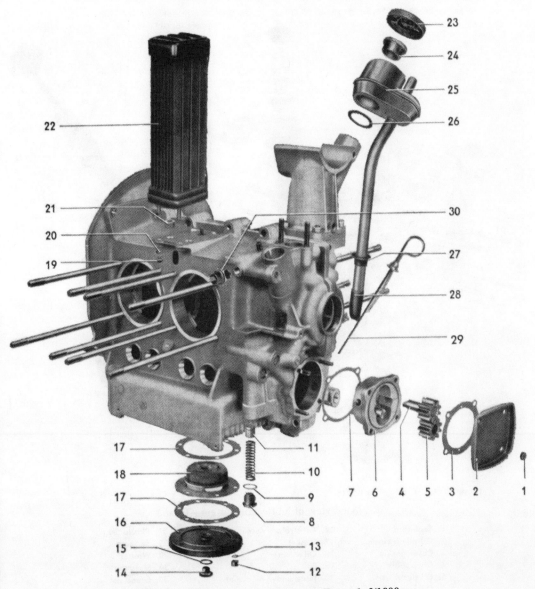

Exploded view of lubrication system—Types 1, 2/1600

1. Sealing nut	11. Relief valve piston	21. Oil cooler seal
2. Oil pump cover	12. Cap nut	22. Oil cooler
3. Pump cover gasket	13. Seal	23. Oil filler neck cap
4. Driveshaft	14. Oil drain plug	24. Breather gland nut
5. Oil pump gear	15. Seal	25. Oil filler and breather assembly
6. Oil pump housing	16. Oil strainer cover	26. Seal
7. Housing gasket	17. Gasket	27. Grommet
8. Plug	18. Oil strainer	28. Breather rubber valve
9. Seal	19. Nut	29. Dipstick
10. Spring	20. Lockwasher	30. Oil pressure switch

three retaining nuts have been taken off. The gaskets should be removed along with the cooler and replaced with new gaskets. If the cooler is leaking, check the oil pressure relief valve. The studs and bracket on the cooler should be checked for tightness. Make certain that the hollow ribs of the cooler do not touch one another. The cooler must not be clogged with dirt. Clean the contact surfaces on the crankcase, install new gaskets, and attach the oil cooler. Types 3 and 4, 2/1700,

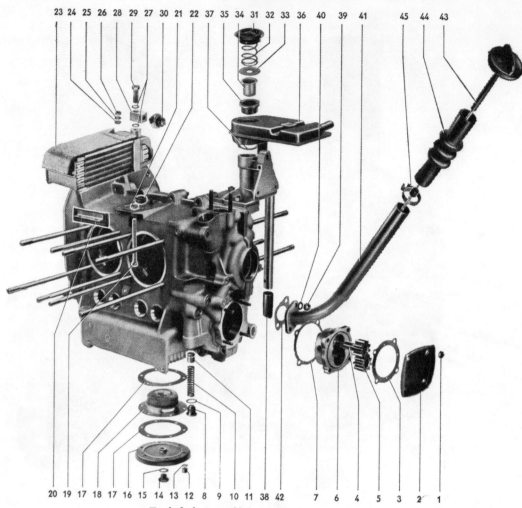

Exploded view of lubrication system—Type 3

1. Sealing nut	16. Oil strainer cover	31. Plastic plug
2. Oil pump cover	17. Gasket	32. Spring
3. Cover gasket	18. Oil strainer	33. Washer
4. Drive shaft	19. Bolt	34. Sleeve
5. Oil pump gear	20. Plate under oil cooler	35. Gland nut
6. Oil pump housing	21. Spacer	36. Oil breather
7. Housing gasket	22. Oil cooler seal	37. Seal
8. Plug	23. Oil cooler	38. Valve for cleaner
9. Seal	24. Washer	39. Nut
10. Spring	25. Lockwasher	40. Lockwasher
11. Relief valve piston	26. Nut	41. Oil filler neck
12. Cap nut	27. Seal	42. Gasket
13. Seal	28. Oil pressure switch connection	43. Dipstick
14. Oil drain plug	29. Gland nut for connection	44. Boot
15. Seal	30. Oil pressure switch	45. Clamp

2/1800 and 2/2000 have a spacer ring between the crankcase and the cooler at each securing screw. If these rings are omitted, the seals may be squeezed too tightly, resulting in oil stoppage and resultant engine damage. Use double retaining nuts and Loctite® on the cooler studs.

Oil Pump Removal and Installation

On Types 1 and 2/1600, the pump can be removed while the engine is in the car, but it is first necessary to remove the cover plate, the crankshaft pulley, and the cover plate under the pulley. On

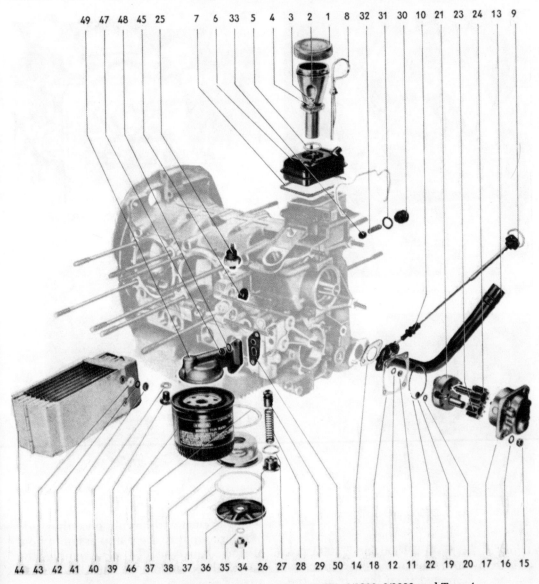

Exploded view of lubrication system—Types 2/1700, 2/1800, 2/2000, and Type 4

1. Oil filter cover	18. Pump housing seal	35. Sealing ring
2. Oil filter	19. Locknut	36. Oil strainer closing cover
3. Nut	20. Spring washer	37. Seal
4. Spring washer	21. Oil pump cover	38. Oil strainer
5. Oil filter seal	22. Pump cover sealing ring	39. Closing screw
6. Oil vent	23. Oil pump gear	40. Sealing ring
7. Seal	24. Driveshaft	41. Nut
8. Oil dipstick	25. Oil pressure switch	42. Spring washer
9. Dipstick	26. Screw	43. Washer
10. Bellows	27. Sealing ring	44. Oil cooler
11. Nut	28. Spring	45. Oil cooler sealing ring
12. Spring washer	29. Piston for oil relief valve	46. Oil filter
13. Oil filler	30. Screw	47. Nut
14. Gasket	31. Sealing ring	48. Spring washer
15. Nut	32. Spring	49. Oil filter intermediate flange
16. Spring washer	33. Piston for oil pressure control valve	50. Seal
17. Oil pump housing	34. Nut	

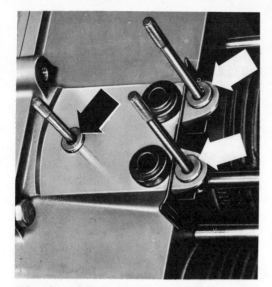

Oil cooler spacers on suitcase engines

Removing Type 1, 2/1600, and 3 oil pump

Removing Type 2/1700, 2/1800, 2/2000, and 4 oil pump

Disassembling Type 2/1700, 2/1800, 2/2000, and 4 oil pump

Types 3, 4, 2/1700, 2/1800 and 2/2000, the oil pump can be taken out only after the engine is removed from the car and the air intake housing, the belt pulley fan housing, and fan are dismantled. On the Automatic Stick Shift models, the torque converter oil pump is driven by the engine oil pump.

NOTE: *The job will be easier if the crankcase halves are loosened.*

On Type 1, 2/1600, and 3 remove the nuts from the oil pump cover and then remove the cover and its gasket. Remove the gears and take out the pump with a special extractor that pulls the body out of the crankcase. Care should be taken so as not to damage the inside of the pump housing.

On Type 4, Type 2/1700, 2/1800, and 2/2000 engines, remove the four pump

securing nuts and, prying on either side of the pump, pry the pump assembly out of the crankcase. To disassemble the pump, the pump cover must be pressed apart.

Prior to assembly, check the oil pump body for wear, especially the gear seating surface. If the pump body is worn, the result will be loss of oil pressure. Check the driven gear shaft for tightness and, if necessary, peen it tightly into place or replace the pump housing. The gears should be checked for excessive wear, backlash, and end-play. Maximum end-play without a gasket is 1 mm (0.004 in.). The end-play can be checked using a T-square and a feeler gauge. Check the mating surfaces of the pump body and the crankcase for damage and cleanliness. Install the pump into the crankcase with a new gasket. Do not use any sealing compound. Turn the camshaft several

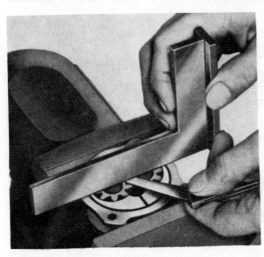

Checking oil pump end-play

revolutions in order to center the pump body opposite the slot in the camshaft. On Type 1, 2/1600, and 3 the cover may now be installed. On Type 4, Type 2/1700, 2/1800, and 2/2000 models, the pump was installed complete. Tighten the securing nuts.

Oil Pressure Relief Valve Removal and Installation

The oil pressure relief valve is removed by unscrewing the end plug and removing the gasket ring, spring, and plunger. If the plunger sticks in its bore, it can be removed by screwing a 10 mm tap into it.

On 1600 cc engines, the valve is located to the left of the oil pump. On Automatic Stick Shift models, it is located in the oil pump housing. On 1700, 1800 and 2000 engines, the valve is located beside the oil filter.

Before installing the valve, check the plunger for any signs of seizure. If necessary, the plunger should be replaced. If

there is any doubt about the condition of the spring, it should also be replaced. When installing the relief valve, be careful that you do not scratch the bore. Reinstall the plug with a new gasket.

Type 4 and Type 2/1700, 2/1800, 2/2000 engines have a second oil pressure relief valve located just to the right of, and below the oil filter.

Engine Cooling

Fan Housing Removal and Installation

TYPE 1 AND 2/1600

1. Remove the two heater hoses and the generator strap.
2. Pull out the lead wire from the coil. Remove the distributor cap and take off the spark plug connectors.
3. Remove the retaining screws that are located on both sides of the fan housing. Remove the rear hood.
4. Remove the outer half of the generator pulley and remove the fan belt.
5. Remove the thermostat securing screw and take out the thermostat.
6. Remove the lower part of the carburetor pre-heater duct.
7. The fan housing can now be removed with the generator. After removal, check the fan housing for damage and for loose air deflector plates.
8. Installation is the reverse of the above.
9. Make sure that the thermostat connecting rod is inserted into its hole in the cylinder head. The fan housing should be fitted properly on the cylinder cover plates so that there is no loss of cooling air.

1. Pulley bolt	16. Lockwasher	31. Spring
2. Dished washer	17. Outer fan cover	32. Washer
3. Crankshaft pulley	18. Reinforcement flange	33. Left cooling air regulator
4. Pulley nut	19. Inner fan cover	34. Right cooling air regulator
5. Special washer	20. Lockwasher	35. Cooling air regulator connecting rod
6. Rear pulley half	21. Nut	36. Washer
7. Spacer washer	22. Fan hub	37. Cheese head screw
8. V-belt	23. Shim	38. Lockwasher
9. Front pulley half	24. Fan	39. Washer
10. Woodruff key	25. Lockwasher	40. Connecting rod
11. Generator	26. Special nut	41. Thermostat bracket
12. Nut	27. Cheese head screw	42. Thermostat
13. Strap	28. Washer	43. Lockwasher
14. Bolt	29. Cheese head screw	44. Bolt
15. Bolt	30. Return spring	

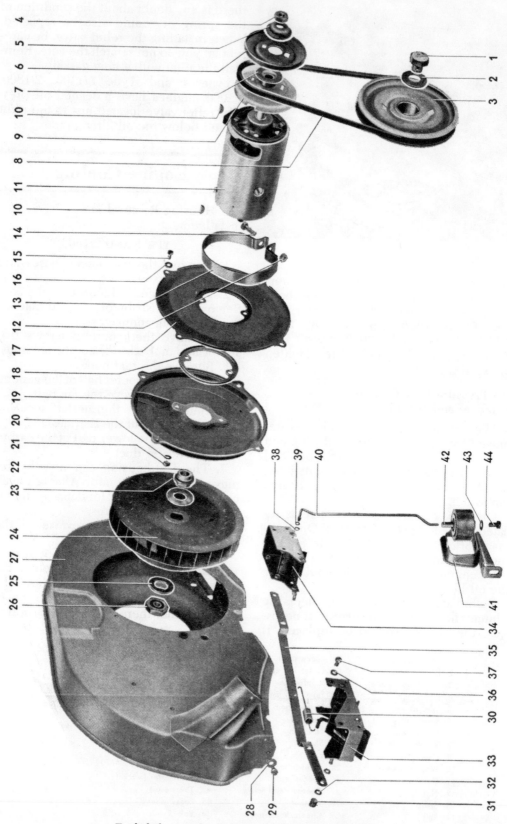

Exploded view of cooling system—Types 1 and 2/1600

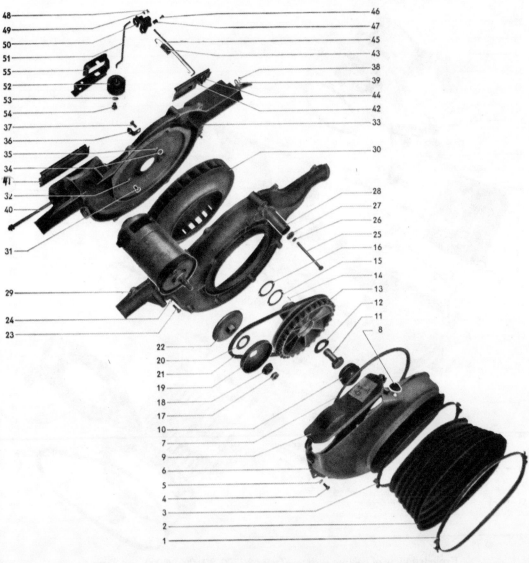

Exploded view of cooling system—Type 3

1. Hose clip
2. Bellows
3. Hose clip
4. Hex bolt
5. Lockwasher
6. Cooling air intake housing
7. Seal
8. Rubber plug
9. Cooling air intake housing cover
10. Cap
11. Bolt
12. Lockwasher
13. Crankshaft pulley
14. Dowel pin
15. Shim
16. Gasket
17. Pulley nut
18. Special washer
19. Rear pulley half

20. Spacer washer
21. Belt
22. Front pulley half
23. Hex bolt
24. Washer
25. Hex bolt
26. Lockwasher
27. Washer
28. Engine mounting tube
29. Rear fan housing half
30. Fan
31. Hex bolt
32. Washer
33. Front fan housing half
34. Nut
35. Washer
36. Center support
37. Hex bolt
38. Lockwasher

39. Washer
40. Throttle valve shaft
41. Left throttle valve
42. Right throttle valve
43. Spring
44. Lockwasher
45. Valve rod
46. Hex bolt
47. Pin
48. C-washer
49. Washer
50. Intermediate lever
51. Connecting rod
52. Thermostat
53. Washer
54. Hex bolt
55. Thermostat bracket

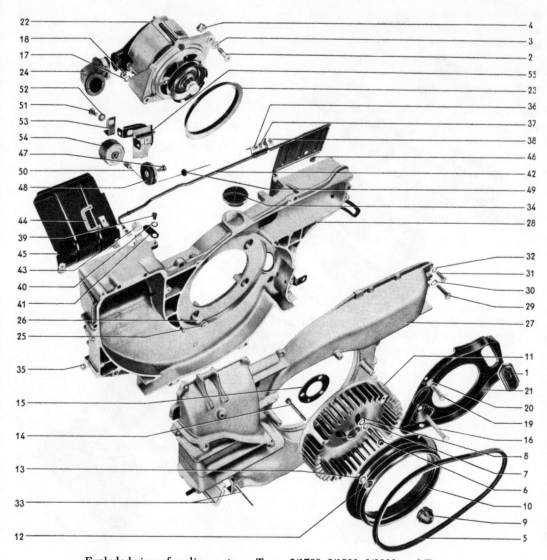

Exploded view of cooling system—Types 2/1700, 2/1800, 2/2000, and Type 4

1. Cover plate insert	21. Alternator cover plate	41. Shaft retaining spring
2. Socket head capscrew	22. Alternator	42. Right flap and shaft
3. Spring washer	23. Alternator sealing ring	43. Bearing
4. Nut	24. Alternator elbow	44. Flap link
5. Belt	25. Nut	45. Left flap
6. Socket head capscrew	26. Spring washer	46. Plug
7. Spring washer	27. Fan housing—rear half	47. Bolt
8. Flat washer	28. Fan housing—front half	48. Cooling air control cable roller
9. Cap	29. Bolt	49. Sealing washer
10. Crankshaft pulley	30. Spring washer	50. Cooling air control cable
11. Fan	31. Screw	51. Bolt
12. Nut	32. Spring washer	52. Washer
13. Spring nut	33. Air non-return flap	53. Thermostat washer
14. Socket head capscrew	34. Inspection hole cover	54. Thermostat
15. Spacer	35. Plug	55. Thermostat bracket
16. Bolt	36. Bolt	
17. Spring washer	37. Washer	
18. Nut	38. Nut	
19. Screw	39. Screw	
20. Spring washer	40. Spring washer	

Fan Removal and Installation

TYPE 1 AND 2/1600

1. Remove the generator and fan assembly as described in the "Generator Removal and Installation" section.

2. While holding the fan, unscrew the fan retaining nut and take off the fan, spacer washers, and the hub.

3. To install, place the hub on the generator shaft, making sure that the woodruff key is securely positioned.

4. Insert the spacer washers. The clearance between the fan and the fan cover is 0.06–0.07 in. Place the fan into position and tighten its retaining nut. Correct the spacing by inserting the proper number of spacer washers. Place any extra washers between the lockwasher and the fan.

5. Reinstall the generator and the fan assembly.

TYPE 2/1700, 2/1800, 2/2000

1. On 1973–74 models, the air injection pump and related parts must first be removed. Loosen the air pump adjusting and retaining bolts, lower the pump and remove the drive belt. Remove the pump and bracket retaining bolts and remove the air pump and retaining brackets. Unbolt and remove the extension shaft and pulley assembly from the fan and fan housing. Using a 12 point allen wrench, loosen the alternator drive belt adjusting bolt. Then, remove the timing scale, fan and crankshaft pulley assembly, and the alternator drive belt.

2. On 1972 and 1975–76 models without the air injection pump, pry out the alternator cover insert, and, using a 12 point allen wrench, loosen the alternator adjusting bolt. Remove the alternator drive belt, the ignition timing scale and the grille over the fan. Remove the three socket head screws attaching the fan and crankshaft assembly to the crankshaft and remove the fan and pulley.

3. Disconnect the cooling air control cable at the flap control shaft.

4. On models so equipped, pull out the rubber elbow for the alternator from the front half of the fan housing.

5. Remove the four nuts retaining the fan housing to the engine crankcase. The assembled fan housing may then be re-moved by pulling it to the rear and off the engine. It is not necessary to separate the fan housing halves or remove the alternator to remove the fan housing.

6. Reverse the above procedure to install, taking care to adjust the alternator and air pump drive belts (1973–74 models) so that moderate thumb pressure deflects the belt about ½ in. when applied at a point midway between the longest run. Also, adjust the cooling air control cable as outlined in this section.

Fan Housing and Fan Removal and Installation

TYPE 3

1. Remove the crankshaft pulley, the rear fan housing half, and the fan.

2. Unhook the linkage and spring at the right-hand air control flap.

3. Remove the screws for the front half of the housing and remove the housing.

4. Install the front half and ensure the correct sealing of the cylinder cover plates.

5. Replace and tighten the two lower mounting screws slightly.

6. Turn the two halves of the fan housing to the left until the left crankcase half is contacted by the front lug.

7. Fully tighten the two lower mounting screws.

8. Loosen the nuts at the breather support until it can be moved.

9. Insert and tighten the mounting screws of the upper fan housing half. Tighten the breather support nuts fully.

Type 3 fan housing nuts

10. Connect the linkage and spring to the right-hand air control flap.

11. Install the fan and the rear half of the fan housing.

TYPE 4, TYPE 2/1700, 2/1800, 2/2000

1. Remove the engine. Remove the fan belt.

2. Remove the allen head screws and remove the belt pulley and fan as an assembly.

NOTE: *It is not necessary to remove the alternator to remove the fan housing.*

3. Remove the spacer and the alternator cover plate.

4. Disconnect the cooling air regulating cable at the shaft.

5. Remove the nuts and remove both halves of the fan housing at the same time.

6. Installation is the reverse of the above.

Air Flap and Thermostat Adjustment

TYPE 1 AND 2/1600

1. Loosen the thermostat bracket securing nut and disconnect the thermostat from the bracket.

2. Push the thermostat upwards to fully open the air flaps.

3. Reposition the thermostat bracket so that the thermostat contacts the bracket at the upper stop, and then tighten the bracket nut.

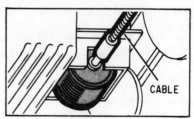

Type 2/1700, 2/1800, 2/2000, and Type 4 thermostat location

Loosening thermostat bracket mounting nut—Types 1, 2/1600, and 3

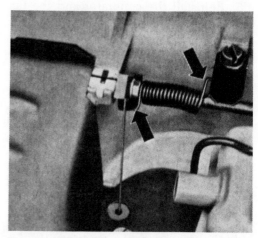

Type 2/1700, 2/1800, 2/2000, and Type 4 air flap cable control

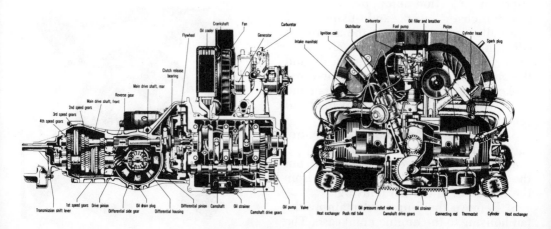

Type 1, 2/1600 upright fan engine and transaxle

4. Reconnect the thermostat to the bracket.

TYPE 3

1. Loosen the clamp screw on the relay lever.

2. Place the air flaps in the closed position. Make sure that the flaps close evenly. To adjust a flap, loosen its securing screw and turn it on its shaft.

3. With the flaps closed, tighten the clamp screw on the relay lever.

TYPE 4, TYPE 2/1700, 2/1800, 2/2000

1. Loosen the cable control.

2. Push the air flaps completely closed.

3. Tighten the cable control.

Engine Rebuilding

This section describes, in detail, the procedures involved in rebuilding a horizontally opposed, air-cooled Volkswagen/Porsche four cylinder engine. It is divided into two sections. The first section, Cylinder Head Reconditioning, assumes that the cylinder head is removed from the engine, all manifolds and sheet metal shrouding is removed, and the cylinder head is on a workbench. The second section, Crankcase Reconditioning, covers the crankcase halves, the connecting rods, crankshaft, camshaft and lifters. It is assumed that the engine is mounted on a work stand (which can be rented), with the cylinder heads, cylinders, pistons, and all accessories removed.

In some cases, a choice of methods is provided. The choice of a method for a procedure is at the descretion of the user. It may be limited by the tools available to a user, or the proximity of a local engine rebuilding or machine shop.

The tools required for the basic rebuilding procedures should, with minor exceptions, be those included in a mechanic's tool kit: An accurate torque wrench (preferably a preset, click type), inside and outside micrometers, electric drill with grinding attachment, valve spring compressor, a set of taps and reamers, a valve lapping tool, and a dial indicator (reading in thousandths of an inch). Special tools, where required, are available from the major tool suppliers (i.e. Zelenda®, Craftsman®, K-D®, Snap-On®). The services of a competent automotive or aviation machine shop must also be readily available.

When assembling the engine, bolts and nuts with no torque specification should be tightened according to size and marking (see chart).

Any parts that will be in frictional contact must be pre-lubricated before assembly to provide protection on initial start-up. Many different pre-lubes are available and each mechanic has his own favorite. However, any product specifically formulated for this purpose, such as Vortex Pre-Lube®, STP®, Wynn's Friction Proofing®, or even a good grade of white grease may be used. NOTE: *Do not use engine oil only, as its viscosity is not sufficient.* Where semi-permanent (locked but removable) installation of nuts or bolts is required, the threads should be cleaned and coated with locking compound. Studs may be permanently installed using a special compound such as Loctite® Stud and Bearing Mount.

Aluminum is used liberally in VW and Porsche engines due to its low weight and excellent heat transfer characteristics. Both the cylinder heads and the crankcase are aluminum alloy castings. However, a few precautions must be observed when handling aluminum engine parts:—Never hot-tank aluminum parts, unless the hot-tanking solution is specified for aluminum application (i.e. Oakite® Aluminum Cleaner 164, or ZEP® Hot Vat Aluminum Cleaner). Most hot-tanking solutions are used for ferrous metals only, and "cook" at much higher temperatures than the 175° F used for aluminum cleaners. The result would be a dissolved head or crankcase. Fizzies anyone?

—Always coat threads lightly with engine oil or anti-seize compound before installation, to prevent seizure.

—Never overtorque bolts or spark plugs in aluminum threads. Should stripping occur, threads can be restored using inserts such as the Heli-Coil®, K-D® Insert or Keenserts® kits.

To install a Heli-Coil® insert, tap drill the hole with the stripped threads to the specified size (see chart). If you are performing this operation on a spark plug hole with the head installed,

Metric

Bolt Diameter (mm)	(5D) 5D	(8G) 8G	(10K) 10K	(12K) 12K	Wrench Size (mm) Bolt and Nut
			Bolt Grade		
6	5	6	8	10	10
8	10	16	22	27	14
10	19	31	40	49	17
12	34	54	70	86	19
14	55	89	117	137	22
16	83	132	175	208	24
18	111	182	236	283	27
22	182	284	394	464	32
24	261	419	570	689	36

*—Torque values are for lightly oiled bolts. CAUTION: Bolts threaded into aluminum require much less torque.

106

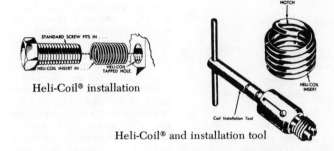

Heli-Coil® installation

Heli-Coil® and installation tool

Heli-Coil Insert		Insert Length (In.)	Drill Size	Tap	Insert Tool	Extracting Tool
Thread Size	Part No.			Part No.	Part No.	Part No.
1/2 -20	1185-4	3/8	17/64 (.266)	4 CPB	528-4N	1227-6
5/16-18	1185-5	15/32	Q (.332)	5 CPB	528-5N	1227-6
3/8 -16	1185-6	9/16	X (.397)	6 CPB	528-6N	1227-6
7/16-14	1185-7	21/32	29/64 (.453)	7 CPB	528-7N	1227-16
1/2 -13	1185-8	3/4	33/64 (.516)	8 CPB	528-8N	1227-16

Heli-Coil Specifications

coat the tap with wheel bearing grease to prevent aluminum shavings from falling into the combustion chamber (it will also help if the engine is rotated so that the exhaust valve of the subject cylinder is open, so that when the engine is initially started, if any chips did fall into the engine, they will be sucked out the exhaust instead of scoring the cylinder walls, and, if compressed air is available, it may be applied through the spark plug hole and the chips blown out the exhaust port).

Using the specified tap (NOTE: *Heli-Coil® tap sizes refer to the size thread being replaced, rather than the actual tap size*), tap the hole for the Heli-Coil®. Place the insert on the proper installation tool (see chart). Apply pressure on the insert while winding it clockwise into the hole, until the top of the insert is one turn below the surface. Remove the installation tool and break the installation tang from the bottom of the insert by moving it up and down. If, for some reason, the Heli-Coil® must be removed, tap the removal tool firmly into the hole, so that it engages the top thread, and turn the tool counterclockwise to extract the insert.

K-D® makes an insert specifically designed for the 14 mm spark plugs used in all VW's. The steel insert is ⅜ in. deep and has a lip which will seat the insert automatically to the correct depth. To install the K-D® insert, screw the combination reamer and tap into the damaged hole to ream the hole to the proper size and cut new threads for the insert. Then, screw the insert onto a spark plug, and torque the plug to 15–18 ft-lbs to seat the insert. NOTE: *Apply locking compound to the threads of the insert (cylinder head side) to make the installation permanent.*

Another spark plug insert that has come into favor is the Keenserts® insert. The special features of this type of insert are the locking keys and gas tight sealing ring. The Keenserts® kit consists of a ream and countersink tool, a tap ¾–16 with pilot point, an installation tool (drift), and the inserts. To install a Keenserts® insert, the following procedure is used:

a. Ream and countersink the damaged spark plug hole.

b. Check the countersink depth. It should be 13/16 in. across the top. Run the tool in until the stop comes into full contact with the head.

c. Tap the hole.

d. Select an insert. Mount the insert on the installation tool.

Keenserts® insert and sealing ring

e. Rotate the tool and insert clockwise until the insert bottoms in the hole.

f. Drive the special anti-rotation keys into the head using the installation tool, sleeve, and a hammer.

g. Remove the installation tool. Check that the insert is flush with the cylinder head surface and that all keys have seated at the undercut portion of the insert.

h. To install the sealing ring, place it squarely around the top of the insert. Then, install a flat seated spark plug, with the plug gasket removed, and torque it to 35 ft-lbs. Remove the plug

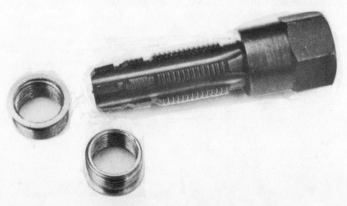

K-D® Tap/reamer and spark plug inserts

INSTALLATION TOOLS

REAM AND COUNTERSINK TOOL. Use this tool to remove the damaged threads, enlarge the hole to the proper size for tapping, and cut the countersink at the top of the hole to accommodate the sealing ring . . . in one operation. Ideally, it should be used in a drill press, however excellent results can be obtained with a hand-held electric drill. Keep the tool well lubricated to extend its life and prevent the adhesion of aluminum to the cutting edges.

TAP This is a conventional ¾-16 tap with a special "pilot point" to assure proper alignment with the newly prepared hole. Thorough lubrication will yield better threads and increase tap life.

— KNURLED SCREW

INSTALLATION TOOL
This tool serves two purposes. It is used to thread the KEENSERTS insert into the cylinder head hole, and to drive the anti-rotation "KEES" into the cylinder head material surrounding the insert. As the insert is threaded into the hole, this tool acts as a depth-stop to assure that the top of the insert is automatically located flush with the upper surface of the cylinder head.

— SLEEVE

— MANDRIL

Keenserts®installation tools

and check the seating of the ring. This should provide a gas tight seal, flush with the insert top.

i. Finally, install the spark plug with its gasket into the insert, and torque it to its normal 18 ft-lbs.

To remove a Keenserts® insert, use a 21/32 drill through the center of the insert to a depth of ¼ in. Remove the locking keys with a punch and remove the insert with an E-Z out® tool.

Snapped bolts or studs may be removed using Vise-Grip® pliers. Penetrating oil (e.g. Liquid Wrench®, CRC®) will often aid in breaking the torque of frozen threads. In cases where the stud or bolt is broken off flush with, or below the surface, the following procedure may be used: Drill a hole (using a hardened bit) in the broken stud or bolt, about ½ of its diameter. Select a screw extractor (e.g. E-Z Out®) of the proper diameter, and tap it into the stud or bolt. Slowly turn the extractor

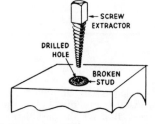

Screw extractor

counterclockwise to remove the stud or bolt.

One of the problems of small displacement, high-revving engines is that they are prone to developing fatigue cracks and

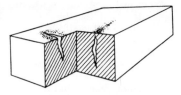

Magnaflux® indication of cracks

other material flaws because they are highly stressed. One of the more popular procedures for checking metal fatigue and stress is Magnafluxing®. Magnafluxing® coats the part with fine magnetic particles, and subjects the part to a magnetic field. Cracks cause breaks in the magnetic field (even cracks below the surface not visible to the eye), which are outlined by the particles. However, since Magnafluxing® is a magnetic process, it applies only to ferrous metals (crankshafts, flywheels, connecting rods, etc.). It will not work with the aluminum heads and crankcases of these engines which are most prone to cracking.

Another process of checking for cracks is the Zyglo® process. This process does work with aluminum alloy. First the part is coated with a flourescent dye penetrant. Then the part is subjected to a blacklight inspection, under which cracks glow brightly, both at or below the surface.

A third method of checking for suspected cracks is the use of spot check dye. This method is quicker, and cheaper to perform, although hidden cracks beneath the surface may escape detection. First, the dye is sprayed onto the suspected area and wiped off. Then, the area is sprayed with a developer. The cracks will show up brightly.

If any of the threaded studs for the rocker arms or manifolds become damaged, and they are not broken off below the surface, they may be removed easily using the following procedure. Lock two nuts on the stud and unscrew the stud using the lower nut. It's as easy as that. Then, to make sure that the new stud remains in place, use locking compound on the threads.

CYLINDER HEAD RECONDITIONING

Procedure	*Method*

Identify the valves:

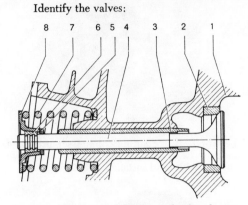

Cross-sectional view of valve and related parts

1. Cylinder head
2. Valve seat insert
3. Valve guide
4. Valve
5. Oil deflector ring (valve stem seal)
6. Valve keeper (key)
7. Valve spring
8. Valve spring cap (retainer)

Keep the valves in order, so that you know which valve (intake and exhaust) goes in which combustion chamber. If the valve faces are not full of carbon, you may number them, front to rear, with a permanent felt tip marker.

Remove the valves and springs:

Lever-type valve spring compressor removing spring from 1600 cylinder head

Overhead-type K-D® valve spring compressor

Using an appropriate valve spring compressor (see illustrations), compress the valve springs and lift out the keepers with needlenose pliers. Then, slowly release the compressor, and remove the valve, spring and spring retainer. On 1972 and earlier engines, a valve stem seal is used beneath the keepers which can be discarded. Check the keeper seating surfaces (see illustration) on the valve stem for burrs which may scratch the valve guide during installation of the valve. Remove any burrs with a fine file.

This section assumes that the cylinder head is removed for this operation. However, if it is desired to remove the valve springs with the head installed, it will be necessary to screw a compressed air adaptor into the subject spark plug hole and maintain a pressure of 85 psi to keep the valve from dropping down.

Inspect the exhaust valves closely. More often than not, the cause of low compression is a burned exhaust valve. The classic burned valve is cracked on the valve face from the edge of the seat to the stem the way you could cut a pie. Remove all carbon, gum and varnish from the valve stem with a hardwood chisel, or with a wire brush and solvent (i.e. carburetor cleaner, lacquer thinner).

Procedure	*Method*

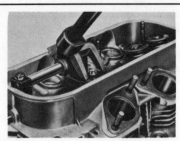

Lever-type valve spring compressor which pivots on bare rocker shaft to remove springs on 1700, 1800 and 2000 cylinder heads

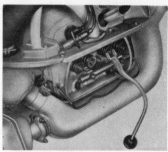

Lever-type valve spring compressor used in conjunction with compressed air chuck to remove springs with head installed—1600 shown

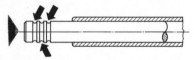

Valve keeper seating surfaces

Burned exhaust valve

Hot-tank the cylinder head:

Cracks in combustion chamber adjoining spark plug hole

Take the head(s) to an engine rebuilding or machine shop and have it (them) hot-tanked to remove grease, corrosion, carbon deposits and scale. NOTE: *Make sure that the hot tanking solution is designed to clean aluminum, not to dissolve it.*

After hot-tanking, inspect the combustion chambers (around the spark plug hole) and the exhaust ports for cracks (see illustration). Also, check the plug threads, manifold studs, and rocker arm studs for damage and looseness.

Degrease the remaining cylinder head parts:

Using solvent (i.e. Gunk® or Zep® carburetor cleaner), clean the rockers, rocker shafts, valve springs, spring retainers, keepers and the pushrods. You may also use solvent to clean the cylinder head although it will not clean as well as hot-tanking. Also clean the sheet metal shrouding at this time. Do not clean the pushrod tubes in solvent.

Procedure	*Method*

De-carbon the cylinder head:

Decarbonizing combustion chamber with power rotary wire brush

Chip carbon away from the combustion chambers and exhaust ports using a chisel made of hardwood. Remove the remaining deposits with a stiff wire brush. You may also use a power brush (drill with wire attachment if you use a very light touch). Remember that you are working with a relatively soft metal (aluminum), and you do not want to grind into the metal. If you have access to a machine shop that works on aluminum heads, ask them about glass-beading the cylinder head.

Check the valve stem-to-guide clearance (valve rock):

VW 689/1

Checking stem-to-guide clearance (valve rock) with dial gauge

Clean the valve stem with lacquer thinner or carburetor cleaner to remove all gum and varnish. Clean the valve guides using solvent and an expanding wire-type valve guide cleaner or brass bristle brush. Mount a dial indicator to the head (see illustration) so that the gauge pin is at a 90° angle to the valve stem, up against the edge of the valve head. Insert the valve by hand so that the stem end is flush with the end of the guide. Move the valve off its seat, and measure the clearance by rocking the stem back and forth to actuate the dial indicator. Check the figure against specifications. Maximum rock should not exceed the wear limit.

To check whether excessive rock is due to worn valve stems or guides (or both), one of two methods may be used. If a new valve is available, you may recheck the valve rock. If rock is still excessive the guide is at fault. Or, you may measure the old valve stem with a micrometer, and determine if it has passed its wear limit.

In any case, most VW and Porsche mechanics will replace the exhaust valve and guides anyway, since they often wear out inside of 50,000 miles.

1600 Engines to '74

	Intake valve guide	Exhaust valve guide	Wear limit
Rock	.008– .009 in. (0.21– 0.23 mm)	.011– .013 in. (0.28– 0.32 mm)	.031 in. (0.8 mm)
Inside diameter	.3149–.3156 in. (8.00–8.02 mm)		.3172 in. (8.06 mm)

Procedure	Method

1700, 1800, 2000 Engines

	Intake valve guide	Exhaust valve guide	Wear limit
Rock	0.45 mm (.018 in.)		0.9 mm (.035 in.)
Inside diameter	8.00–8.02 mm (.3149–.3156 in.)	8.98–8.99 mm (.3534–.3538 in.)	8.06 or 9.06 mm (.3172 or .3566 in.)

1975–76 1600 Engines

	Intake valve guide	Exhaust valve guide	Wear limit
Rock	.008–.009 in. (0.21–0.23 mm)	.018 in. (0.45 mm)	.032 or .035 in. (0.8 or 0.9 mm)
Inside diameter	.3149–.3156 in. (8.00–8.02 mm)	.3534–.3538 in. (8.98–8.99 mm)	.3172 or .3566 in. (8.06 or 9.06 mm)

VW does not make available oversize valve stems to clean up excessive valve rock. Therefore, if excessive clearance is evident, replace the guides.

Knurling the valve guides:

Knurling is a process whereby metal is displaced and raised, thereby reducing clearance. It is a procedure used in engines where the guides are shrunk in making replacement a costly procedure. Although this operation can be performed on VW and Porsche engines, it is not recommended, since the exhaust guides will eventually need replacement anyway.

Replacing the valve guides:

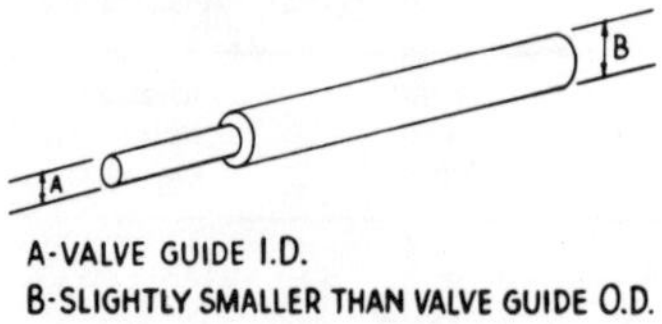

A-VALVE GUIDE I.D.
B-SLIGHTLY SMALLER THAN VALVE GUIDE O.D.

Valve guide removal tool

The valve guides are a press fit into the head. NOTE: *If your replacement valve guides do not have a collar at the top, measure the distance the old guides protrude above the head.* Several different methods may be used to remove worn valve guides. One method is to press or tap the guides out of the head using a stepped drift (see illustration). The problem with this method is the risk of cracking the head. Another method, which reduces this risk, is to first drill out the guide about ⅔ of the length of the guide so that the walls of the guide at the top are paper thin (¹⁄₃₂ in. or so). This relieves most of the tension from the cylinder head guide bore, but still provides a solid base at the bottom of the guide to drift out the guide from the top. A third method of removing guides is to tap threads into the guide and pull it out

Procedure | *Method*

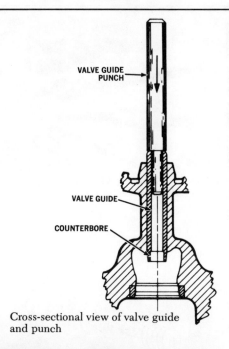

Cross-sectional view of valve guide and punch

Guide drilled out to relieve tension for removal

Tapping guide for removal using wrist pin method

from the top. After tapping the guide, place an old wrist pin (or some other type of sleeve) over the guide, so that the wrist pin rests squarely on the boss on the cylinder head around the guide. Then, take a long bolt (about 4 or 5 inches long with threads running all the way up to the bolt head) and thread a nut about half way up the bolt. Place a washer on top of the wrist pin (see illustration) and thread the bolt into the valve guide until the nut contacts the washer and wrist pin. Finally, screw the nut down against the washer and wrist pin to pull out the guide.

If you are installing the guides without the aid of a press, using only hand tools, it will help to place the new valve guides in the freezer for an hour or so, and the clean, bare cylinder head in the oven at 350–400° F for ½ hour to 45 minutes. Controlling the temperature of the metals in this manner will slightly shrink the valve guides and slightly expand the guide bore in the cylinder head, allowing easier installation and lessening the risk of cracking the head in the process.

Most replacement valve guides, other than those manufactured by VW, have a collar at the top which provides a positive stop to seat the guides in the head. However, VW guides have no such collar. Therefore, on these guides, you will have to determine the height above the cylinder head boss that the guide must extend (about ¼ in.). Then, obtain a stack of washers, their inner diameter slightly larger than the outer diameter of the guide at the top of the guide. If the guide should extend ¼ in., use a ¼ in. thick stack of washers around the guide.

To install the valve guides in the head, use a collared drift, or a special valve guide installation tool of the proper outer diameter (see illustration). CAUTION: *If you have heated the head in the oven to aid installation, be extremely careful handling metal of this temperature. Use pot holders, or asbestos gloves with thick insulation. Do not set the head down on any surface that may be affected by the heat.* If the replacement guide is collared, drive in the guide until it seats against the boss on the cylinder head. If the guide is not collared, drive in the guide until the installation tool butts against the stack of washers (approx. ¼ in. thick) on the head. NOTE: *If you do not heat the head to aid installation, use penetrating lubricant in the guide bore, instead.*

Procedure	Method

Valve guide removal kit

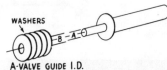

WASHERS

A-VALVE GUIDE I.D.
B-LARGER THAN THE VALVE GUIDE O.D.

Valve guide removal using long
bolt, washer, nut, and wrist pin

Valve guide installation tool

Resurfacing (grinding) the valve face:

Using a valve grinding machine, have the
valves resurfaced according to specifications
(see chart).

Grinding a valve

Intake valves: 1600

A	B	C	D
1.259 in.	4.4 in.	.3130–3126 in.	44°
(32.0 mm)	(112 mm)	(7.95–7.94 mm)	

Exhaust valves: 1600

A	B	C	D
1.259 in.	4.4 in.	1970–'74	45°
(32.0 mm)	(112 mm)	.3114–.3118 in.	
		(7.91–7.92 mm)	
		1975–'76	
		.3500–.3510 in.	
		(8.91–8.92 mm)	

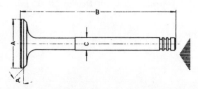

Critical valve dimensions (see chart)

1700, 1800, 2000	Intake valve	Exhaust valve
A (1700)	39.1–39.3 mm dia (1.5394–1.5472 in.)	32.7–33.0 mm dia (1.2874–1.2992 in.)
A (1800)	41 mm dia (1.614 in.)	34 mm dia (1.338 in.)
A (2000)	37.5 mm dia (1.475 in.)	34 mm dia (1.338 in.)

Procedure	Method

1700, 1800, 2000	Intake valve	Exhaust valve
B	116.8–117.3 mm (4.5984–4.6181 in.)	117.0–117.5 mm (4.6063–4.6260 in.)
C	7.94–7.95 mm dia (.3126–.3130 in.)	8.91–8.92 mm dia (.3508–.3512 in.)
D	29° 30′	45°

The valve stem tip should also be squared and resurfaced, by placing the stem in the V-block of the grinder, and turning it while pressing lightly against the grinding wheel. NOTE: *After grinding, the minimum valve head margin must be 0.50 mm (.020 in.). The valve head margin is the straight surface on the edge of the valve head, parallel with the valve stem.*

Replacing valve seat inserts:

This operation is not normally performed on VW and Porsche engines due to its expense and special shrink fit of the insert in the head. Usually, if the seat is destroyed, the head is also in bad shape (i.e. cracked, or hammered from a broken valve or piston). Some high-performance engine builders will replace the inserts to accommodate larger diameter valve heads. Otherwise, the operation will usually cost more than replacement of the head. Also, a replacement insert, if not installed correctly, could come out of the head, damaging the engine.

Resurfacing the valve seats:

Most valve seats can be reconditioned by resurfacing. This is done with a reamer or grinder. First, a pilot is installed in the valve guide (a worn valve guide will allow the pilot to wobble, causing an inaccurate seat cut). When using a reamer, apply steady pressure while rotating clockwise. The seat should clean up in about four complete turns, taking care to remove only as much metal as necessary. NOTE: *Never rotate a reamer counterclockwise.* When using a grinder, lift the cutting stone on and off the seat at approximately two cycles per second, until all flaws are removed.

It takes three separate cuts to recondition a VW or Porsche valve seat. After each cut, check the position of the valve seat using Prussian blue dye (see illustration). First, you cut the center of the seat using a 45° cutter (30° cutter on 1700, 1800 and 2000 cc intake valve seats). Then, you cut the bottom of the seat with a 75° cutter and narrow the top of the seat with a 15° stone. The center of the seat (seat width "a") must be maintained as per the following chart:

Installing pilot in valve guide

Procedure	Method		
	Engine	Intake	Exhaust
	1600	.051–.063 in. (1.3–1.6 mm)	.067–.079 in. (1.7–2.0 mm)
	1700, 1800, 2000	1.8–2.2 mm (.071–.087 in.)	2.0–2.5 mm (.079–.098 in.)

Cutting valve seat using reamer

Equally as important as the width of the seat is its location in relation to the valve. Using a caliper, measure the distance between the center of the valve face on both sides of a valve. Then, place the caliper on the valve seat, and check that the pointers of the caliper locate in the center of the seat.

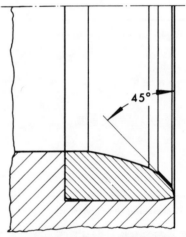

45° contact facing on seat of all 1600 valves and on 1700, 1800 and 2000 exhaust valves

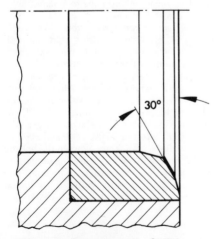

Cutting valve seat using grinder

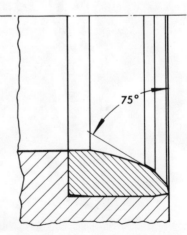

30° contact facing on seat of 1700, 1800 and 2000 intake valves

75° cut on lower edge of seat

Procedure	Method

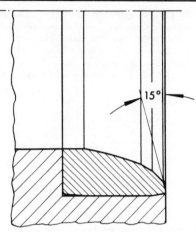

15° finish cut on upper (outer) edge of seat

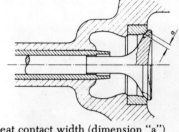

Seat contact width (dimension "a")

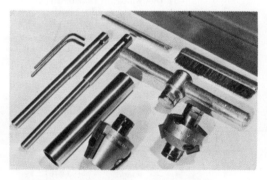

Valve seat reaming kit

Checking contact facing location and width

Checking valve seat concentricity:	In order for the valve to seat perfectly in its seat, providing a gas tight seal, the valve seat must be concentric with the valve guide. To check concentricity, coat the valve face with Prussian blue dye and install the valve in its guide. Applying light pressure, rotate the valve ¼ turn in its valve seat. If the entire valve seat face becomes coated, and the valve is known to be concentric, the seat is concentric.

Lapping the valves:

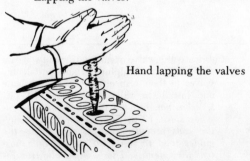

Hand lapping the valves

With accurately refaced valve seat inserts and new valves, it is not usually necessary to lap the valves. Valve lapping alone is not recommended for use as a resurfacing procedure.

Prior to lapping, invert the cylinder head, lightly lubricate the valve stem and install the valves in their respective guides. Coat the valve seats with fine Carborundum® grinding compound, and attach the lapping tool suction cup (moistened for adhesion) to the valve head. Then, rotate the tool (see illustration) between your palms, changing direction and lifting the tool often

Procedure	Method

Suction cup end of lapping tool on valve face

to prevent grooving. Lap the valve until a smooth, polished seat is evident. Finally, remove the tool and thoroughly wash away all traces of grinding compound. Make sure that no compound accumulates in the guides as rapid wear would result.

Check the valve springs:

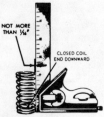

NOT MORE THAN 1/16"

CLOSED COIL END DOWNWARD

Checking valve spring free-length and squareness

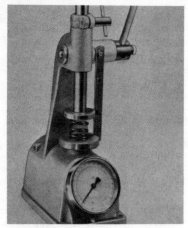

Checking valve spring loaded-length and tension

Place the spring on a flat surface next to a square. Measure the height of the spring and compare that value to that of the other 7 springs. All springs should be the same height. Rotate the spring against the edge of the square to measure distortion. Replace any spring that varies (in both height and distortion) more than 1/16 in.

If you have access to a valve spring tester, you may use the following specifications to check the springs under a load (which is the only specification VW gives).

Type	Loaded length	Load
1600	1.2 in. (31.0 mm)	117.5–134.9 lb (53.2–61.2 kg)
1700, 1800, 2000	1.141 in. (29.0 mm)	168.0–186.0 lb (76.5–84.5 kg)

If any doubt exists as to the condition of the springs, and a spring tester is not available, replace them, they're cheap.

Install the valves:

Lubricate the valve stems with white grease (molybdenum-disulphide), and install the valves in their respective guides. Lubricate and install the valve stem seals (NOTE: *VW has not installed stem seals on new engines since 1972. The reason is, although the seals provide excellent oil control, the guides tend to run "dry" which only hastens their demise. This is especially true for*

Procedure	Method

	exhaust valves which run at much greater temperatures). Position the valve springs on the head. The spring is positioned with the closely coiled end facing the head. Check the valve stem keys (keepers) for burrs or scoring. The keys should be machined so that the valve may still rotate with the keys held together. Finally, install the spring retainers, compress the springs (using a valve spring compressor), and insert the keys using needlenose pliers or a special tool designed for this purpose. NOTE: *You can retain the keys with wheel bearing grease during installation.*
Inspect the rocker shafts and rocker arms:	Remove the rocker arms, springs and washers from the rocker shaft. NOTE: *Lay out the parts in the order they are removed.* Inspect the rocker arms for pitting or wear on the valve stem contact point, and check for excessive rocker arm bushing wear where the arm rides on the shaft. If the shaft is grooved noticeably, replace it. Use the following chart to check the rocker arm inner diameter and the rocker shaft outer diameter.

1700, 1800, 2000		1600
.7874–.7882 in. (20.00–20.02 mm)	rocker arms inner diameter (new)	.7086–.7093 in. (18.00–18.02 mm)
.7890 in. (20.04 mm)	wear limit	.710 in. (18.04 mm)
.7854–.7861 in. (19.95–19.97 mm)	rocker arm shaft outer diameter (new)	.7073–.7077 in. (17.97–17.98 mm)
.7846 in. (19.93 mm)	wear limit	.7066 in. (17.95 mm)

Minor scoring may be removed with an emery cloth. If the valve stem contact point of the rocker arm is worn, grind it smooth, removing as little metal as necessary. If it is noticed at this point that the valve stem is worn concave where it contacts the rocker arm, and it is not desired to disassemble the valve from the head, a cap (see illustration) may be installed over the stem prior to installing the rocker shaft assembly.

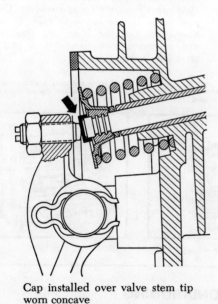

Cap installed over valve stem tip worn concave

Inspect the pushrods and pushrod tubes:	After soaking the pushrods in solvent, clean out the oil passages using fine wire, then blow through them to make sure there are no obstructions. Roll each pushrod over a

Procedure	Method

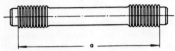

Pushrod tube required length "a"

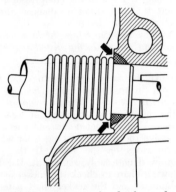

Silicone seal at pushrod tube ends

piece of clean, flat glass. Check for runout. If a distinct, clicking sound is heard as the pushrod rolls, the rod is bent, necessitating replacement. All pushrods must be of equal length.

Inspect the pushrod tubes for cracks or other damage to the tube that would let oil out and dirt into the engine. The tubes on the 1600 engine are particularly susceptible to damage at the stretchable bellows. Also, on the 1600 engine, the tubes must be maintained at length "a" (see illustration) which is 190–191 mm or 7.4–7.52 in. If a tube is too short, it may be carefully stretched, taking care to avoid cracking. However, if the bellows are damaged or if a gritty, rusty sound occurs when stretching the tube, replace it. Always use new seals. When installing tubes in a 1600 engine, rotate the tubes so that the seams face upwards. When installing tubes in a 1700, 1800 or 2000 engine, make sure the retaining wire for the tubes engages the slots in the supports and rests on the lower edges of the tubes.

If, on an assembled, installed 1600 engine, it is desired to replace a damaged or leaky pushrod tube without pulling the engine, it may be accomplished using a "quick-change" pushrod tube available from several different specialty manufacturers. The special two-piece aluminum replacement tube is installed after removing the valve cover, rocker arm assembly and pushrod of the subject cylinder. The old tube is then pried loose with a screwdriver. Using new seals, the replacement tube is positioned between the head and crankcase, and expanded into place, via a pair of threaded, locking nuts.

Remove cover. Shove affected rocker arm to one side and pull out push rod.

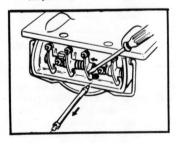

Pry loose the damaged tube (don't lose seals from either end).

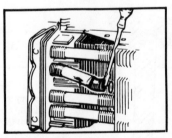

Using old seals, position new tube with gold end toward spark plug. Tighten.

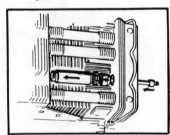

Quick-change tube installation

CRANKCASE RECONDITIONING

Procedure	Method
Disassembling crankcase:	See "Crankcase Disassembly and Assembly" earlier in this chapter.

Procedure	*Method*
Hot tank the crankcase:	Using only a hot-tanking solution formulated for aluminum or magnesium alloy, clean the crankcase to remove all sludge, scale, or foreign particles. You may also cold-tank the case, using a strong degreasing solvent, but you will have to use a brush and a lot of elbow grease to get the same results. After cleaning, blow out all oil passages with compressed air. Remove all old gasket sealing compound from the mating surfaces.

Inspect the crankcase:  Checking tightness of oil suction pipe	Check the case for cracks using the Zyglo or spot-check method described earlier in this section. Inspect all sealing or mating surfaces, especially along the crankcase seam, as the crankcase halves are machined in pairs and use no gasket. Check the tightness of the oil suction pipe. The pipe must be centered over the strainer opening. On 1600 engines, peen over the crankcase where the suction pipe enters the camshaft bearing web. Check all studs for tightness. Replace any defective studs as mentioned earlier in this section. Check all bearing bores for nicks and scratches. Remove light marks with a file. Deeper scratches and scoring must be removed by align boring the crankshaft bearing bores.

Align bore the crankcase:  Ridged main bearing bores prior to align boring	There are two surfaces on a VW crankcase that take quite a hammering in normal service. One is the main bearing saddles and the other the thrust flange of #1 bearing (at the flywheel end). Because the case is constructed of softer metal than the bearings, it is more malleable. The main bearing saddles are slowly hammered in by the rotation of the heavy crankshaft working against the bearings. This is especially true for an out-of-round crankshaft. The thrust flange of #1 main bearing receives its beating trying to control the end play of the crankshaft. This beating is more severe in cases of a driver with a heavy clutch foot. Popping the clutch bangs the pressure plate against the clutch disc, against the flywheel, against the crankcase flange, and finally against the thrust flange. All of this hammering leaves its mark on the case, but can be cleaned up by align boring. Most VW engine rebuilders who want their engines to stay together will align bore the case. This assures proper bearing bore alignment. Then, main bearings with the correct oversize outer diameter (and oversize thrust shoulder on #1) are installed. Also, as the split crankcase is constructed of light aluminum and magnesium alloy, it is particularly susceptible to warpage due to overheating. Align boring the case will clean up any bearing saddle misalignment due to warpage.

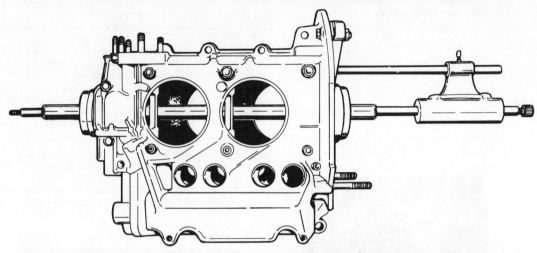

Align boring apparatus installed on crankcase

No. 1 main bearing thrust flange

Crankcase after align boring

Procedure	Method
Check connecting rod side clearance, and check connecting rods for straightness:	Before removing the connecting rods from the crankshaft, check the clearance between the rod and the crank throw using a feeler gauge. Replace any rod exceeding the wear limit. Proper side clearance (also known as end play or axial play) is .004–.016 in. (0.10–0.40 mm). Also, prior to removing the rods from the crankshaft, check them for straightness. This is accomplished easily using an old wrist pin, and sliding the wrist pin through each connecting rod (small end) in succession. Position each rod, in turn, so that as the pin begins to leave one rod, it is entering the next rod. Any binding indicates a scored wrist pin bushing or misaligned (bent) connecting rod. If the wrist pin absolutely will not slide from one adjacent rod to another, then you've got a really bent rod. Be ready for bent rods on any engine which has dropped a valve and damaged a piston.
Disassemble crankshaft:	Number the connecting rods (1 through 4 from the flywheel side) and matchmark their bearing halves. Remove the connecting rod retaining nuts (do not remove the bolts) from the big end and remove the rods. Slide off the oil thrower (1600 only) and #4 main bearing. Slide off #1 main bearing from the flywheel end. Remove the snap-ring (circlip) using snap-ring pliers. #2 main bearing is the split type, each half of which should remain in its respective crankcase half. Using a large gear puller, or an arbor or hydraulic press, remove the distributor drive gear and crankshaft timing gear and spacer. Don't loose the woodruff key(s). NOTE: *The 1600 engine has two woodruff keys. The 1700, 1800 and 2000 engines have only one.* Finally, slide off #3 main bearing.
Inspect the crankshaft:	Clean the crankshaft with solvent. Run all oil holes through with a brass bristle brush. Blow them through with compressed air. Lightly oil the crankshaft to prevent rusting. Using a micrometer of known accuracy, measure the crankshaft journals for wear. The maximum wear limit for all journals is .0012 in. (0.03 mm). Check the micrometer reading against those specifications listed under "Crankshaft and Connecting Rod Specifications" which appears earlier in this chapter. Check the crankshaft runout. With main bearing journals #1 and #3 supported on V-blocks and a dial gauge set up perpendicular to the crankshaft, measure the runout at #2 and #4 main bearing journals. Maximum permissable runout is .0008 in. (0.02 mm). Inspect the crankshaft journals for scratches, ridges, scoring and nicks. All small nicks and scratches necessitate re-

Procedure	*Method*

grinding of the crankshaft at a machine shop. Journals worn to a taper or slightly out-of-round must also be reground. Standard undersizes are .010, .020, .030 in. (0.25, 0.50, 0.75 mm).

Inspect connecting rods:	Check the connecting rods for cracks, bends and burns. Check the rod bolts for damage; replace any rod with a damaged bolt. If possible, take the rods to a machine shop and have them checked for twists and magnafluxed for hidden stress cracks. Also, the rods must be checked for straightness, using the wrist pin method described earlier. If you did not perform this check before removing the rods from the crankshaft, definitely do so before dropping the assembled crankshaft into the case.

Weigh the rods on a gram scale. On 1600 engines, the rods should all weigh within 10 grams (lightest to heaviest); on 1700, 1800 and 2000 engines, within 6 grams. All rods should ideally weigh the same. If not, find the lightest rod and lighten the others to match. Up to 8 grams of metal can be removed from a rod by filing or grinding at the low stress points shown in the illustration.

Check the fit of the wrist pin bushing. At 72° F, the pin should slide through the bushing with only light thumb pressure.

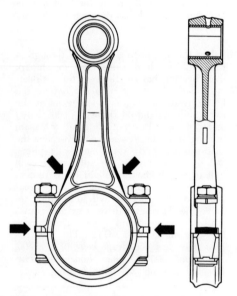

To lighten connecting rods, metal can be removed at the locations indicated by the arrows

Checking wrist pin fit

Check connecting rod bearing (oil) clearance:	It is always good practice to replace the connecting rod bearings at every teardown. The bearing size is stamped on the back of the inserts. However, if it is desired to reuse the bearings, two methods may be used to determine bearing clearance.

One tedious method is to measure the crankshaft journals using a micrometer to determine what size bearing inserts to use on reassembly (see Crankshaft and Connecting Rod Specifications) to obtain the required 0.0008–0.0027 in. oil clearance.

Another method of checking bearing clearance is the Plastigage method. This method can only be used on the split-type bearings and not on the ring-type bearings used to support the crankshaft. First, clean

Procedure	Method

all oil from the bearing surface and crankshaft journal being checked. Plastigage is soluble in oil. Then, cut a piece of Plastigage the width of the rod bearing and insert it between the journal and bearing insert. NOTE: *Do not rotate the rod on the crankshaft.* Tighten the rod cap nuts to 22–25 ft-lbs. Remove the bearing insert and check the thickness of the flattened Plastigage using the Plastigage scale. Journal taper is determined by comparing the width of the Plastigage strip near its ends. To check for journal eccentricity, rotate the crankshaft 90° and retest. After checking all four connecting rod bearings in this manner, remove all traces of Plastigage from the journal and bearing. Oil the crankshaft to prevent rusting.

If the oil clearance is .006 in. (0.15 mm) or greater, it will be necessary to have the crankshaft ground to the nearest undersize (.010 in.) and use oversize connecting rod bearings.

Check main bearing (oil) clearance:

It is also good practice to replace the main bearings at every engine teardown as their replacement cost is minimal compared to the replacement cost of a crankshaft or short block. However, if it becomes necessary to reuse the bearings, you may do so after checking the bearing clearance.

Main bearings #1, 3 and 4 are ring-type bearings that slip over the crankshaft. These bearings cannot be checked using the Plastigage method. Only the split-type #2 main bearing can be checked using Plastigage. However, since this involves bolting together and unbolting the crankcase halves several times, it is not recommended. Therefore, the main bearings are checked using a micrometer. Use the following chart to determine if the bearing (oil) clearance exceeds its wear limit.

Main Bearing Clearance

	New	Wear limit
Crankshaft bearings 1 + 3 (1600 engine)	0.04–0.10 mm (.0016–.004 in.)	0.18 mm (.007 in.)
Crankshaft bearings 1 + 3 (1700, 1800, 2000 engine)	0.05–0.10 mm (.002–.004 in.)	0.18 mm (.007 in.)
Crankshaft bearing 2 (all models)	0.03–0.09 mm (.001–.0035 in.)	0.17 mm (.0067 in.)
Crankshaft bearing 4 (all models)	0.05–0.10 mm (.002–.004 in.)	0.19 mm (.0075 in.)

Procedure	*Method*
	Never reuse a bearing that shows signs of wear, scoring or blueing. If the bearing clearance exceeds its wear limit, it will be necessary to regrind the crankshaft to the nearest undersize and use oversize main bearings.
Clean and inspect the camshaft: Camshaft lobe measurement  Checking camshaft run-out  Checking axial play of camshaft and timing gear	Degrease the camshaft using solvent. Clean out all oil holes and blow through with compressed air. Visually inspect the cam lobes and bearing journals for excessive wear. The edges of the camshaft lobes should be square. Slight damage can be removed with silicone carbide oilstone. To check for lobe wear not visible to the eye, mike the camshaft diameter from the tip of the lobe to base (distance A) and then mike the diameter of the camshaft at a 90° angle to the previous measurement (distance B) (see illustration). This will give you camshaft lift. Measure lift for each lobe. If any lobe differs more than .025 in., replace the camshaft. Check the camshaft for runout. Place the #1 and #3 journals in V-blocks and rest a dial indicator on #2 journal. Rotate the camshaft and check the reading. Runout must not exceed 0.0015 in. (0.04 mm). Repair is by replacement. Check the camshaft timing gear rivets for tightness. If any of the gear rivets are loose, or if the gear teeth show a poor contact pattern, replace the camshaft and timing gear assembly. Check the axial (end) play of the timing gear. Place the camshaft in the left crankcase halve. The wear limit is .0063 in. (0.16 mm). If the end play is excessive, the thrust shoulder of #3 camshaft bearing is probably worn, necessitating replacement of the cam bearings.
Check the camshaft bearings:	The camshaft bearings are the split-type. #3 camshaft bearing has shoulders on it to control axial play. Since there is no load on the camshaft, the bearings are not normally replaced. However, if the bearings are scored or imbedded with dirt, if the camshaft itself is being replaced, or if the thrust shoulders of #3 bearing are worn (permitting excessive axial play), the bearings should be replaced. In all cases, clean the bearing saddles and check the oil feed holes for cleanliness. Make sure that the oil holes for the bear-

Procedure	Method

Camshaft bearing inserts

ing inserts align with those in the crankcase. Coat the bearing surfaces with prelube.

Check the lifters (tappets):

Checking lifter face for wear

Remove all gum and varnish from the lifters using a tooth brush and carburetor cleaner. The cam following surface of the lifters is slightly convex when new. In service, this surface will wear flat which is OK to reinstall. However, if the cam following surface of the lifter is worn concave, the lifter should be replaced. To check this, place the cam following surface of one lifter against the side of another (as illustrated), using the one lifter as a straightedge. After checking, coat the lifters with oil to prevent rusting.

Assemble crankshaft:

NOTE: *All dowel pin holes in the main bearings must locate to the flywheel end of the bearing saddles.*
Coat #3 main bearing journal with assembly lubricant. Slide the #3 bearing onto the pulley side of the crankshaft and install the large woodruff key in its recess (the hole in the bearing should be nearest to the flywheel end of the crankshaft). In the meantime, heat both the crankshaft timing gear and distributor drive gears to 176° F in an oil bath. If a hydraulic or an arbor press is available, press on the timing gear, taking care to keep the slot for the woodruff key aligned, the timing marks facing away from the flywheel, and the chamfer in the gear bore facing #3 main bearing journal. CAUTION: *Use protective gloves when handling the heated gears.* NOTE: *Be careful not to scratch the crankshaft journals.* Or, if a press is not available, you may drive on the gear using a 2 in. diameter length of pipe and a hammer, taking care to protect the flywheel end of the crankshaft with a piece of wood. The woodruff key must lie flat in its recess. Then, slide on the spacer ring and align it with the woodruff key. On 1600 engines, install the smaller woodruff key. Now, press or drive on the distributor drive gear in the same manner as the crankshaft timing gear. Make sure it seats against the spacer ring. Install the snap-ring (cir-

Procedure	*Method*
	clip) using snap-ring pliers. Take care not to scratch #4 main bearing journal. Prelube main bearings #1 and #4 and slide them on the crankshaft. On 1600 engines, install the oil slinger, concave side out. NOTE: *Make sure crankshaft timing gear and distributor drive gear fit snugly on the crankshaft once they return to room temperature.*
	Install the bearing inserts for the connecting rods and rod caps by pressing in on bearing ends with both thumbs. Make sure the tangs fit in the notches. Don't press in the middle as the inserts may soil or crack. Prelube the connecting rod bearings and journals. Then, install the connecting rods on the crankshaft, making sure the forge marks are up (as they would be installed in the crankcase [3, 1, 4, 2 from flywheel end]), and the rod and bearing cap matchmarks align. Use new connecting rod nuts. After tightening the nuts, make sure that each rod swings freely 180° on the crankshaft by its own weight. NOTE: *A slight pretension (binding) of the rod on the crankshaft may be relieved by lightly rapping on the flat side of the big end of the rod with a hammer.* If the connecting rod nuts are not of the self-locking type (very rare), peen the nuts into the slot on the rods to lock them in place and prevent the possibility of throwing a rod.
Installing crankshaft and camshaft:	Pencil mark a line on the edge of each ring-type main bearing to indicate the location of the dowel pin hole. Install the lower half of #2 main bearing in the left side of the crankcase so that the shell fits securely over its dowel pin. Pre-lube the bearing surface.
	Lift the crankshaft by two of the connecting rods and lower the assembly into the left crankcase halve. Make sure the other connecting rods protrude through their corresponding cylinder openings. Then, rotate each ring-type main bearing (#1, then #3, then #4) until the pencil marks made previously align with the center of the bearing bore. As each bearing is aligned with its dowel pin, a distinctive click should be heard and the crankshaft should be felt dropping into position. After each bearing is seated, you should not be able to rock any of the main bearings or the crankshaft in the case. Just to be sure, check the bearing installation by placing the other half of #2 main bearing over the top of its crankshaft journal. If the upper half rocks, the bearing or bearings are not seated properly on their dowels. Then, install the other half of #2 main bearing in the right crankcase halve. Pre-lube the bearing surface.
	Rotate the crankshaft until the timing

Procedure	Method

Aligning timing marks

Camshaft end plug installation

marks (twin punch marks on two adjacent teeth) on the timing gear point towards the camshaft side of the case. Lubricate and install the lifters. Coat the lifters for the right half of the case with grease to keep them from falling out during assembly. Coat the camshaft journals and bearing surfaces with assembly lubricant. Install the camshaft so that the single timing mark (0) on the camshaft timing gear aligns (lies between) with the two on the crankshaft timing gear. This is critical as it establishes valve timing.

Install the camshaft end plug using oil-resistant sealer. On cars with manual transmission, the hollow end of the plug faces in toward the engine. On cars equipped with automatic or automatic stick shift transmission, the hollow end faces out towards the front of the car to provide clearance for the torque converter drive plate retaining bolts.

The timing gear mesh is correct if the camshaft does not lift from its bearings when the crankshaft is rotated backwards (opposite normal direction of rotation).

Check timing gear backlash:

Checking timing gear backlash

Mount a dial indicator to the crankcase with its stem resting on a tooth of the camshaft gear. Rotate the gear until all slack is removed, and zero the indicator. Then, rotate the gear in the opposite direction until all slack is removed and record gear backlash. The reading should be between .000 and .002 in. (0.00 and 0.05 mm).

Assembling crankcase:

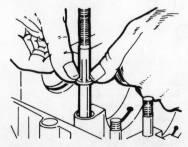

Installing crankcase stud seals

See "Crankcase Assembly and Disassembly" earlier in this chapter. Use the following installation notes;

a. Make sure all bearing surfaces are pre-lubed.
b. Always install new crankcase stud seals.
c. Apply only non-hardening oil resistant sealer to all crankcase mating surfaces.
d. Always use new case nuts. Self-sealing nuts must be installed with the red coated side down.
e. All small crankcase retaining nuts are first torqued to 10 ft-lbs, then 14 ft-lbs. All large crankcase retaining nuts are torqued to 20 ft-lbs, then 25 ft-lbs (ex-

Procedure	*Method*
	cept self-sealing large nuts [red plastic insert], which are torqued to a single figure of 18 ft lbs). Use a criss-cross torque sequence. On 1700, 1800 and 2000 engines, you will have to keep the long case bolt heads from turning.
	f. While assembling the crankcase halves, always rotate the crankshaft periodically to check for binding. If any binding occurs, immediately disassemble and investigate the case. Usually, a main bearing has come off its dowel pin, or maybe you forgot to align bore that warped crankcase.
Check crankshaft end-play:	After assembling the case, crankshaft end-play can be checked. End-play is controlled by the thickness of 3 shims located between the flywheel and #1 main bearing flange. End-play is checked with the flywheel installed as follows. Attach a dial indicator to the crankcase with the stem positioned on the face of the flywheel. Move the flywheel in and out and check the reading. End-play should be between .003–.005 in. (0.07–0.13 mm). The wear limit is .006 in. (0.15 mm).
	To adjust end-play, remove the flywheel and reinstall, this time using only two shims. Remeasure the end-play. The differ-

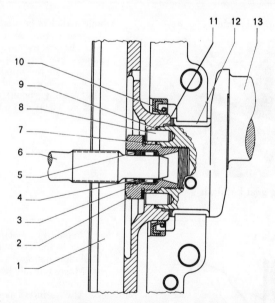

Cross-section of 1600 flywheel, crankshaft, oil seal, and related parts

1. Flywheel	8. Dowel pin
2. Gland nut	9. Rubber sealing ring
3. Needle bearing	10. Crankshaft oil seal
4. Felt ring	11. Shims
5. Retaining ring	12. Crankshaft bearing
6. Rear driveshaft	13. Crankshaft
7. Lockwasher	

Procedure	Method

Checking crankshaft end-play

ence between the second reading and the .003–.005 in. figure is the required thickness of the third shim. Shims come in the following sizes;
0.24 mm—.0095 in.
0.30 mm—.0118 in.
0.32 mm—.0126 in.
0.34 mm—.0134 in.
0.36 mm—.0142 in.
0.38 mm—.0150 in. (1700, 1800 and 2000 only)

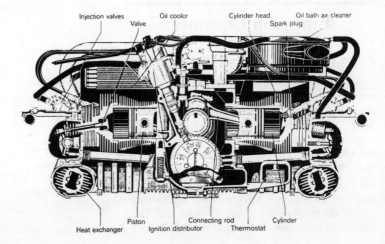

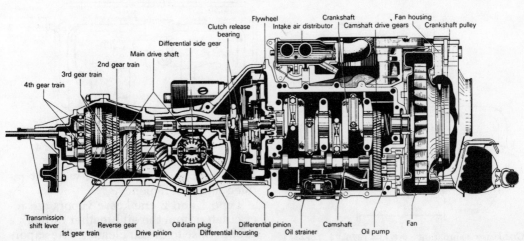

Type 4 suitcase engine and transaxle

Chapter Four

Emission Controls and Fuel System

Emission Controls

CRANKCASE VENTILATION SYSTEM

All models are equipped with a crankcase ventilation system. The purpose of the crankcase ventilation system is twofold. It keeps harmful vapors from escaping into the atmosphere and prevents the buildup of crankcase pressure. Prior to the 1960s, most cars employed a vented oil filler cap and road draft tube to dispose of crankcase vapor. The crankcase ventilation systems now in use are improvement over the old method and, provement over the old method and,

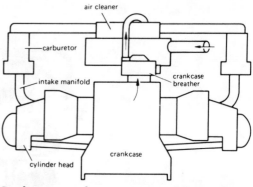

Crankcase ventilation system—1972–74 Types 2/1700, 2/1800

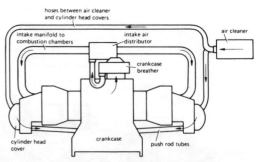

Crankcase ventilation system—Types 3 and 4

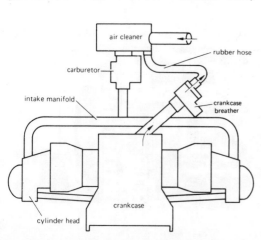

Crankcase ventilation system—1970–74 Types 1, 2/1600

when functioning properly, will not reduce engine efficiency.

Type 1 and 2 crankcase vapors are recirculated from the oil breather through a rubber hose to the air cleaner. The vapors then join the air/fuel mixture and are burned in the engine. Fuel injected cars mix crankcase vapors into the air/fuel mixture to be burned in the combustion chambers. Fresh air is forced through the engine to evacuate vapors and recirculate them into the oil breather, intake air distributor, and then to be burned.

Crankcase Ventilation System Service

The only maintenance required on the crankcase ventilation system is a periodic check. At every tune-up, examine the hoses for clogging or deterioration. Clean or replace the hoses as required.

EVAPORATIVE EMISSION CONTROL SYSTEM

Required by law since 1971, this system prevents raw fuel vapors from entering the atmosphere. The various systems for different models are similar. They consist of an expansion chamber, activated charcoal filter, and connecting lines. Fuel vapors are vented to the charcoal filter where hydrocarbons are deposited on the element. The engine fan forces fresh air into the filter when the engine is running. The air purges the

filter and the hydrocarbons are forced into the air cleaner to become part of the air/fuel mixture and burned.

Evaporative Emission Control Service

See Chapter One under "Routine Maintenance."

AIR INJECTION SYSTEM 1973–74

Type 2 vehicles are equipped with the air injection system, or air pump as it is sometimes called. In this system, an engine driven air pump delivers fresh air to the engine exhaust ports. The additional air is used to promote after-burning of any unburned mixture as it leaves the combustion chamber. In addition, the system supplies fresh air to the intake manifold during gear changes to provide more complete combustion of the air/fuel mixture.

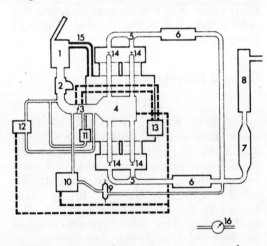

1975–76 Type 1 and Type 2 emission control systems

1. Air cleaner
2. Air sensor
3. Throttle valve
4. Intake air distributor
5. Exhaust manifold
6. Heat exchanger
7. Catalytic converter
8. Muffler
9. EGR filter
10. EGR valve
11. Auxiliary air regulator
12. Throttle switch
13. Ignition distributor
14. Fuel injector
15. Crankcase ventilation
16. Indicator light for EGR

Exhaust and air lines
– – – – – – – – – –
Control lines (vacuum)

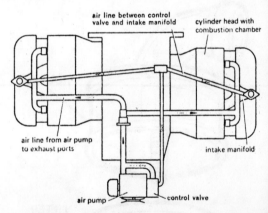

Air injection (exhaust manifold afterburning) system—1973 Type 2/1700

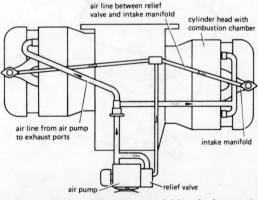

Air injection (exhaust manifold afterburning) system—1974 Type 2/1800

Check the air pump belt tension and examine the hoses for deterioration as a regular part of your tune-up procedure.

Air Injection System Service

The only maintenance required for the system is an air pump belt tension check at 6,000 mile intervals and an air pump filter element replacement at 18,000 mile or 2 year intervals. See Chapter One for the belt tension check.

The air pump filter element is located in a housing adjacent to the pump. To remove the element, loosen the hose clamp and disconnect the filter housing from the pump. Then, loosen the wing nut and draw out the element. Never attempt to clean the old element. Install a new paper element and assemble the filter housing.

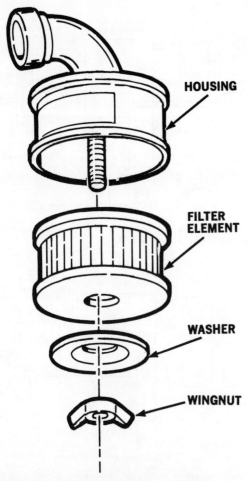

HOUSING

FILTER ELEMENT

WASHER

WINGNUT

Type 2 air injection pump filter assembly

EXHAUST GAS RECIRCULATION SYSTEM

In order to control exhaust emissions of oxides of nitrogen (NO_x), an exhaust gas recirculation (EGR) system is employed on 1972 Type 1 and Type 3 models equipped with automatic transmission and sold in California, on 1973 Type 1 and Type 3 models equipped with automatic transmission sold nationwide, on all 1973–76 Type 2 models, on all 1974 Type 4 models equipped with automatic transmission, and on all 1974–76 Type 1 models. The system lowers peak flame temperature during combustion by introducing a small (about 10%) percentage of relatively inert exhaust gas into the intake charge. Since the exhaust gas contains little or no oxygen, it cannot react with nor influence the air/fuel mixture. However, the exhaust gas does (by volume) take up space in the combustion chambers (space that would otherwise be occupied by a heat-producing, explosive air/fuel mixture), and does serve to lower peak combustion chamber temperature. The amount of exhaust gas directed to the combustion chambers is infinitely variable by means of a vacuum operated EGR valve. For system specifics, see the vehicle type breakdown under "General Description."

General Description

TYPE 1

For 1972, EGR is used only on automatic stick shift models sold in California. Exhaust gas is drawn from the left hand rear exhaust flange and then cooled in a cooling coil. From here, the gas is filtered in a cyclone filter and finally channelled to the intake manifold, via the EGR valve. The valve permits exhaust gas recirculation during part throttle applications, but not during idling or wide open throttle.

All 1973 models (nationwide) equipped with the automatic stick shift transmission use an EGR system. As in '72, the gas is drawn from the left rear exhaust flange. However, instead of the cooling coil and cyclone filter, a replaceable element type filter is used. The remainder of the system remains unchanged from 1972.

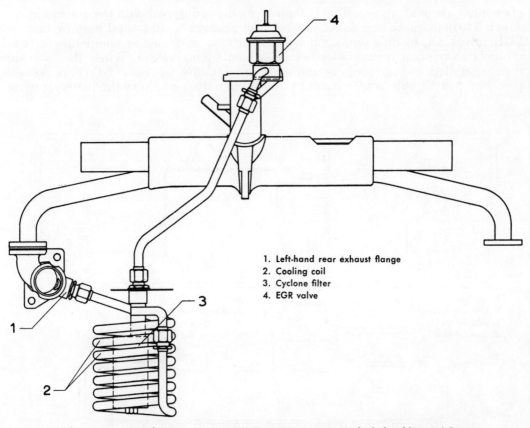

1. Left-hand rear exhaust flange
2. Cooling coil
3. Cyclone filter
4. EGR valve

Exhaust gas recirculation system—1972 Type 1 automatic stick shift sold in California

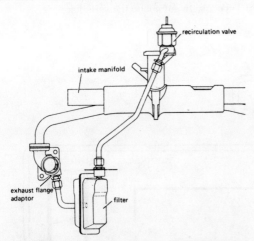

Exhaust gas recirculation system—1973–74 Type 1

All 1974 Type 1 cars, regardless of equipment, are equipped with EGR. The system uses the element type filter and EGR valve which recirculates exhaust gases during part throttle applications as before. However, to improve driveability, all California models use a two stage EGR valve (one stage in the 49 states), and California models equipped with an automatic use an electric throttle valve switch to further limit exhaust gas recirculation to part throttle applications (EGR permitted only between 12° to 72° on a scale of 90° throttle valve rotation).

EGR is installed on all 1975–77 models. All applications use the element type filter and single stage EGR valve. Recirculation occurs during part throttle applications as before. The system is controlled by a throttle valve switch which measures throttle position, and an intake air sensor which reacts to engine vacuum. Beginning in 1975, an odometer actuated EGR reminder light (on the dashboard) is used to inform the driver that it is time to service the EGR system. The reminder light measures elapsed mileage and lights at 15,000 mile intervals. A reset button is located behind the switch.

TYPE 2

Type 2 models use an EGR system beginning in 1973. All models use two valves; one at each manifold. Exhaust gas is taken from the muffler, cleaned in a replaceable element type filter, then directed to both intake manifolds, via the EGR valves. On models equipped with manual transmission, recirculation is vacuum controlled and occurs *both* during part *and* full throttle applications. On models equipped with the automatic, recirculation is controlled both by throttle position and engine compartment (ambient) temperature. When the ambient temperature exceeds 54° F, a sensor switch (located above the battery) opens,

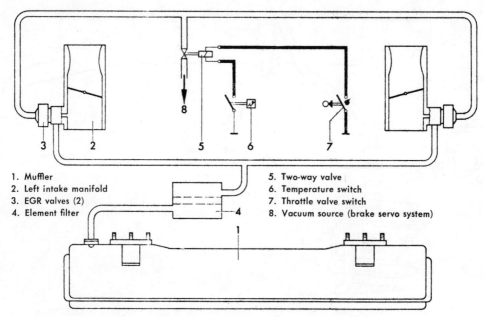

1. Muffler
2. Left intake manifold
3. EGR valves (2)
4. Element filter

5. Two-way valve
6. Temperature switch
7. Throttle valve switch
8. Vacuum source (brake servo system)

Exhaust gas recirculation system—1973 Type 2 with automatic transmission

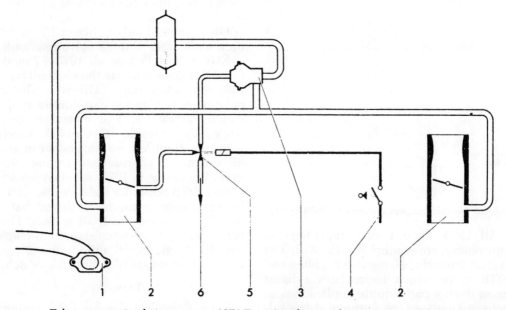

Exhaust gas recirculation system—1974 Type 2 with manual transmission sold in California

1. No. 1 exhaust port
2. Intake manifolds
3. EGR valve

4. Throttle micro-switch
5. Two-way valve
6. Vacuum source (brake servo system)

permitting EGR during part throttle applications.

All 1974 Type 2 models use EGR, but there are three different systems used. All models use one central EGR valve. Exhaust gas is taken from #4 exhaust port, cleaned in an element type filter, and then directed to both intake manifolds via the single EGR valve. Models equipped with manual transmission and sold in the 49 states use a single stage EGR valve which allows recirculation according to the vacuum signal in the left carburetor during part throttle applications. Models equipped with manual transmission and sold in California use a two stage EGR valve which recirculates exhaust gases during part throttle openings in two steps. During the first stage, EGR is controlled by the vacuum in the left carburetor. The second stage controls EGR according to the throttle position of the right carburetor. Finally, all models equipped with automatic transmission (nationwide) use a single stage EGR valve which controls recirculation according to throttle valve position and engine cooling air temperature. When the cooling system air reaches 185° F, a sensor switch (located between the coil and distributor) opens, permitting EGR during part throttle applications.

All 1975–77 Type 2 models utilize an EGR system. A single stage EGR valve and element type filter are used on all applications. Recirculation occurs during part throttle openings, and is controlled by throttle position, engine vacuum, and engine compartment temperature (54° F cutoff as in 1973). At 15,000 mile intervals, a dash mounted EGR service reminder light is activated to warn the driver that EGR service is now due. A reset button is located behind the switch.

TYPE 3

EGR is first used in the 1972 Type 3 models destined for California and equipped with automatic transmission. Exhaust gas is drawn from the front right hand exhaust flange to the EGR valve via a container and cyclone filter. The EGR valve then delivers the exhaust gases to the intake air distributor under the following conditions; Under part throttle (not full throttle or idling) conditions when the ambient air temperature

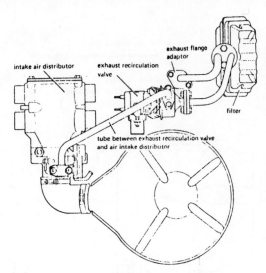

Exhaust gas recirculation system—1973 Type 3 with automatic transmission

reaches 65° F *and* only first or second gears are selected.

All 1973 Type 3 models equipped with automatic transmission use an EGR system. The exhaust gases are cleaned in a replaceable element type filter in 1973 instead of the cyclone filter and container of the previous year. The EGR valve then delivers the gases according to an electromagnetic valve which permits recirculation above 54° F.

TYPE 4

EGR appears only on 1974 models (nationwide) equipped with automatic transmission. On this system, exhaust gas is drawn from the muffler to a single EGR valve via an element type filter. The gases are delivered to the intake air distributor under part throttle conditions.

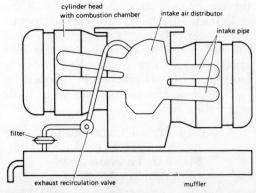

Exhaust gas recirculation system—1974 Type 4 with automatic transmission

A. Intake distributor
B. Exhaust gas recirculating valve
C. Pipeline
D. Cyclone filter
E. Cyclone filter container
F. Throttle valve switch

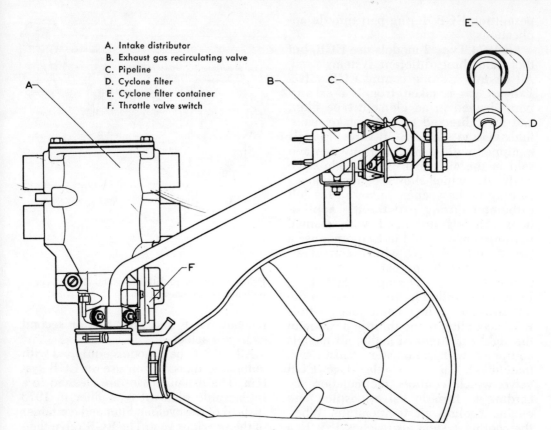

Exhaust gas recirculation system—1972 Type 3 with automatic transmission sold in California

EGR Valve Checking

1972–74 TYPE 1 (EXCEPT 1974 CALIFORNIA MODELS)

1. With the engine idling at operating temperature (176° F), pull off the vacuum hose from the EGR valve and push on the black hose from the intake air preheating thermostat instead.

2. If the idle speed drops off sharply or stalls, recirculation is taking place and the valve is OK. If, however, the idle speed does not change, the EGR valve is faulty or a hose is cracked or blocked.

3. Replace the vacuum hoses to their original locations.

1974 TYPE 1 CALIFORNIA AND 1974 TYPE 2 MANUAL TRANSMISSION CALIFORNIA MODELS

On these 1974 California models, a two-stage EGR valve with a visible pin is used. To check the valve operation, simply make sure that the pin moves in and out relative to engine rpm. If the pin does not move, check the hoses and/or replace the EGR valve.

1974 TYPE 2 w/MANUAL TRANSMISSION (EXCEPT CALIFORNIA MODELS)

1. With the engine idling at operating temperature, pull off the vacuum hose at the tee-fitting for the EGR valve and push on the hose from the flow valve of the air pump to the fitting instead.

2. If idle speed drops sharply or stalls, the valve is OK. If the rpm does not change, a hose is blocked or the valve is faulty.

3. Replace the hoses to their original locations.

1972–73 Type 3

1. Remove the EGR valve.
2. Reconnect the vacuum hose and place the valve on the base.
3. Start the engine. If it doesn't stall, the vacuum line between the valve base and the intake manifold is clogged and must be cleaned.
4. Run the engine at 2000–3000 rpm. The closing pin of the EGR valve should pull in 0.15 in. (4 mm) and immediately return to its original position at idle. Replace the EGR valve if it doesn't operate correctly.
5. Install the EGR valve using new seals.

1973 Type 2

1. Remove the EGR valve.
2. Inspect the valve for cleanliness.
3. Check the valve for freedom of movement by pressing in on the valve pin.
4. Connect the valve to the vacuum hose of another engine or vacuum source and start the engine. At 1500–2000 rpm the valve pin should be pulled in and when the speed is reduced it should return to its original position. Replace the EGR valve if it doesn't operate correctly.
5. Replace the washer and install the valve.
6. Repeat this operation on the second valve.

CATALYTIC CONVERTER SYSTEM

All 1975–77 Type 1 and 2 models sold in California and in 1977 in the other 49 states, are equipped with a catalytic converter. The converter is installed in the exhaust system, upstream and adjacent to the muffler.

Catalytic converters change noxious emissions of hydrocarbons (HC) and carbon monoxide (CO) into harmless carbon dioxide and water vapor. The reaction takes place inside the converter at great heat using platinum and palladium metals as the catalyst. If the engine is operated on lead-free fuel, they are designed to last 50,000 miles before replacement.

DECELERATION CONTROL

All 1975–77 Type 2 models, as well as those 1975–77 Type 1 models equipped with manual transmission, are equipped with deceleration control to prevent an overly rich fuel mixture from reaching the exhaust. During deceleration, a vacuum valve (manual transmission) or electrical transmission switch (automatic transmission) opens, bypassing the closed throttle plate and allowing air to enter the combustion chambers.

THROTTLE VALVE POSITIONER

All 1970–71 Type 1 and 2/1600 models equipped with manual transmission, and 1972 Type 1 models with manual transmission sold in California use a throttle valve positioner to hold the throttle butterfly slightly open during deceleration to prevent an excessively rich mixture from reaching the combustion chambers. The throttle valve positioner consists of two parts connected by a hose. The operating part is mounted on the carburetor, connected to the throttle valve arm. It regulates fast idle speed. The control section (altitude corrector) is located at the left side of the engine compartment. It controls throttle valve closing time.

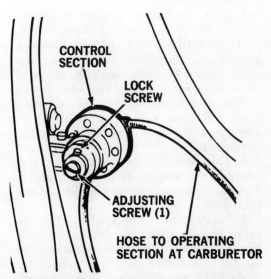

CONTROL SECTION

LOCK SCREW

ADJUSTING SCREW (1)

HOSE TO OPERATING SECTION AT CARBURETOR

1970–72 Throttle valve positioner adjustment showing adjusting screw (1) on control section (altitude corrector) located at left rear of engine compartment on Type 1 and 2/1600 models

Operating section of 1970–72 two-piece throttle valve positioner showing mounting screws and hose connections

Adjustment

NOTE: *The car should first be warmed to operating temperature (122–158° F) for this adjustment. Make sure the choke plate is open.*

1. Hook up a tachometer (0–3000 rpm sweep minimum) to the engine with the positive lead to the distributor side of the coil and the negative lead to a good ground. You will also need a stop watch or a good wristwatch with a second hand.

CAUTION: *Keep yourself, any clothing, jewelry, long locks (of hair), or tools etc. well clear of the engine belts and pulleys. Make sure you are in a well ventilated area.*

2. Start the engine and let it idle in neutral. Make a check of the fast idle speed by pulling the fast idle lever back so that it contacts the lever stop on the carburetor. The tachometer should read 1450–1650 rpm. If the fast idle is not within specifications, turn the adjusting screw (on the lever stop, not on the lever you dummy) as required. Disconnect the tachometer.

3. Take the car for a warmup drive. Recheck the fast idle as in steps 1 and 2. The tachometer reading should not exceed 1700 rpm.

4. Now, make a check of the throttle valve closing time and get your watch handy. Pull the throttle lever away from the fast idle lever until the tachometer reads 3000 rpm. While keeping an eye on the second hand of your watch, release the throttle lever and check the time elapsed until the engine reaches idle

speed (800–900 rpm). The closing time should be 2.5–4.5 seconds. If the closing time is not within specifications, adjust the control section at the left side of the engine compartment. After loosening the lock screw, turn the adjusting screw (1) clockwise to increase closing time and counterclockwise to decrease closing time. Recheck the adjustment. If it is within specifications, tighten the lock screw and disconnect the tachometer.

5. Take the car for another test drive (isn't this fun?). Once again, recheck the closing time as in step 4. The closing time now must not exceed 6 seconds. If it does, go back to step 4. If it doesn't, shut off the engine, disconnect the tachometer, and have a cigar.

Fuel System

MECHANICAL FUEL PUMP

All 1970–74 Type 1 and 2 models utilize a mechanical fuel pump. The pump is located to the left of the generator/alternator on Type 1 and 2/1600 models, and located next to the flywheel on dual carburetor Type 2 models. On Type 1 and 2/1600 models the pump is pushrod operated by an eccentric on the distributor driveshaft. On Type 2/1700 and 2/1800 twin carb models the pump is operated by a pushrod which rides on a camshaft eccentric.

Removal and Installation

TYPES 1, 2/1600

1. Disconnect the fuel lines at the pump and plug them to prevent leakage.

2. Remove the two securing nuts.

3. Remove the fuel pump. If necessary, the pushrod, gaskets, and intermediate flange may also be removed.

4. When installing the fuel pump, it is necessary to check the fuel pump pushrod stroke. This is done by measuring the distance that the pushrod projects above the intermediate flange when both gaskets are in place. The rod must project ½ inch.

5. Fill the cavity in the lower part of

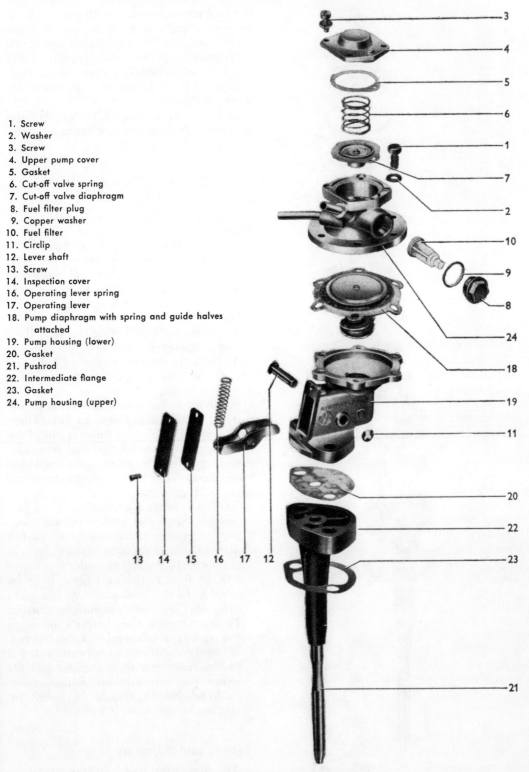

1. Screw
2. Washer
3. Screw
4. Upper pump cover
5. Gasket
6. Cut-off valve spring
7. Cut-off valve diaphragm
8. Fuel filter plug
9. Copper washer
10. Fuel filter
11. Circlip
12. Lever shaft
13. Screw
14. Inspection cover
16. Operating lever spring
17. Operating lever
18. Pump diaphragm with spring and guide halves attached
19. Pump housing (lower)
20. Gasket
21. Pushrod
22. Intermediate flange
23. Gasket
24. Pump housing (upper)

Exploded view of fuel pump—1970 Type 1

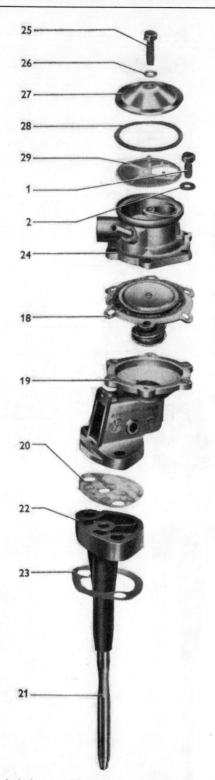

25
26
27
28
29
1
2
24
18
19
20
22
23
21

Exploded view of fuel pump—1970 Type 2

18. Pump diaphragm with	22. Intermediate flange
spring and guide halves	27. Fuel filter cover
attached	28. Fuel filter cover gasket
21. Pushrod	29. Fuel filter screen

the fuel pump housing with grease. Total pushrod length is 4.252 in. for all Type 2/1600 and for Type 1 models equipped with generators. Pushrod length is 3.937 in. for all 1973–74 Type 1 models equipped with alternators. Replace any worn pushrod.

6. Using new gaskets, install the fuel pump and tighten the two securing nuts.

7. Install the fuel hoses.

TYPES 2/1700 AND 2/1800 TWIN CARB

1. Believe it or not, remove the engine.

2. Once the engine is removed, remove the upper and lower deflector plates and the carburetor preheater connection to gain access to the pump mounting bolts (adjacent to the flywheel).

3. Disconnect and plug the fuel lines to the carburetors.

4. Remove the two retaining bolts and lift off the fuel pump, gaskets and intermediate flange.

5. Reverse the above laborious procedure to install, using new gaskets. However, since the blasted thing is out of the bus already, you might as well rebuild it referring to the accompanying exploded view. Remember to coat the pushrod and lever with grease.

NOTE: *Prior to installation of the fuel pump, check the action of the camshaft eccentric driven pushrod. Install just the intermediate flange on the engine with 2 gaskets underneath and one on top. Turn the engine over by hand until the pushrod is on the highest point of the camshaft eccentric. Then, measure the distance between the tip of the pushrod and the top gasket surface. Adjust, as necessary, to 0.2 in. by removing or installing gaskets under the intermediate flange. Total pushrod length should be 5.492 in. minimum. Replace, if worn.*

Testing and Adjusting

The maximum fuel pump pressure developed by the Type 1 and 2/1600 fuel pump is 3.5 psi at 3,400 rpm for the Type 1 and 4,000 rpm for the Type 2. The maximum fuel pump pressure developed by

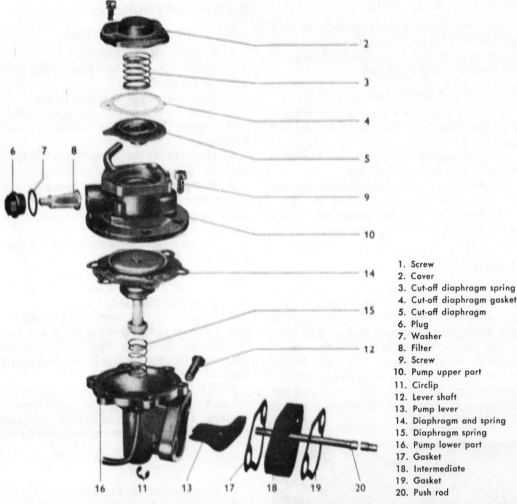

1. Screw
2. Cover
3. Cut-off diaphragm spring
4. Cut-off diaphragm gasket
5. Cut-off diaphragm
6. Plug
7. Washer
8. Filter
9. Screw
10. Pump upper part
11. Circlip
12. Lever shaft
13. Pump lever
14. Diaphragm and spring
15. Diaphragm spring
16. Pump lower part
17. Gasket
18. Intermediate
19. Gasket
20. Push rod

Exploded view of fuel pump—1972–74 Type 2 twin carb

the Type 2 Twin carb fuel pump is 5 psi at 3800 rpm.

All fuel pumps deliver 400 cc of fuel per minute.

The only adjustment possible is performed by varying the thickness of the fuel pump flange gaskets. Varying the thickness of the gaskets will change the stroke of the fuel pump pushrod. This adjustment is not meant to compensate for a pump in bad condition; therefore, do not attempt to vary the height of the pushrod to any great extent.

The fuel pumps used on 1970 Type 1 and 2 models, and 1972–74 Type 2 models may be disassembled for cleaning or repairs. All other mechanical pumps are permanently sealed and must be replaced if found defective.

Electric fuel pump showing fuel filter mounting bracket

ELECTRIC FUEL PUMP

All Type 3 and Type 4 models, as well as 1975–77 Type 1 and Type 2 models have an electric pump. The fuel pump is located near the front axle.

Removal and Installation

1. Disconnect the fuel pump wiring. Pull the plug from the pump but do not pull on the wiring.
2. Disconnect the fuel hoses and plug them to prevent any leakage.
3. Remove the two nuts which secure the pump and then remove the pump.
4. Reconnect the fuel pump hoses and wiring and install the pump on the vehicle.

Adjustments

Electric fuel pump pressure is 28 psi. Fuel pump pressure is determined by a pressure regulator which diverts part of the fuel pump output to the gas tank when 28 psi is reached. The regulator, located on the engine firewall, has a screw and lock nut on its end. Loosen the lock nut and adjust the screw to adjust the pressure. Do not force the screw in or out if it does not turn.

Fuel injection fuel pressure regulator with locknut and adjusting screw (small arrow) at left end of regulator

CARBURETORS

Carburetors are used on all 1970–74 Type 1 and 2 models. A single downdraft unit is used on all Type 1 models and on 1970–71 Type 2 models. Beginning with the 1972 model year, the Type 2 utilizes twin carburetion.

Removal and Installation

TYPE 1 AND 2/1600

1. Remove the air cleaner.
2. Disconnect the fuel hose. Plug it to prevent leakage.
3. Disconnect the vacuum hoses.
4. Remove the automatic choke cable and remove the wire for the electromagnetic pilot jet.
5. Disconnect the accelerator cable at the throttle valve lever.
6. Remove the two nuts securing the carburetor on the intake manifold and then remove the carburetor from the engine.
7. Using a new gasket, install the carburetor on the manifold.
8. Reconnect the fuel and vacuum hoses, the automatic choke cable, and the wiring for the pilot jet.
9. Reconnect the throttle cable and adjust it so that at full throttle there is a gap of 0.04 in. between the throttle valve lever and its stop on the lower portion of the carburetor body.

NOTE: *Open the throttle valve by hand and tighten the adjustment screw, then have an assistant open the throttle and recheck the adjustment.*

TYPE 2/1700 AND 2/1800 TWIN CARB

1. Remove the air cleaner.
2. Disconnect and plug the fuel line(s).
3. Disconnect the electrical leads for

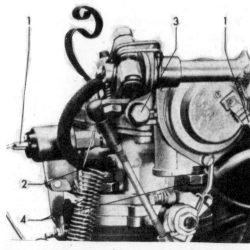

Type 2 twin carb connections for left carburetor

Carburetor Overhaul

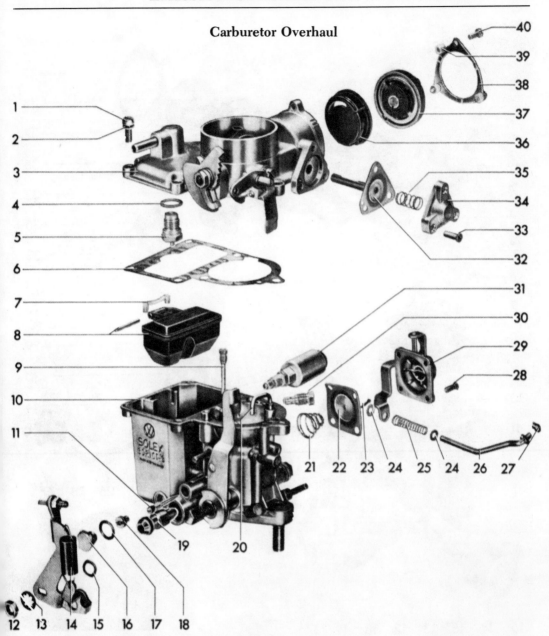

Exploded view of Solex 30 PICT-3 carburetor used on 1970 Type 1 and 2/1600 models

1. Carburetor screw, upper part
2. Spring washer
3. Carburetor upper part
4. Float needle valve washer
5. Float needle valve
6. Washer
7. Float pin retainer
8. Float and pin
9. Air correction jet
10. Carburetor lower part
11. Volume control screw
12. Nut
13. Lock washer
14. Accelerator cable spring

16. Plug
15. Spring
17. Plug seal
18. Main jet
19. By-pass air screw
20. Accelerator pump injector tube
21. Pump diaphragm spring
22. Pump diaphragm
23. Cotter pin
24. Washer
25. Connecting rod spring
26. Connecting rod
27. Clip
28. Screw

29. Pump cover
30. Pilot jet
31. By-pass mixture cut-off valve
32. Vacuum diaphragm
33. Screw
34. Vacuum diaphragm cover
35. Vacuum diaphragm spring
36. Cap (plastic)
37. Automatic choke
38. Cover retaining ring
39. Cover spacer
40. Retaining ring screw

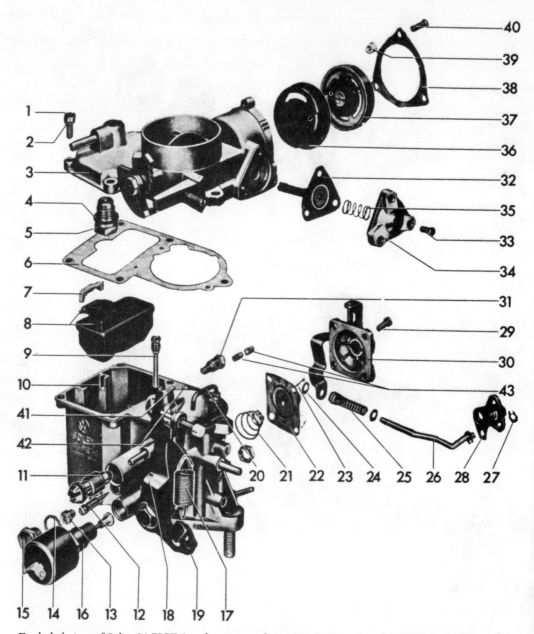

Exploded view of Solex 34 PICT-3 carburetor used on 1971–74 Type 1 and 1971 Type 2/1600 models

1. Carburetor screw, upper part
2. Spring washer
3. Carburetor upper part
4. Float needle valve washer
5. Float needle valve
6. Washer
7. Float pin retainer
8. Float and pin
9. Air correction jet and emulsion tube
10. Carburetor lower part
11. By-pass screw
12. Volume control screw
13. Main jet
14. Plug washer
15. Plug
16. By-pass air cut-off valve
17. Return spring
18. Fast idling lever
19. Throttle valve lever and stop screw
20. Accelerator pump injection pipe
21. Diaphragm spring
22. Accelerator pump diaphragm
23. Cotter pin
24. Washer
25. Connecting rod spring
26. Connecting rod
27. Clip
28. Bell crank lever
29. Countersunk head screw
30. Pump cover
31. Pilot jet
32. Vacuum-diaphragm
33. Countersunk head screw
34. Vacuum diaphragm cover
35. Vacuum diaphragm spring
36. Plastic cap
37. Insert with spring and heater element
38. Cover retaining ring
39. Retaining ring spacer
40. Retaining ring screw
41. Pilot air drilling
42. Auxiliary air drilling
43. Auxiliary fuel jet and plug

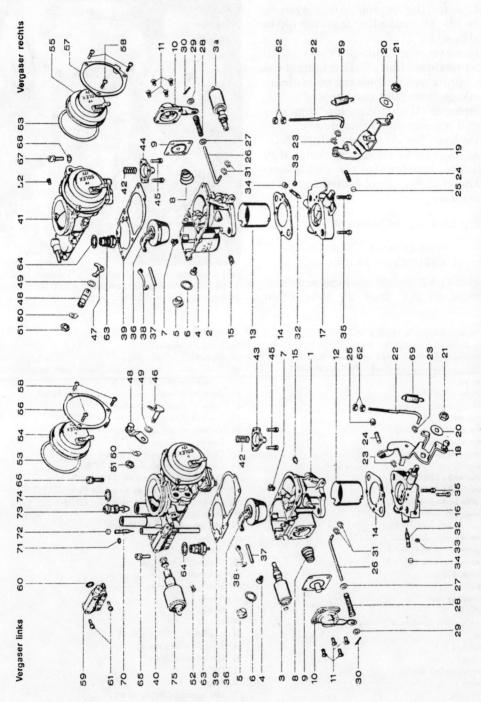

Exploded view of Solex 34 PDSIT 2/3 carburetors used on 1972–74 Type 2/1700, 2/1800 models

the automatic choke, pilot jet cut-off valve, and idle mixture cut-off valve.

4. If removing the left carburetor, disconnect the vacuum line (2), the idle mixture line for the central idling system, and the idle air intake line from the top of the carburetor.

5. Remove the linkage cross shaft bracket retaining bolt (3). Disconnect the return spring and the pull rod and release the linkage from both carburetors.

6. Remove the carburetor retaining nuts and remove the carburetor(s).

7. Reverse the above procedure to install, taking care to use new gaskets. After installation, synchronize the carburetors as outlined under "Fuel Adjustments" in Chapter Two.

Throttle Linkage Adjustment

SINGLE AND TWIN
CARBURETOR MODELS

1. Have an assistant hold the accelerator pedal to the floor at wide open

throttle. Measure the distance (a) between the throttle valve lever and the stop

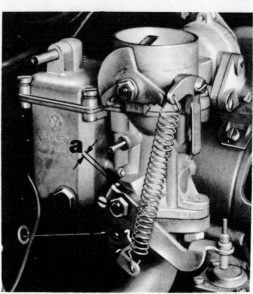

Full throttle clearance (distance "a") should be 0.04 in. on Type 1 and 2/1600 engines, and 0.04–0.06 in. on Type 2/1700 and 2/1800 engines

1. Carburetor body—34 PDSIT-2
2. Carburetor body—34 PDSIT-3
3. Electromagnetic idling cutoff valve—34 PDSIT-2
3a. Electromagnetic idling cutoff valve—34 PDSIT-3
4. Main jet
5. Main jet cover plug
6. Main jet cover plug seal
7. Air correction jet
8. Pump diaphragm spring
9. Pump diaphragm
10. Accelerator pump cover
11. Screws
12. Venturi—34 PDSIT-2
13. Venturi—34 PDSIT-3
14. Throttle body gasket
15. Venturi setscrew
16. Throttle body—34 PDSIT-2
17. Throttle body—34 PDSIT-3
18. Throttle arm—34 PDSIT-2
19. Throttle arm—34 PDSIT-3
20. Special washer
21. Nut
22. Connecting rod
23. Circlip
24. Throttle valve opening adjusting screw
25. Plug
26. Conecting link
27. Washer
28. Connecting link spring
29. Washer
30. Cotter pin
31. Circlip
32. Idle mixture screw
33. O-ring
34. Plug
35. Throttle body screws
36. Float

37. Float pin
38. Float pin retainer
39. Gasket
40. Carburetor upper part (air horn) with idle mixture enrichment—34 PDSIT-2
41. Carburetor upper part (air horn)—34 PDSIT-3
42. Vacuum diaphragm spring
43. Vacuum diaphragm cover—34 PDSIT-2
44. Vacuum diaphragm cover—34 PDSIT-3
45. Screws
53. Choke heating element gasket
54. Choke heating element—34 PDSIT-2
55. Choke heating element—34 PDSIT-3
56. Choke cover retaining ring—34 PDSIT-2
57. Choke cover retaining ring—34 PDSIT-3
58. Screws
59. Idle mixture enrichment unit
60. O-ring
61. Screws
62. Connecting rod locknuts
63. Float valve
64. Float valve washer
65. Screws
66. Screws
67. Screws
68. Washer
69. Throttle return spring
70. Idle mixture screw
71. O-ring
72. Plug
73. Idle speed adjusting screw
74. O-ring
75. Central idling system electromagnetic cutoff valve
Vergaser links—left carburetor (34 PDSIT-2)
Vergaser rechts—right carburetor (34 PDSIT-3)

on the carburetor body. Proper distance (a) is 0.04 in. minimum.

2. To adjust, loosen the cable adjusting screw found in the bottom on the throttle lever.

3. The throttle lever has a rigid cylinder attached to its end. Move the rigid portion in or out of the end of the throttle lever to obtain the proper adjustment and tighten the adjusting screw. The proper adjustment is reached when there is a gap of 0.04 in. (single carb) or 0.04–0.06 in (twin carb) between the throttle valve lever and its stop on the lower portion of the carburetor body. See the note at the end of the "Carburetor Removal and Installation" procedure.

Float and Fuel Level Adjustment

NOTE: *The carburetor or car must be on a level surface to obtain an accurate reading.*

A properly asembled carburetor has a preset float level. For the float level to be correct the fiber washer under the needle valve seat must be installed and be of the proper thickness. See the "Carburetor Specifications Chart."

The only way to adjust the float level, if it is absolutely necessary, and still retain proper seating of the needle in the needle valve seat, is to vary the thickness of the fiber washer beneath the seat.

Washers are available in thicknesses of 0.50 mm, 0.80 mm, 1.00 mm, and 1.50 mm.

Throttle Valve Gap

34 PDSIT 2/3 CARBURETORS

Carburetor Removed

1. Remove the carburetor from the car.

2. Loosen the two nuts (A) on the automatic choke connecting rod and insert a 0.028 in. wire gauge or drill between the throttle valve and the side of the venturi.

3. Move the two nuts (A) up or down on the connecting rod until the throttle valve gap is adjusted and tighten the two nuts (A).

NOTE: *The choke valve must be closed for proper adjustment.*

Carburetor Installed

1. Back out the idle speed screw until the throttle valve is completely closed.

Adjusting throttle valve gap with adjusting nuts (A) —34 PDSIT 2/3 carburetors

2. Turn the idle speed screw until it just touches the throttle lever.

3. Close the choke valve.

4. Place a 0.09 in. drill or wire gauge between the idle screw and the throttle valve lever. Adjust the two nuts on the automatic choke connecting rod either up or down until the drill can be easily pulled out.

5. It will be necessary to rebalance the carburetors.

Accelerator Pump Adjustment

ALL CARBURETOR TYPES

Improper accelerator pump adjustment is characterized by flat spots during acceleration or a severe hesitation when the throttle is first depressed.

NOTE: *VW now has a special tool available that allows you to check accelerator pump injection quantity without removing the top of the carburetor (air horn). It consists of a measuring glass, and injection pipe and a choke plate retainer. The part number is VW 119.*

1. Remove the carburetor from the engine and remove the upper half of the carburetor.

2. Support the carburetor securely in a vise without damaging the carburetor body.

3. Fill the float chamber with gasoline and attach a rubber tube to the injector

Measuring accelerator pump injection quantity

tube. Place the open end of the tube into a milliliter measuring tube.

4. Move the throttle lever several strokes until all of the air is forced out of the tube. Move the throttle lever an additional ten full strokes and measure the quantity of gas in the measuring tube. Multiply the accelerator pump quantity injected specification by 10 and compare this figure to the amount of gas in the measuring tube.

5a. On 30 PICT-3 and 34 PDSIT 2/3 carburetors, the injection quantity is de-

Accelerator pump injection quantity adjusting segment for 1973–74 Type 1 models with alternator. Dotted line shows position of adjusting segment for 1971–73 Type 1 models with generator (Solex 34 PICT-3).

creased by moving the cotter pin to the outer hole in the connecting link, and increased by moving it to the inner hole.

5b. On 34 PICT-3 carburetors, the injection quantity is decreased by loosening the retaining screw and turning the adjusting segment clockwise, and increased by loosening the retaining screw and turning the adjusting segment clockwise. After adjusting, always tighten the retaining screw.

5c. On 34 PICT-4 carburetors (used on 1973–74 Type 1 models sold in California), the injection quantity is adjusted by turning the adjusting screw (spring loaded) on the pump operating rod.

NOTE: *Below 70° F, injection quantity is 1.7 cm³ per stroke. Above 78° F, injector quantity is 1.1 cm³ per stroke.*

Accelerator pump injection quantity adjusting nut for 1973–74 Type 1 models sold in California (Solex 34 PICT-4)

Fast Idle Adjustment

The fast idle speed is adjusted by means of a screw located at the upper end of the throttle valve arm. This screw rests against a cam with steps cut into its edge.

To adjust the fast idle, start the engine and rotate the cam so that the fast idle screw is resting against the highest step on the fast idle cam. The fast idle speed should be approximately 1500 rpm. Turn the fast idle screw either in or out until the proper idle speed is obtained.

On dual carburetor engines it is necessary to adjust the fast idle on only the left carburetor. There is a direct connection between the two carburetors and if the left carburetor is adjusted the right will automatically be adjusted.

Accelerator Cable Replacement

1. Disconnect the cable from the accelerator pedal.

2. Disconnect the cable from the throttle lever.

3. Pull the cable from the accelerator pedal end and then remove it from the car.

4. Grease the cable before sliding it into its housing.

5. Slide the cable into its housing and push it through its guide tubes. It may be necessary to raise the car and start the cable into the segments of guide tube found under the car.

6. Install one cable end into the accelerator cable. Slip the other end into the throttle valve lever and adjust the cable.

NOTE: *Make sure that the rubber boot at the rear end of the cable is properly seated so that water will not enter the guide tubes.*

Dashpot Adjustment

1972–74 Type 1 with Manual Transmission

NOTE: *The car must be fully warmed up and the choke plate open.*

1. Check that the distance (a) between the tip of the dashpot and the throttle lever is 0.040 in. with the dashpot plunger fully retracted and the throttle fully closed on the warm running position of the fast idle cam.

2. To adjust, loosen the two locknuts on the dashpot mounting bracket, and raise or lower the dashpot as needed.

1972–74 Type 2 Twin Carb

NOTE: *This adjustment is required only if the dashpot has been removed or the linkage disassembled.*

1. Check that the distance between

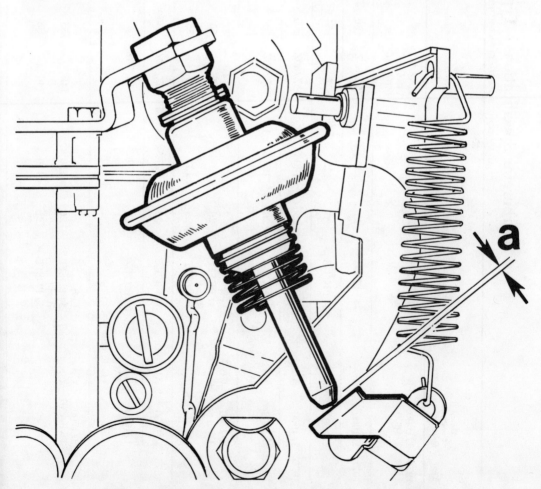

Dashpot adjustment on 1972–74 Type 1 models. Distance "A" is 0.040 in.

Carburetor Specifications—Types 1 and 2
(All measurements are in metric units)

Year	Type/ Common Designation	Engine Code	Carburetor (Solex)	Venturi Diameter (mm)	Main Jet	Air Correction Jet	Pilot Jet	Aux Fuel Jet	Aux Air Jet	Power Fuel Jet	Needle Valve Washer Thickness (mm)	Accelerator Pump Injection Quantity (cc³ stroke)	Throttle Valve Gap (mm)	Fuel Level (mm)
1970	1/1600, 2/1600	B	30 PICT-3	24	x 112.5	125Z-MT 140Z-AT 140Z-Bus	65	45.0	130	100/100	1.5	1.05–1.35	—	19.5–20.5
1971	1/1600	AE	34 PICT-3	26	x 130	75Z/80Z	g60	47.5	90	100/100	0.5	1.45–1.75	—	17–19
	2/1600	AE	34 PICT-3	26	x 125	60Z	g57.5	42.5	90	95/95	0.5	1.45–1.75	—	17–19
1972	1/1600	AE	34 PICT-3	26	x 130	75Z/80Z	g60	47.5	90	100/100	0.5	1.45–1.75	—	17–19
	1/1600	AH (Calif only)	34 PICT-3	26	x 127.5/ x 130	75Z/80Z	g55	42.5	90	100	0.5	1.3–1.6	—	17–19
	2/1700 Twin carb	CB	Left 34 PDSIT-2	26	x 137.5	155	55	45.0	0.7	—	0.5	0.8–1.0	0.6	12–14
			Right 34 PDSIT-3	26	x 137.5	155	55	—	—	—	0.5	0.8–1.0	0.6	12–14
1973	1/1600	AK	34 PICT-3	26	x 127.5/ x 127.5	75Z/80Z	g55	42.5	90	100	0.5	1.3–1.6	—	17–19
	1/1600	AH, AM (Calif only)	34 PICT-4	26	x 112.5	75Z/70Z	g55	42.5	90	100	0.5	1.3–1.6	—	17–19
	2/1700 Twin carb (man trans)	CB	Left 34 PDSIT-2	26	x 130	140	55	45.0	0.7	—	1.0	0.6–0.8	0.6	12–14
			Right 34 PDSIT-3	26	x 130	140	55	—	—	—	1.0	0.6–0.8	0.6	12–14

Engine	Code	Carburetor											
2/1700 Twin carb	CD (AT)	Left 34 PDSIT-2	26	x 132.5	155	50	45.0	0.7	—	1.0	0.7-1.2	0.6	12-14
		Right 34 PDSIT-3	26	x 132.5	155	50	—	—	—	1.0	0.7-1.2	0.6	12-14
1974 1/1600	AK	34 PICT-3	26	x 127.5/ x 127.5	75Z/80Z	g55	42.5	90	100	0.5	1.3-1.6	—	17-19
1/1600	AH, AM (Calif only)	34 PICT-4	26	x 127.5	75Z-MT 70Z-AT	g55	42.5	90	100	0.5	1.1-1.7	—	17-19
2/1800 Twin carb	AW	Left 34 PDSIT-2	26	x 130	175	52.5	45.0	0.7	—	1.0	1.3-1.7	0.7	12-14
		Right 34 PDSIT-3	26	x 130	175	52.5	—	—	—	1.0	1.3-1.7	0.7	12-14
1975-77		Air flow controlled electronic fuel injection											

MT—Manual Transmission
AT—Automatic Transmission
— Not Applicable

the tip of the plunger and the tab on the linkage is 0.0015 in. while holding the dashpot plunger in the retracted position.

2. To adjust, loosen the two locknuts on the dashpot mounting bracket, and raise or lower the dashpot as required.

ELECTRONIC FUEL INJECTION— NON-AIR FLOW CONTROLLED

The Bosch Electronic fuel injection system used on all Type 3 models, and on 1971–74 Type 4 models (except 1974 models equipped with an automatic), consists of two parts. One part consists of the actual injection components: the injectors, the fuel pump, pressure regulator, and related wiring and hoses. The second part consists of the injection controls and engine operating characteristics sensors: a manifold vacuum sensor that monitors engine load, trigger contacts used to determine when and which pair of injectors will operate, three temperature sensors used to control air fuel mixture enrichment, a cold starting valve for additional cold starting fuel enrichment, a throttle valve switch used to cut off fuel during deceleration, and the brain box used to analyze information about engine operating characteristics and, after processing this information, to control the electrically operated injectors.

It is absolutely imperative that no adjustments other than those found in the following pages be performed. The controls for this fuel injection system are extremely sensitive and easily damaged when subject to abuse. Never attempt to test the brain box without proper training and the proper equipment. The dealer is the best place to have any needed work performed.

CAUTION: *Whenever a fuel injection component is to be removed or installed, the battery should be disconnected and the ignition turned OFF.*

It is not recommended that the inexperienced mechanic work on any portion of the fuel injection system.

AIR FLOW CONTROLLED ELECTRONIC FUEL INJECTION

1974 Type 4 models equipped with automatic transmission, as well as all 1975–77 Type 1 and Type 2 models, are equipped with an improved system known as the Air Flow Controlled Electronic Fuel Injection System. With this system, some of the electronic sensors and wiring are eliminated, and the control box is smaller. Instead fuel is metered according to intake air flow.

The system consists of the following components;

Intake air sensor—measures intake air volume and temperature and sends voltage signals to the control unit (brain box). It also controls the electric fuel pump by shutting it off when intake air stops. It is

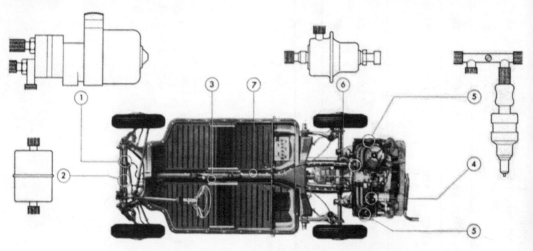

Location of fuel injection components—Type 3

1. Fuel pump
2. Fuel filter
3. Pressure line
4. Ring main
5. Injectors
6. Pressure regulator
7. Return line (not pressurized)

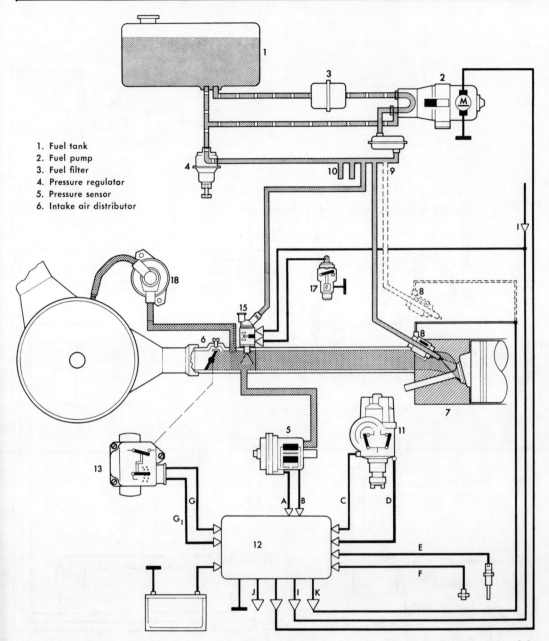

1. Fuel tank
2. Fuel pump
3. Fuel filter
4. Pressure regulator
5. Pressure sensor
6. Intake air distributor

Schematic of electronic fuel injection system—1970 and later 49 states models, 1970–71 California models

7. Cylinder head
8. Injectors
9. Fuel distributor pipe
10. Fuel distributor pipe with connection for cold starting device
11. Distributor with trigger contacts (distributor contact I, distributor contact II)
12. Control unit
13. Throttle valve switch with acceleration enrichment
15. Cold starting valve
17. Thermostat for cold starting device
18. Auxiliary air regulator

A + B. from pressure sensor (load condition signal)
C + D. from distributor contacts (engine speed and releasing signal)
E + F. from temperature sensors (warmup signal)
G. from throttle valve switch (fuel supply cut-off when coasting)
G 1. Acceleration enrichment
I. from starter, terminal 50 solenoid switch (signal for enrichment mixture when starting)
J. to the injectors, cylinders 1 and 4
K. to the injectors, cylinders 2 and 3

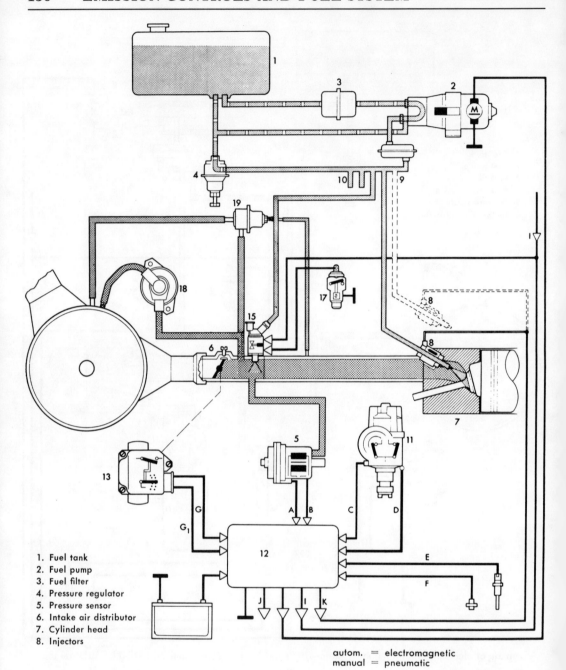

autom. = electromagnetic
manual = pneumatic

Schematic of electronic fuel injection system—1972–74 California models

1. Fuel tank
2. Fuel pump
3. Fuel filter
4. Pressure regulator
5. Pressure sensor
6. Intake air distributor
7. Cylinder head
8. Injectors

9. Fuel distributor pipe
10. Fuel distributor pipe with connection for cold starting device
11. Distributor with trigger contacts (contacts I and II)
12. Electronic control unit
13. Throttle valve switch with acceleration enrichment
14. Pressure switch
15. Cold starting valve
17. Thermostat for cold starting device
18. Auxiliary air regulator
19. Deceleration mixture control valve

A + B. from pressure sensor (load condition signal)
C + D. from distributor contacts (engine speed and releasing signal)
E + F. from temperature sensors (warmup signal)
G. from throttle valve switch (full throttle signal. Type 3 only)
G 1. Acceleration enrichment
I. from starter, terminal 50 solenoid switch (signal for enrichment mixture when starting)
J. to injectors, cylinders 1 and 4
K. to the injectors, cylinders 2 and 3

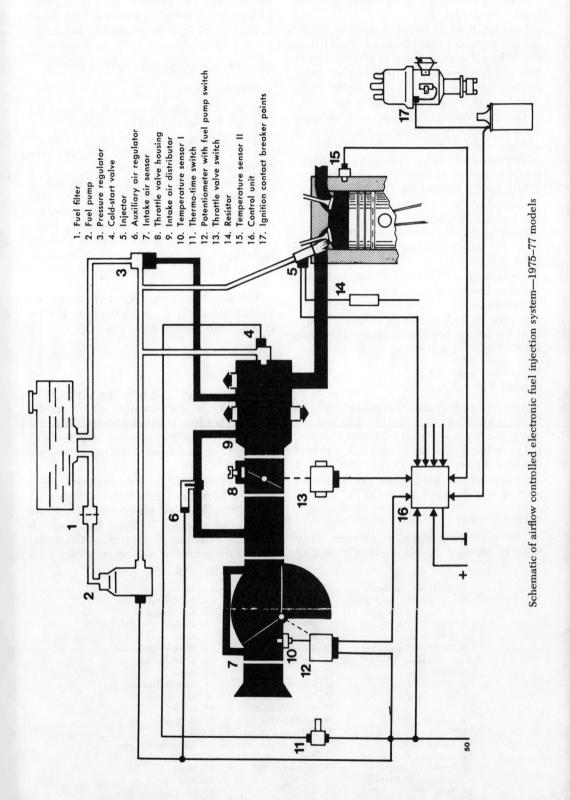

1. Fuel filter
2. Fuel pump
3. Pressure regulator
4. Cold-start valve
5. Injector
6. Auxiliary air regulator
7. Intake air sensor
8. Throttle valve housing
9. Intake air distributor
10. Temperature sensor I
11. Thermo-time switch
12. Potentiometer with fuel pump switch
13. Throttle valve switch
14. Resistor
15. Temperature sensor II
16. Control unit
17. Ignition contact breaker points

Schematic of airflow controlled electronic fuel injection system—1975–77 models

located between the air cleaner and the intake air distributor.

Ignition contact breaker points—these are the regular points inside the distributor. When the points open, all four injectors are triggered. The points also send engine speed signals to the control unit. No separate triggering contacts are used.

Throttle valve switch—provides only for full load enrichment. This switch is not adjustable.

Temperature sensor I—senses intake temperature as before. It is now located in the intake air sensor.

Temperature sensor II—senses cylinder head temperature as before.

Control unit (brain box)—contains only 80 components compared to the old systems 300.

Pressure regulator—is connected by a vacuum hose to the intake air distributor and is no longer adjustable. It adjusts fuel pressure according to manifold vacuum.

Auxiliary air regulator—provides more air during cold warmup.

Electronic Control (Brain) Box

All work concerning the brain box is to be performed by the dealer. Do not remove the brain box and take it to a dealer because the dealer will not be able to test it without the vehicle. Do not disconnect the brain box unless the battery is disconnected and the ignition is OFF.

Fuel Injectors

There are two types of injectors. One type is secured in place by a ring that holds a single injector. The second type of injector is secured to the intake manifold in pairs by a common bracket.

REMOVAL AND INSTALLATION

Single Injectors

1. Remove the nut which secures the injector bracket to the manifold.

2. If the injector is not going to be replaced, do not disconnect the fuel line. Disconnect the injector wiring.

3. Gently slide the injector bracket up the injector and pull the injector from the intake manifold. Be careful not to damage the inner and outer rubber sealing rings. These sealing rings are used to seal the injector to the manifold and must be replaced if they show any sign of deterioration.

4. Installation is the reverse of removal. Be careful not to damage the injector tip or contaminate the injector with dirt.

Paired Injectors

1. Disconnect the injector wiring.

2. Remove the two nuts which secure the injector bracket to the manifold. Slide the bracket up the injector. Do not disconnect the fuel lines if the injector is not going to be replaced.

3. Gently slide the pair of injectors out of their bores along with the rubber sealing rings, injector plate, and the inner and outer injector locating bushings. It may be necessary to remove the inner bushings from the intake manifold after

1. Intake air distributor (right-side) assembly	18. Connecting hose	37. Tee
2. Stud	19. By-pass air screw	38. Auxiliary air regulator
3. Stud	20. Washer	39. Spring washer
4. Stud	21. Gasket	40. Screw
5. Throttle valve housing assembly	22. Intake manifold	41. Hose
6. Stud	23. Gasket	42. Throttle valve switch
7. Washer	24. Spring washer	43. Spring washer
8. Spring washer	25. Nut	44. Screw
9. Nut	26. Connecting hose	45. Cold-start valve
10. Gasket	27. Tee	46. Spring washer
11. Gasket	28. Bellcrank assembly	47. Screw
12. Spring washer	29. Spring washer	48–52. Hoses
13. Nut	30. Nut	53. Pipe
14. Intake air distributor (left-side) assembly	31. Spring washer	54. Flat connector plug (two-prong)
15. Stud	32. Nut	55. Boot
16. Spring washer	33. Connecting rod	56. Boot
17. By-pass air screw	34. Pin	57. Flat connector plug (five-prong)
	35. Circlip	
	36. Spring	

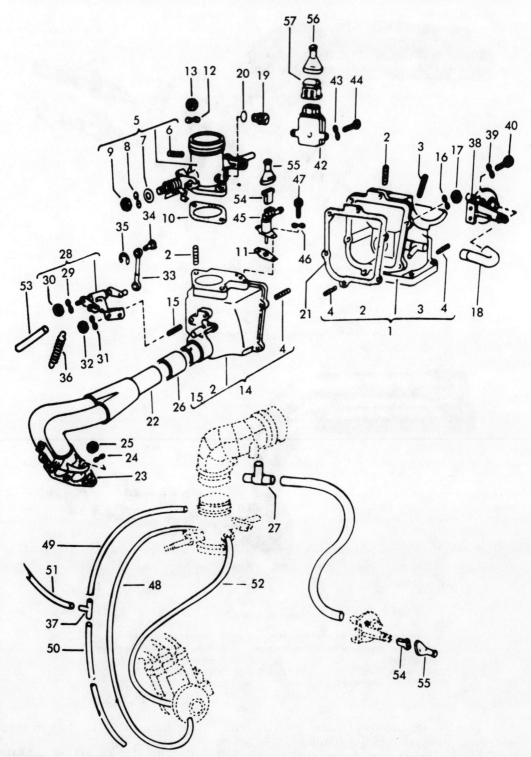

Exploded view of airflow controlled electronic fuel injection system components—1975–77 Type 1 shown, Type 2 similar

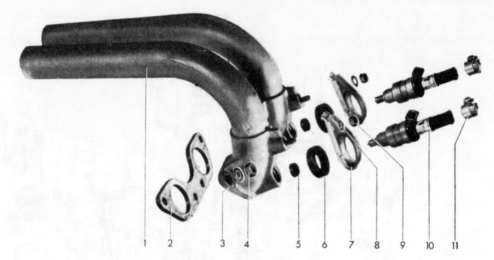

Individually mounted fuel injectors

1. Intake manifold
2. Intake manifold gasket
3. Lockwasher
5. Inner sealing bushing
6. Outer sealing bushing

7. Retainer
8. Lockwasher
9. Nut
10. Fuel injector
11. Hose connection with clamp

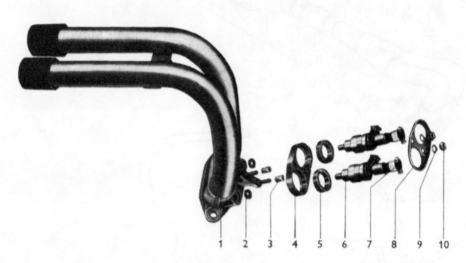

Paired fuel injectors

1. Intake manifolds with injector seats
2. Injector inner locating sealing bushings
3. Sleeves
4. Injector plate
5. Injector outer locating bushings

6. Electromagnetic fuel injector
7. Hose connection with clamp
8. Injector retainer
9. Lockwasher
10. Nut

the injectors are removed since they sometimes lodge within the manifold.

NOTE: *There are two sleeves that fit over the injector bracket studs. Be careful not to lose them.*

4. Upon installation, place the injector bracket, the outer locating bushings, the injector plate, and the inner locating bushings on the pair of injectors in that order.

5. Gently slip the injector assembly into the manifold and install the bracket nuts. Be careful not to damage the injector tips or contaminate the injectors with dirt.

6. Reconnect the injector wiring.

Throttle Valve Switch

REMOVAL AND INSTALLATION

1. Remove the air filter.
2. The switch is located on the throttle valve housing. Disconnect the throttle valve return spring.
3. Remove the throttle valve assembly but do not disconnect the bowden wire for the throttle valve or the connecting hoses to the ignition distributor.
4. Remove the throttle valve switch securing screws and remove the switch.
5. Reverse the above steps to install. It will be necessary to adjust the switch after installation.

Throttle valve switch—1970–72 Type 3, 1972–74 Type 4

Throttle valve switch—1971 Type 4 shown. Note securing screws (a) and direction of adjustment (b).

ADJUSTMENT (NON-AIR FLOW CONTROLLED ONLY)

The throttle valve switch is used to shut off the fuel supply during deceleration. The switch is supposed to operate when the throttle valve is opened 2°. A degree scale is stamped into the attachment plate for adjustment purposes.

1. Completely close the throttle valve.
2. Loosen the switch attaching screws and turn the switch carefully to the right until it hits its stop.
3. Turn the switch slowly to the left until it can be heard to click and then note the position of the switch according to the degree scale.
4. Continue to turn the switch another 2°. The distance between any two marks on the degree scale is 2°.

5. Tighten the screws and recheck the adjustment.

Cold Start Valve

REMOVAL AND INSTALLATION

The cold start valve is located near the thermo-switch and is secured to the air intake distributor by two screws. This valve sometimes jams open and causes excessive consumption, rough idle, and low power output.

Cold start valve location—Type 1

Trigger Contacts (Non-Air Flow Controlled Only)

REMOVAL AND INSTALLATION

The trigger contacts are located in the base of the distributor and are secured by two screws. These contacts are supplied

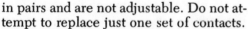

Removing trigger contacts—Non-airflow controlled only

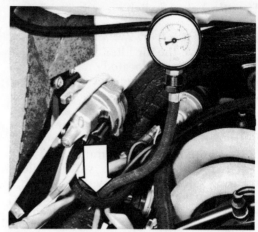

Fuel pressure regulator test gauge installation

in pairs and are not adjustable. Do not attempt to replace just one set of contacts.

One set of contacts controls a pair of injectors and tells the injectors when to fire.

Fuel Pressure Regulator

REMOVAL AND INSTALLATION

Disconnect the hoses from the regulator and remove the regulator from its bracket. The fuel pump pressure is adjustable; however, lack of fuel pressure is usually due to other defects in the system and the regulator should be adjusted only as a last resort.

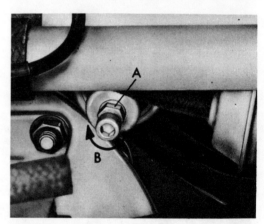

Fuel pressure regulator adjustment—Type 3

ADJUSTMENT (NON-AIR FLOW CONTROLLED ONLY)

1. Remove the air cleaner.
2. Connect a fuel pressure gauge as shown.
3. Start the engine and operate at idle.
4. Loosen locknut "A" and adjust fuel pressure to 28 psi with screw "B."

Temperature Sensors I and II

REMOVAL AND INSTALLATION

The air temperature sensor is located in the air distributor housing and may be unscrewed from the housing. The second temperature switch is located in the cylinder head on the left side and senses cylinder head temperature. It is removed with a special wrench. To test these switches, attach an ohmmeter and measure the resistance of the switch as the

Fuel pressure regulator adjustment—Type 4

temperature is raised gradually to 212°. As the temperature rises, the resistance of the first switch should drop from about 200 ohms to 80 ohms. The cylinder head switch resistance should drop from about 1700 ohms to 190 ohms at 212°.

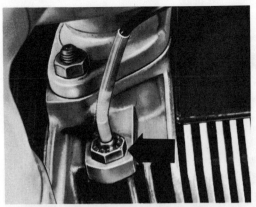

Cylinder head temperature sensing switch

Thermo (air temperature) switch location—Type 1

The third switch is actually a thermoswitch and is an ON/OFF type switch. Below 41° it is ON to activate the cold starting valve. The switch is located next to the distributor and may be removed with a 24 mm wrench.

Pressure Sensor (Non-Air Flow Controlled Only)

REMOVAL AND INSTALLATION

The sensor is secured to the firewall by two screws. Remove the screws and disconnect the wiring.

Pressure sensor retaining screws—Types 3 and 4 only

Remove the pressure connection and immediately plug the connection into the sensor. Always keep the connection plugged as the bellows inside the sensor is sensitive to the smallest pieces of dirt. Reverse the above steps to install.

Do not disassemble the sensor. There are no adjustments possible for the sensor.

NOTE: *Do not reverse the square electrical plug when reconnecting the sensor wiring.*

Troubleshooting

There are very few items to check without the special tester used by the dealer.

It is possible to check the fuel pressure by inserting a fuel pressure gauge in the line after the pressure regulator. Insert the gauge using a T-fitting. Turn on the key and check the pressure. If the pressure is low, check for leaking injectors, restricted lines, clogged fuel filters, damaged pressure regulator, bad fuel pump, water in the gas and resultant corrosion of the injectors, or a leaking or jammed cold start valve.

Chapter Five

Chassis Electrical

Heater

The Volkswagen heating system has no electrical blower. The engine cooling fan blows air over the engine and out through the cooling ducts. If the heater flaps are opened, then a portion of the heated air from the engine is diverted to the passenger compartment. An auxiliary gas heater is optional on Types 1, 2, and 3, and standard on Type 4.

Procedures for removing the heat exchangers and heater flap assemblies are given in Chapter Three.

CABLE FOR HEATER OUTLET

Removal and Installation

TYPES 1, 2, 3

1. Remove the rear air outlet, hose, and heater pipe as an assembly.
2. Remove the hose from the outlet and from the pipe.
3. Remove the pin which attaches the cable to the flap in the heater pipe.
NOTE: *The pin is push-fit.*
4. Remove the heater pipe from the outlet.
5. Bend up the tabs which secure the cable shielding to the outlet.

6. Disconnect the opposite end from the heater controls and remove the cable.
7. Reverse the above steps to install.

Windshield Wipers

Motor Removal and Installation

TYPE 1

1. Disconnect the battery ground cable.
2. Loosen the clamp screws and remove the wiper arms.

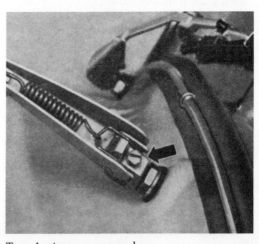

Type 1 wiper arm removal

3. Remove the wiper bearing nuts as well as the washers. Take off the outer bearing seals.

4. Remove the back of the instrument panel from the luggage compartment.

5. Disconnect the cable from the wiper motor.

6. Remove the glove compartment box.

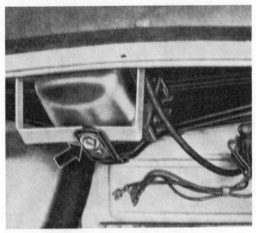

Type 1 wiper motor and frame removal

7. Remove the screw which secures the wiper frame to the body.

8. Remove the frame and motor with the linkage.

NOTE: *The ball joints at the ends of the linkage may be slipped apart by*

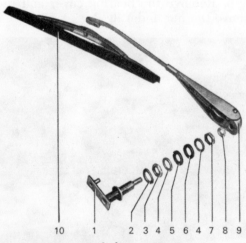

Type 1 wiper motor linkage

1. Wiper shaft with crank
2. Spring washer
3. Brass nut
4. Washer
5. Inner bearing seal
6. Outer bearing seal
7. Nut
8. Wiper shaft seal
9. Bracket and arm
10. Windshield wiper blade

gently popping the ball and socket apart with a screwdriver. Always lubricate the joints upon reassembly.

9. Remove the lock and spring washers from the motor drive shaft and remove the connecting rod. Matchmark the motor and frame to ensure proper realignment when the motor is reinstalled.

10. Remove the nut located at the base of the motor driveshaft, and the nut at the side of the driveshaft, and remove the motor from the frame.

11. To install, reverse the above steps and heed the following reminders.

12. The pressed lug on the wiper frame must engage the groove in the wiper bearing. Make sure that the wiper spindles are perpendicular to the plane of the windshield.

13. Check the linkage bushings for wear.

14. The hollow side of the links must face toward the frame with the angled end of the driving link toward the right bearing.

15. The inner bearing seal should be placed so that the shoulder of the rubber molding faces the wiper arm.

TYPE 2

1. Disconnect the ground wire from the battery.

2. Remove both wiper arms.

3. Remove the bearing cover and nut.

4. Remove the heater branch connections under the instrument panel.

5. Disconnect the wiper motor wiring.

6. Remove the wiper motor securing screw and remove the motor.

7. Reverse the above steps to install.

Type 2 wiper motor location

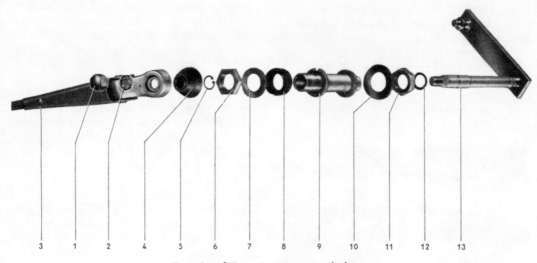

Type 2 and Type 4 wiper motor linkage

1. Cap nut
2. Lock washer
3. Wiper arm
4. Bearing cover
5. Circlip
6. Nut
7. Washer
8. Seal
9. Shaft bearing
10. Spring washer
11. Brass nut
12. Spring washer
13. Wiper shaft

TYPE 3

1. Disconnect the negative battery cable.

2. Remove the ashtray and glove compartment.

3. Remove the fresh air controls.

4. Remove the cover for the heater and water drainage hoses.

5. Disconnect the motor wiring.

6. Remove the wiper arms.

7. Remove the bearing covers and nuts, washers, and outer bearing seals.

8. Remove the wiper motor securing screws and remove the motor.

9. Reverse the above steps to install.

TYPE 4

1. Disconnect the negative battery cable.

2. Remove the wiper arms.

3. Remove the bearing cover and remove the nut under it.

Removing Type 3 wiper motor from bracket

Typical wiper linkage ball joint—Type 4 shown

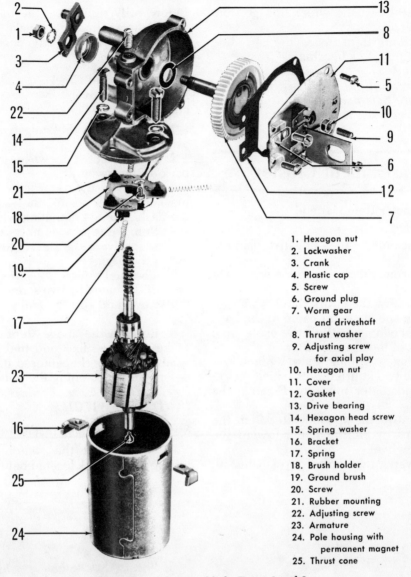

1. Hexagon nut
2. Lockwasher
3. Crank
4. Plastic cap
5. Screw
6. Ground plug
7. Worm gear
   and driveshaft
8. Thrust washer
9. Adjusting screw
   for axial play
10. Hexagon nut
11. Cover
12. Gasket
13. Drive bearing
14. Hexagon head screw
15. Spring washer
16. Bracket
17. Spring
18. Brush holder
19. Ground brush
20. Screw
21. Rubber mounting
22. Adjusting screw
23. Armature
24. Pole housing with
    permanent magnet
25. Thrust cone

Wiper motor disassembled—Types 1 and 3

4. Remove the steering column cover and the hoses running between the fresh air control box and the vents.

5. Remove the clock but do not disconnect the wiring.

6. Remove the left fresh air and defroster vent. Disconnect the air hose from the vent.

7. Disconnect the wiring for the motor at the windshield wiper switch. Remove the ground wire from the motor gear cover.

8. Remove the motor securing screw and remove the motor frame and motor assembly downward and to the right.

9. Reverse the above steps to install.

Linkage Removal and Installation

The windshield wiper linkage is secured at the ends by a ball and socket type joint. The ball and joint may be gently pryed apart with the aid of a screwdriver. Always lubricate the joints with grease before reassembly.

WIPER ARM SHAFT

1. Remove the wiper arm.

2. Remove the bearing cover or the shaft seal depending on the type.

3. On Type 4, remove the shaft circlip.

4. Remove the large wiper shaft bearing securing nut and remove the accompanying washer and rubber seal.

5. Disconnect the wiper linkage from the wiper arm shaft.

6. Working from inside the car, slide the shaft out of its bearing.

NOTE: *It may be necessary to lightly tap the shaft out of its bearing. Use a soft face hammer.*

7. Reverse the above steps to install.

Instrument Cluster

Speedometer Removal and Installation

1. Disconnect the negative battery cable.

2. Disconnect the speedometer light bulb wires.

3. Unscrew the knurled nut which secures the speedometer cable to the back of the speedometer. Pull the cable from the back of the speedometer.

4. Using a 4 mm allen wrench, remove the two knurled nuts which secure the speedometer brackets. Remove the brackets.

5. Remove the speedometer from the dashboard by sliding it out toward the steering wheel.

6. Reverse the above steps to install.

Before fully tightening the nuts for the speedometer brackets, make sure the speedometer is correctly positioned in the dash.

Fuel Gauge and Clock Assembly Removal and Installation

1. Disconnect the negative battery cable.

2. Disconnect the wiring from the back of the assembly.

3. Remove the knurled nuts and brackets which secure the assembly in the dash. Use a 4 mm allen wrench.

4. Remove the assembly by gently sliding it toward the steering wheel and out of the dash.

5. The fuel gauge is secured into the base of the clock by two screws. Remove the screws and slip the fuel gauge out of the clock.

6. Reverse the above steps to install. Make sure the clock and fuel gauge assembly is properly centered in the dash before fully tightening the nuts.

IGNITION SWITCH

Switch Removal and Installation

1. Disconnect the steering column wiring at the block located behind the in-

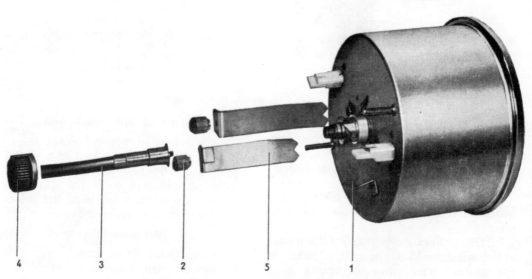

Speedometer and brackets—Type 1 Beetle

1. Speedometer
2. Knurled nut
3. Drive cable
4. Union nut
5. Bracket

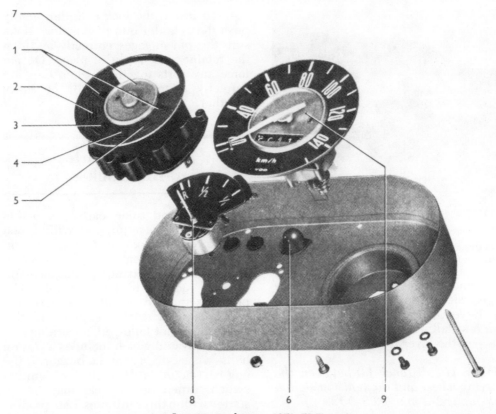

Instrument cluster—1970–72 Type 2

1. Turn signal warning lights
2. Generator warning light
3. High beam warning light
4. Parking light warning light
5. Oil pressure warning light
6. Instrument lighting
7. Warning light holder
8. Fuel gauge
9. Speedometer

strument panel and pull the column wiring harness into the passenger compartment.

2. Remove the steering wheel.

3. Remove the circlip on the steering shaft.

4. Disconnect the negative battery cable.

5. Insert the key and turn the switch to the ON position. On Type 3 vehicles it is necessary to remove the fuse box.

6. Remove the three securing screws and slide the switch assembly from the steering column tube.

NOTE: *It is not necessary to remove the turn signal switch at this time. If it is necessary to remove the switch from the housing, continue with the disassembly procedure.*

7. Remove the turn signal switch.

8. After removing the wiring retainer, press the ignition switch wiring block

Removing turn signal switch

upward and out of the housing and disconnect the wiring.

9. Remove the lock cylinder and the steering lock mechanism.

Correct distance (a) between ignition switch housing and steering wheel is 0.08–0.12 in.

10. Remove the ignition switch screw and pull the ignition switch rearward.

11. Reverse the above steps to install. When reinstalling the turn signal switch, make sure the lever is in the center position.

NOTE: *The distance (a) between the steering wheel and the ignition switch housing is 2–3 mm (0.08–0.12 in.).*

Ignition Lock Cylinder
Removal and Installation

1. Proceed with Steps 1–8 in the "Ignition Switch" procedure.

2. With the key in the cylinder and turned to the ON position, pull the lock cylinder out far enough so the securing pin can be depressed through a hole in the side of the lock cylinder housing. Use a steel wire to depress the pin.

3. As the pin is depressed, pull the lock cylinder out of its housing.

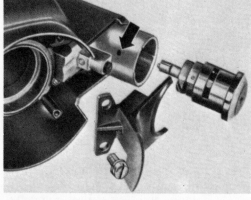

Access hole for depressing lock cylinder retaining pin

4. To install the lock cylinder, gently push the cylinder into its housing. Make sure the pin engages correctly and that the retainer fits easily in place. Do not force any parts together; when they are correctly aligned, they will fit easily together.

Seat Belt/Starter Interlock

All 1974 and some early production 1975 models are equipped with a seat belt/starter interlock system to prevent the driver and front seat passenger (if applicable) from starting the engine without first buckling his/her seat belts. The proper sequence is; sit in the seat(s), buckle up, start the engine. If this sequence is not followed, a warning system is activated which includes a "fasten belts" visual display and a buzzer. If the engine should stall with the ignition switch turned on, the car may be restarted within three minutes. Late production 1975 models are not equipped with this system.

Headlights

Removal and Installation
TYPE 1, 2, AND 3

1. Remove the screw which secures the headlight ring and remove the ring.

2. The sealed beam is held in place by a ring secured by three screws. Remove the screws and the ring. Do not confuse the headlight aiming screws with the

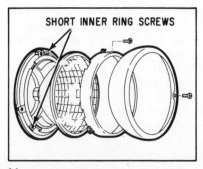

Sealed beam retaining screws

screws for the ring. There are only two screws used for aiming.

3. Pull the wiring off the back of the sealed beam and remove the beam.

4. Reverse the above steps to install.

TYPE 4

This is the same procedure as above except that the headlight ring is secured by two screws.

Fuses

All major circuits are protected from overloading or short circuiting by fuses. A 12 position fusebox is located beneath the dashboard near the steering column, or located in the luggage compartment on some air conditioned models.

When a fuse blows, the cause should be investigated. Never install a fuse of a larger capacity than specified (see "Fuse Specifications"), and never use foil or a bolt or nail in place of a fuse. However, always carry a few spares in case of emergency. There are 10 8 amp (white) fuses and two 16 amp (red) fuses in the VW fusebox. Circuits number 9 and 10 use the 16 amp fuses. To replace a fuse, pry off the clear plastic cover for the fusebox and depress a contact at either end of the subject fuse.

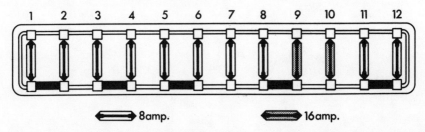

Typical fuse box layout

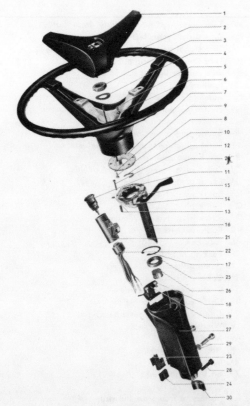

1. Padded cover
2. Steering wheel
3. Nut
4. Spring washer
5. Screw
6. Clip
7. Contact ring with cancelling cam
8. Fillister head screw
9. Toothed washer
10. Circlip for steering column
11. Turn signal switch spring
12. Turn signal switch screw
13. Spacer sleeve and washer
14. Turn signal switch with horn contact
15. Hand dimmer contact
16. Cable guide rail
17. Ball bearing circlip
18. Screw
19. Retainer
20. Lock cylinder
21. Steering lock with buzzer contact
22. Starter switch
23. Plug for starter switch
24. Wire guide
25. Ball bearing for steering column switch
26. Contact ring
27. Steering column switch
28. Clamp screw for steering column switch
29. Socket head capscrew with lockwasher
30. Plug for turn signal switch

Typical steering column assembly—Type 4 shown

Wiring Diagrams

A. Battery
B. Starter
C. Generator
C^1. Regulator
D. Ignition/starter switch
E. Windshield wiper switch
E^1. Light switch
E^2. Turn signal and headlight dimmer switch
E^3. Emergency flasher switch
F. Brake light switch and warning switch
F^1. Oil pressure switch
F^2. Door contact switch, left, with contact for buzzer H^5
F^3. Door contact switch, right
F^4. Back-up light switch
G. Fuel gauge sending unit
G^1. Fuel gauge
H. Horn button
H^1. Horn
H^5. Ignition key warning buzzer
J. Dimmer relay
J^2. Emergency flasher relay
J^3. Vibrator for fuel gauge
K^1. High beam warning light
K^2. Generator charging warning light
K^3. Oil pressure warning light
K^5. Turn signal warning light
K^6. Emergency flasher warning light
K^7. Dual circuit brake system warning light
L^1. Sealed beam unit, left headlight
L^2. Sealed beam unit, right headlight
L^{10}. Instrument panel light
M^2. Tail and brake light, right
M^4. Tail and brake light, left

M^5. Turn signal and parking light, front, left
M^6. Turn signal, rear, left
M^7. Turn signal and parking light, front, right
M^8. Turn signal, rear, right
M^{11}. Side marker light, front
N. Ignition coil
N^1. Automatic choke
N^3. Electro-magnetic pilot jet
O. Ignition distributor
P^1. Spark plug connector, No. 1 cylinder
P^2. Spark plug connector, No. 2 cylinder
P^3. Spark plug connector, No. 3 cylinder
P^4. Spark plug connector, No. 4 cylinder
Q^1. Spark plug, No. 1 cylinder
Q^2. Spark plug, No. 2 cylinder
Q^3. Spark plug, No. 3 cylinder
Q^6. Spark plug, No. 4 cylinder
R. Radio connection
S. Fuse box
S^1. Back-up light fuse
T. Cable adapter
T^1. Cable connector, single
T^2. Cable connector, double
T^3. Cable connector, triple
T^4. Cable connector (four connections)
V. Windshield wiper motor
W. Interior light
X. License plate light
X^1. Back-up light, left
X^2. Back-up light, right

① Battery to frame ground strap
② Transmission to frame ground strap

Wiring diagram—1970–71 Type 1 Beetle

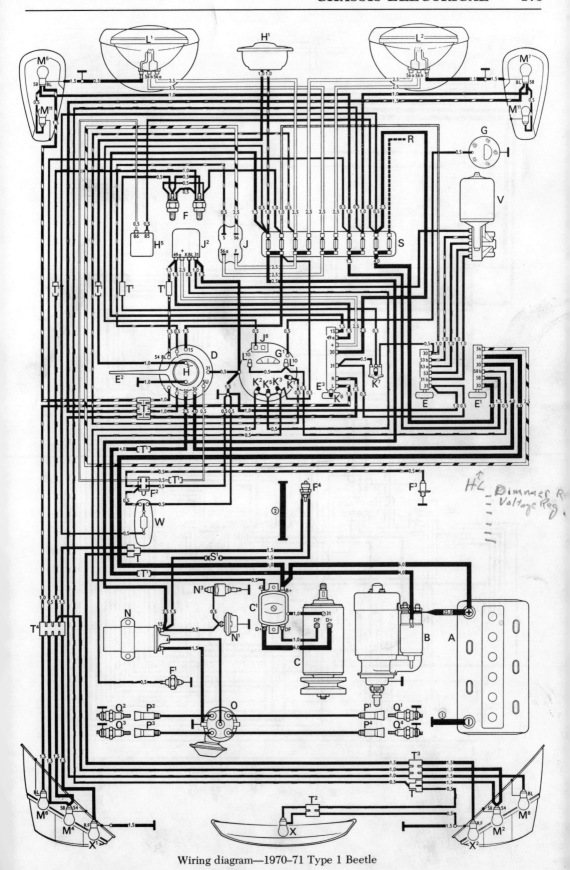

Wiring diagram—1970–71 Type 1 Beetle

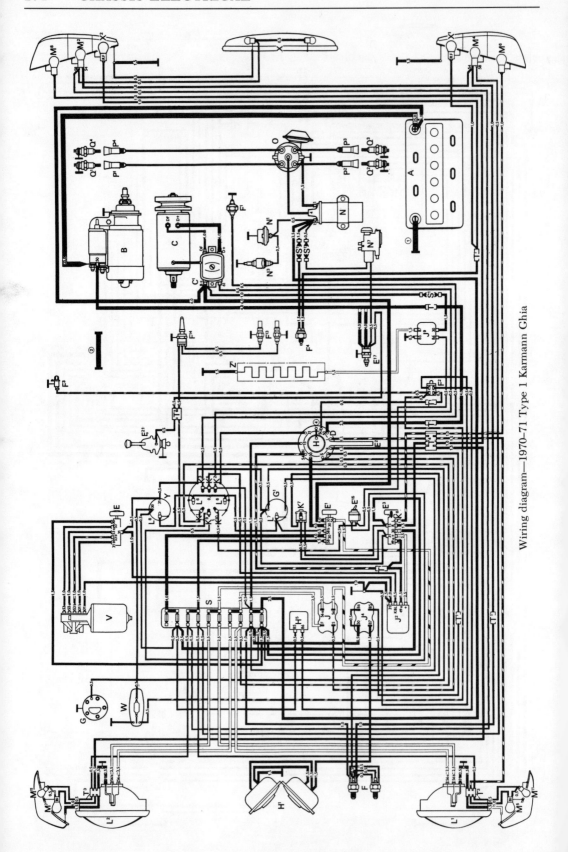

Wiring diagram—1970-71 Type 1 Karmann Ghia

A. Battery
B. Starter
C. Generator
C[1]. Regulator
D. Ignition/starter switch
E. Windshield wiper switch
E[1]. Light switch
E[2]. Turn signal and headlight dimmer switch
E[3]. Emergency flasher switch
E[15]. Switch for rear window defogger
E[17]. Starter cut-out switch
E[21]. Contact at selector lever
F. Brake light switch with warning switch
F[1]. Oil pressure switch
F[2]. Door contact switch, left,
      with contact for buzzer
F[3]. Door contact switch, right
F[4]. Back-up light switch
F[13]. Temperature sensor
F[14]. ATF temperature sensor selector
G. Fuel gauge sending unit
G[1]. Fuel gauge
H. Horn button
H[1]. Twin horns
H[5]. Ignition key warning buzzer
J. Dimmer relay
J[2]. Emergency flasher relay
J[4]. Relay for twin horns
J[9]. Rear window defogger relay
K[1]. High beam warning light
K[2]. Generator charging warning light
K[3]. Oil pressure warning light
K[5]. Turn signal warning light
K[6]. Emergency flasher warning light
K[7]. Dual circuit brake system warning light
K[9]. ATF temperature warning light
K[10]. Rear window defogger warning light
L[1]. Sealed beam unit, left headlight
L[2]. Sealed beam unit, right headlight
L[6]. Speedometer light
L[7]. Fuel gauge light

L[8]. Clock light
M[2]. Tail and brake light, right
M[4]. Tail and brake light, left
M[5]. Turn signal and parking light, front, left
M[6]. Turn signal, rear, left
M[7]. Turn signal and parking light, front, right
M[8]. Turn signal, rear, right
M[11]. Side marker light, front
N. Ignition coil
N[1]. Automatic choke
N[3]. Electro-magnetic pilot jet
N[7]. Automatic Stick Shift control valve
O. Ignition distributor
P[1]. Spark plug connector, No. 1 cylinder
P[2]. Spark plug connector, No. 2 cylinder
P[3]. Spark plug connector, No. 3 cylinder
P[4]. Spark plug connector, No. 4 cylinder
Q[1]. Spark plug, No. 1 cylinder
Q[2]. Spark plug, No. 2 cylinder
Q[3]. Spark plug, No. 3 cylinder
Q[4]. Spark plug, No. 4 cylinder
S. Fuse box
S[1]. Fuse for rear window defogger,
      back-up lights, Automatic
      Stick Shift control valve
T[1]. Cable connector, single
T[2]. Cable connector, double
T[3]. Cable connector, triple
T[4]. Cable connector, four connections
V. Windshield wiper motor
W. Interior light
X. License plate light
X[1]. Back-up light, left
X[2]. Back-up light, right
Y. Clock
Z[1]. Rear window defogger heating element

① Ground strap battery to engine
② Ground strap transmission to frame
④ Ground strap steering column

Wiring diagram—1970–71 Type 1 Karmann Ghia

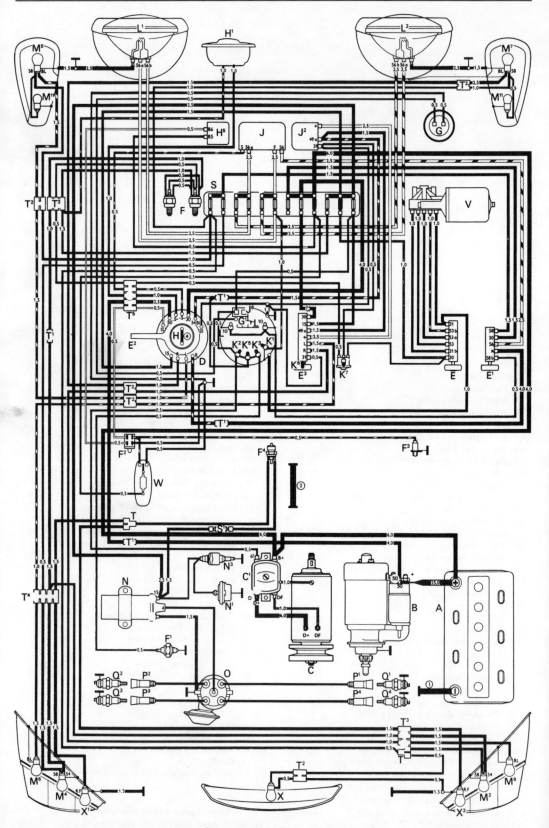

Wiring diagram—1971 Type 1 Super Beetle

A. Battery
B. Starter
C. Generator
C^1. Regulator
D. Ignition/starter switch
E. Windshield wiper switch
E^1. Light switch
E^2. Turn signal and headlight dimmer switch
E^3. Emergency flasher switch
F. Brake light switch
F^1. Oil pressure switch
F^2. Door contact and buzzer alarm switch, left
F^3. Door contact switch, right
F^4. Back-up switch
G. Fuel gauge sending unit
G^1. Fuel gauge
H. Horn button
H^1. Horn
H^5. Ignition key warning buzzer
J. Dimmer relay
J^2. Emergency flasher relay
J^6. Fuel gauge vibrator
K^1. High beam warning light
K^2. Generator charging warning light
K^3. Oil pressure warning light
K^5. Turn signal warning light
K^6. Emergency flasher warning light
K^7. Dual circuit brake warning light
L^1. Sealed Beam unit, left headlight
L^2. Sealed Beam unit, right headlight
L^{10}. Instrument panel light
M^1. Parking light, left
M^2. Tail/brake light, right
M^4. Tail/brake light, left

M^5. Turn signal and parking light front left
M^6. Turn signal, rear, left
M^7. Turn signal and parking light front right
M^8. Turn signal, rear, right
M^{11}. Side marker light, front
N. Ignition coil
N^1. Automatic choke
N^3. Electro-magnetic pilot jet
O. Distributor
P^1. Spark plug connector, No. 1 cylinder
P^2. Spark plug connector, No. 2 cylinder
P^3. Spark plug connector, No. 3 cylinder
P^4. Spark plug connector, No. 4 cylinder
Q^1. Spark plug, No. 1 cylinder
Q^2. Spark plug, No. 2 cylinder
Q^3. Spark plug, No. 3 cylinder
Q^4. Spark plug, No. 4 cylinder
S. Fuse box
S^1. Back-up light in-line fuse
T. Cable adapter
T^1. Cable connector, single
T^2. Cable connector, double
T^3. Cable connector, triple
T^4. Cable connector (four connections)
T^5. Cable connector (five connections)
V. Windshield wiper motor
W. Interior light
X. License plate light
X^1. Back-up light, left
X^2. Back-up light, right

① Ground strap from battery to frame
② Ground strap from transmission to frame
④ Ground cable from front axle to frame

Wiring diagram—1971 Type 1 Super Beetle

B. Starter
C^1. Regulator
D. Ignition/starter switch
d. To ignition/starter switch, terminal 50
E^1. Light switch
E^2. Turn signal and headlight dimmer switch

E^9. Fan motor switch
E^{15}. Rear window defogger switch
E^{17}. Starter cut-out switch
E^{21}. Contact at selector lever
F^{13}. ATF temperature sensor
J^9. Rear window defogger relay

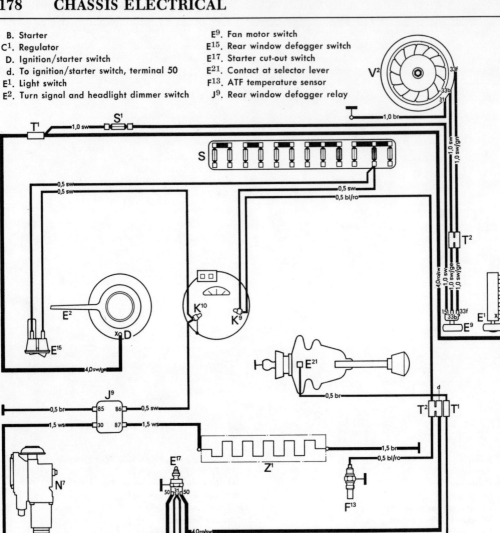

Supplemental wiring diagram—1971 Super Beetle; automatic stick shift, rear window defroster, and fresh air fan circuits

K^9. ATF temperature warning light
K^{10}. Rear window defogger warning light
N. Ignition coil
N^7. Automatic Stick Shift control valve
S. Fuse box
S^1. Fuse for:
    rear window defogger,

Automatic Stick Shift control valve,
    fan motor
T^1. Cable connector, single
T^2. Cable connector, double
V^2. Fan motor
Z^1. Rear window defogger heating element

Color of cables:

sw = black
ro = red
ws = white
br = brown
bl = blue
gn = green
ge = yellow

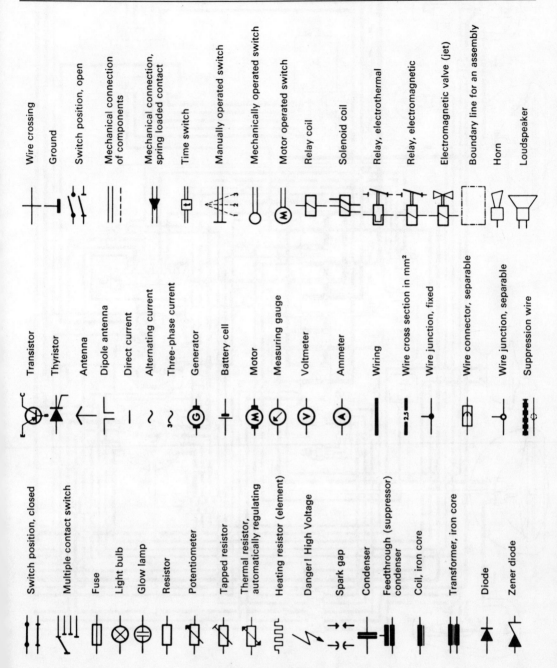

Legend for current flow diagrams

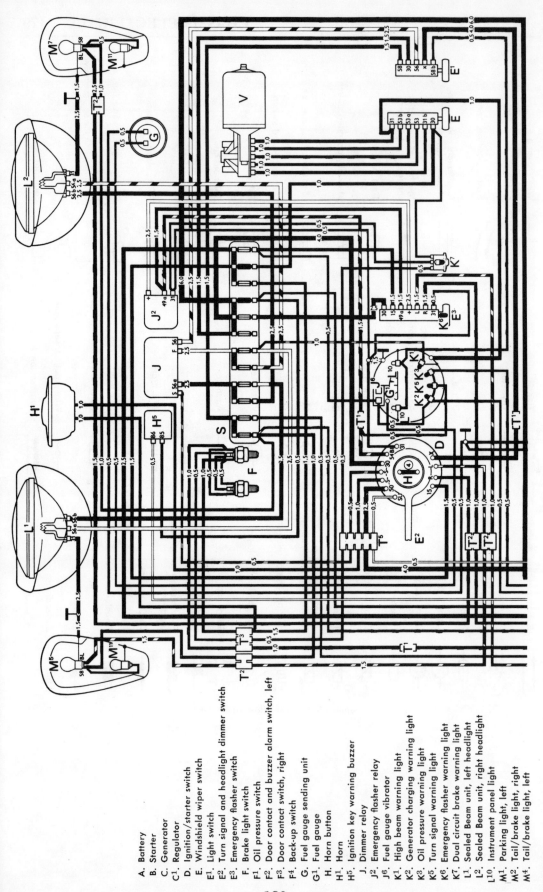

A. Battery
B. Starter
C. Generator
C1. Regulator
D. Ignition/starter switch
E. Windshield wiper switch
E1. Light switch
E2. Turn signal and headlight dimmer switch
E3. Emergency flasher switch
F. Brake light switch
F1. Oil pressure switch
F2. Door contact and buzzer alarm switch, left
F3. Door contact switch, right
F4. Back-up switch
G. Fuel gauge sending unit
G1. Fuel gauge
H. Horn button
H1. Horn
H5. Ignition key warning buzzer
J. Dimmer relay
J2. Emergency flasher relay
J6. Fuel gauge vibrator
K1. High beam warning light
K2. Generator charging warning light
K3. Oil pressure warning light
K5. Turn signal warning light
K6. Emergency flasher warning light
K7. Dual circuit brake warning light
L1. Sealed Beam unit, left headlight
L2. Sealed Beam unit, right headlight
L10. Instrument panel light
M1. Parking light, left
M2. Tail/brake light, right
M4. Tail/brake light, left

180

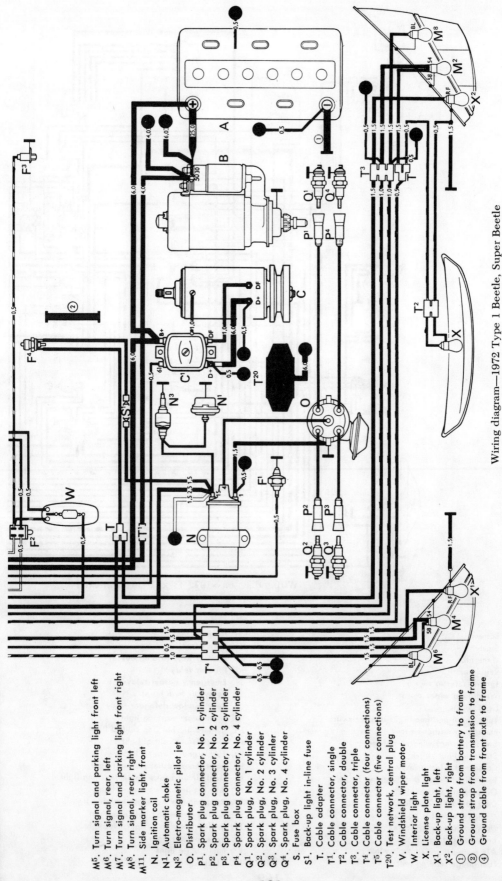

M5. Turn signal and parking light front left
M6. Turn signal, rear, left
M7. Turn signal and parking light front right
M8. Turn signal, rear, right
M11. Side marker light, front
N. Ignition coil
N1. Automatic choke
N3. Electro-magnetic pilot jet
O. Distributor
P1. Spark plug connector, No. 1 cylinder
P2. Spark plug connector, No. 2 cylinder
P3. Spark plug connector, No. 3 cylinder
P4. Spark plug connector, No. 4 cylinder
Q1. Spark plug, No. 1 cylinder
Q2. Spark plug, No. 2 cylinder
Q3. Spark plug, No. 3 cylinder
Q4. Spark plug, No. 4 cylinder
S. Fuse box
S1. Back-up light in-line fuse
T. Cable adapter
T1. Cable connector, single
T2. Cable connector, double
T3. Cable connector, triple
T4. Cable connector (four connections)
T5. Cable connector (five connections)
T20. Test network, central plug
V. Windshield wiper motor
W. Interior light
X. License plate light
X1. Back-up light, left
X2. Back-up light, right
① Ground strap from battery to frame
② Ground strap from transmission to frame
④ Ground cable from front axle to frame

Wiring diagram—1972 Type 1 Beetle, Super Beetle

181

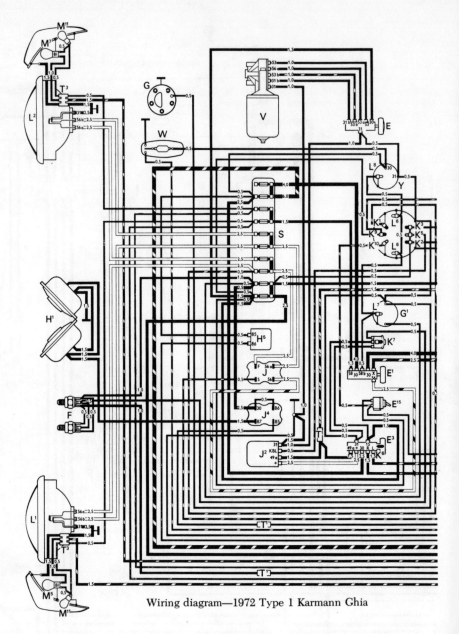

Wiring diagram—1972 Type 1 Karmann Ghia

A. Battery	G^1. Fuel gauge
B. Starter	H. Horn button
C. Generator	H^1. Twin horns
C^1. Regulator	H^5. Ignition key warning buzzer
D. Ignition/starter switch	J. Dimmer relay
E. Windshield wiper switch	J^2. Emergency flasher relay
E^1. Light switch	J^4. Relay for twin horns
E^2. Turn signal and headlight dimmer switch	J^9. Rear window defogger relay
E^3. Emergency flasher switch	K^1. High beam warning light
E^{15}. Switch for rear window defogger	K^2. Generator charging control light
E^{17}. Starter cut-out switch	K^3. Oil pressure control light
E^{21}. Contact at selector lever	K^5. Turn signal warning light
F. Brake light switch with warning switch	K^6. Emergency flasher warning light
F^1. Oil pressure switch	K^7. Dual circuit brake system warning light
F^2. Door contact switch, left, with contact for buzzer	K^9. ATF temperature warning light
F^3. Door contact switch, right	K^{10}. Rear window defogger warning light
F^4. Back-up light switch	L^1. Sealed beam unit, left headlight
F^{13}. ATF temperature control switch	L^2. Sealed beam unit, right headlight
G. Fuel gauge sending unit	L^6. Speedometer light
	L^7. Fuel gauge light
	L^8. Clock light

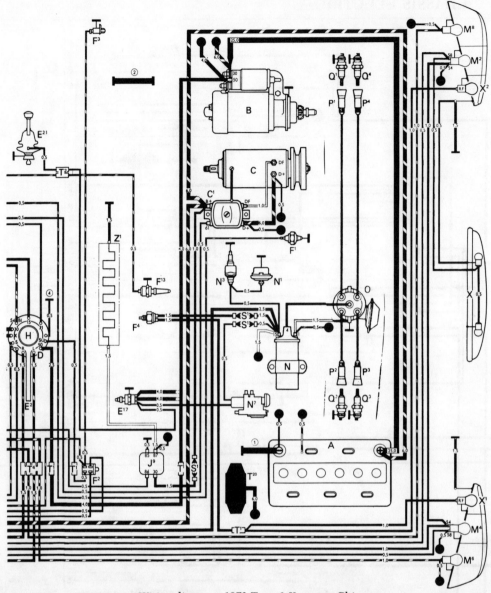

Wiring diagram—1972 Type 1 Karmann Ghia

M². Tail and brake light, right
M⁴. Tail and brake light, left
M⁵. Turn signal and parking light, front, left
M⁶. Turn signal, rear, left
M⁷. Turn signal and parking light, front, right
M⁸. Turn signal, rear, right
M¹¹. Side marker light, front
N. Ignition coil
N¹. Automatic choke
N³. Electromagnetic pilot jet
N⁷. Automatic Stick Shift control valve
O. Ignition distributor
P¹. Spark plug connector, No. 1 cylinder
P². Spark plug connector, No. 2 cylinder
P³. Spark plug connector, No. 3 cylinder
P⁴. Spark plug connector, No. 4 cylinder
Q¹. Spark plug, No. 1 cylinder
Q². Spark plug, No. 2 cylinder
Q³. Spark plug, No. 3 cylinder
Q⁴. Spark plug, No. 4 cylinder
S. Fuse box

S¹. Fuse for rear window defogger
     back-up lights, Automatic
     Stick Shift control valve
T¹. Cable connector, single
T². Cable connector, double
T³. Cable connector, triple
T⁴. Cable connector, four connections
T²⁰. Test network, central plug
V. Windshield wiper motor
W. Interior light
X. License plate light
X. Back-up light, left
X². Back-up light, right
Y. Clock
Z¹. Rear window defogger heating element

① Ground strap battery to engine
② Ground strap transmission to frame
④ Ground strap steering column

183

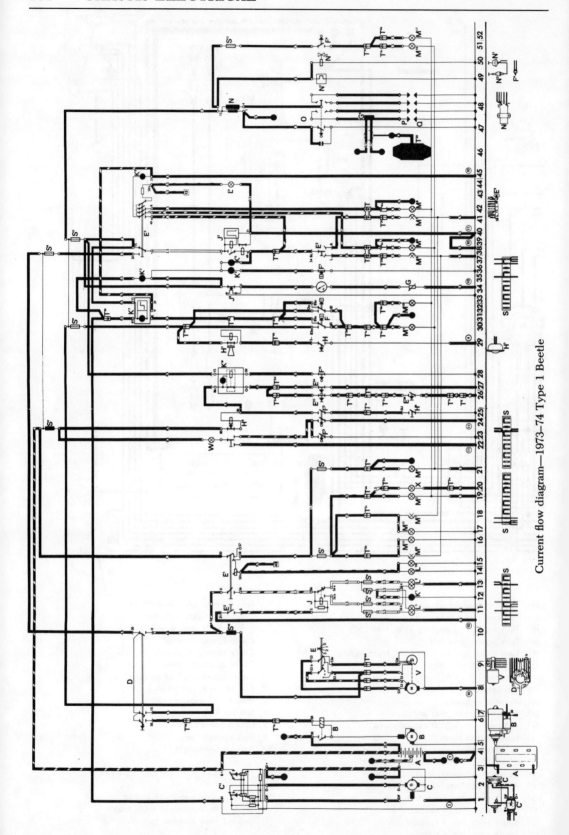

Current flow diagram—1973–74 Type 1 Beetle

Description	current track	Description	current track
A. Battery	4	M7. Turn signal and parking	18, 41
B. Starter	5, 6	light front right	
C. Generator	1, 2, 3	M8. Turn signal, rear, right	42
C1. Regulator	1, 2, 3	M9. Brake light, left	30
D. Ignition/starter switch	6, 7, 10, 25	M10. Brake light, right	33
E. Windshield wiper switch	9	M11. Side marker light, front	16, 17
E1. Light switch	12, 14, 15	M16. Backup light, left	51
E2. Turn signal and headlight	11, 38, 39	M17. Backup light, right	52
dimmer switch		N. Ignition coil	48
E3. Emergency flasher switch	38, 39, 42,	N1. Automatic choke	49
	44, 45	N3. Electromagnetic pilot jet	50
E24. Safety belt lock, left	27	O. Distributor	48
E25. Safety belt lock, right	26	P. Spark plug connectors	48
E26. Contact strip in passenger seat	26	Q. Spark plugs	48
F. Brake light switch	30, 31, 32,	S1.	10, 11, 13,
	33	to Fuse box	15, 21, 24,
F1. Oil pressure switch	36	S12.	30, 38, 40
F2. Door contact and buzzer alarm	24, 25	S13. Fuse for backup light (8 Amp)	51
switch, left		T. Wire connector (close to fuse box)	
F3. Door contact switch, right	23	T1. Wire connector, single	
F4. Backup light switch	51	a. close to fuse box	
F15. Transmission switch for safety	28	b. below rear seat bench	
belt warning system		c. behind the engine compartment	
G. Fuel gauge sending unit	34	insulation, front	
G1. Fuel gauge	34	T2. Wire connector, double	
G4. Ignition timing sensor	47	a. in engine compartment lid	
H. Horn button	29	b. in luggage compartment, front, left	
H1. Horn	29	c. in passenger seat	
H5. Ignition key warning buzzer	24, 25	d. below rear seat bench	
H6. Steering lock contact for	25	T3. Wire connector, triple	
ignition key warning system		a. in luggage compartment, front, left	
J. Dimmer relay	11, 13	T4. Wire connector, four connections	
J2. Emergency flasher relay	39, 40	a. close to fuse box	
J6. Fuel gauge vibrator	34	b. behind engine compartment	
K1. High beam warning light	12	insulation, right	
K2. Generator charging warning light	35	c. behind engine compartment	
K3. Oil pressure warning light	36	insulation, left	
K5. Turn signal warning light	37	T5. Wire connector, double on passenger	
K6. Emergency flasher warning light	45	seat rail	
K7. Dual circuit brake warning light	31, 33	T20. Test network, test socket	46
K19. Safety belt warning system light	27, 28	V. Windshield wiper motor	8, 9
L1. Sealed beam unit, left headlight	11	W. Interior light	23
L2. Sealed beam unit, right headlight	13	X. License plate light	20
L10. Instrument panel light	14, 15		
L21. Light for heater lever illumination	44	① Ground strap from battery to frame	4
M2. Tail light, right	19	② Ground strap from transmission	1
M4. Tail light, left	21	to frame	
M5. Turn signal and parking light	15, 38	④ Ground wire on steering coupling	29
front left		⑩ Ground connector, dashboard	
M6. Turn signal, rear, left	39	⑪ Ground connector, speedometer	

Current flow diagram—1973–74 Type 1 Beetle

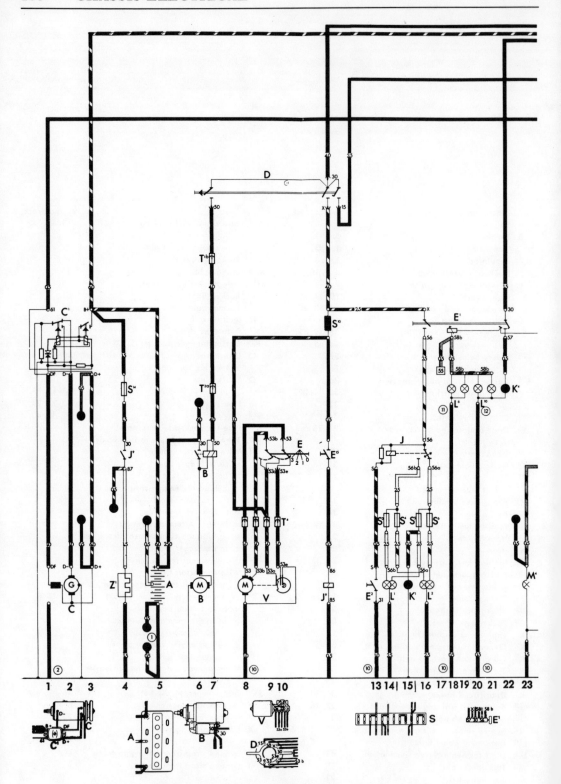

Current flow diagram—1973–74 Type 1 Karmann Ghia

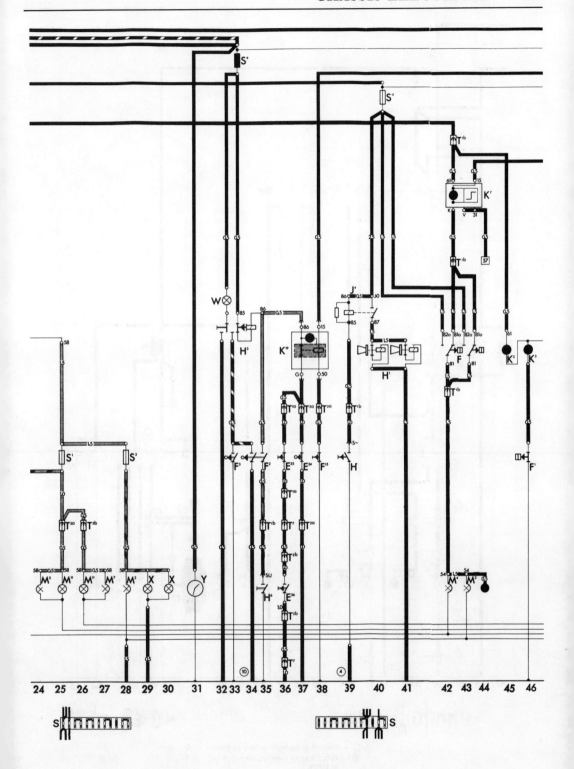

Current flow diagram—1973–74 Type 1 Karmann Ghia

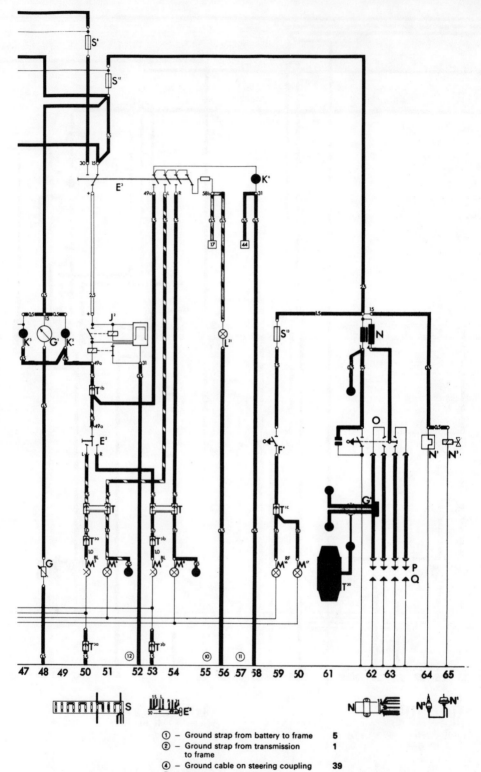

① – Ground strap from battery to frame   **5**
② – Ground strap from transmission   **1**
    to frame
④ – Ground cable on steering coupling   **39**
⑩ – Ground connector, dashboard
⑪ – Ground connector, speedometer
    housing
⑫ – Ground connector, clock

Current flow diagram—1973–74 Type 1 Karmann Ghia

Description	current track
A. Battery	5
B. Starter	6, 7
C. Generator	1, 2, 3
C^1. Regulator	1, 2, 3
D. Ignition/starter switch	7, 11, 12
E. Windshield wiper switch	9, 10
E^1. Light switch	16, 18, 22
E^2. Turn signal and headlight dimmer switch	13, 50
E^3. Emergency flasher switch	50, 53, 54, 56, 58
E^{15}. Rear window defogger switch	11
E^{24}. Safety belt lock, left	37
E^{25}. Safety belt lock, right	36
E^{26}. Contact strip in passenger seat	36
F. Brake light and dual circuit warning light switch	42, 43
F^1. Oil pressure switch	46
F^2. Door contact and buzzer alarm switch, left	34, 35
F^3. Door contact switch, right	33
F^4. Backup light switch	59
F^{15}. Transmission switch for safety belt warning system	38
G. Fuel gauge sending unit	48
G^1. Fuel gauge	48
G^4. Ignition timing sensor	62
H. Horn button	39
H^1. Twin horns	40, 41
H^5. Ignition key warning buzzer	33, 35
H^6. Steering lock contact for ignition key warning system	35
J. Dimmer relay	13, 16
J^2. Emergency flasher relay	50, 52
J^4. Relay for twin horns	39
J^9. Rear window defogger relay	4, 11
K^1. High beam warning light	15
K^2. Generator charging warning light	45
K^3. Oil pressure warning light	46
K^4. Parking light warning light	22
K^5. Turn signal warning light	47, 49
K^6. Emergency flasher warning light	58
K^7. Dual circuit brake warning light	42, 43
K^{19}. Safety belt warning system light	37, 38
L^1. Sealed beam unit, left headlight	14
L^2. Sealed beam unit, right headlight	16
L^6. Speedometer light	18, 19
L^{10}. Instrument panel light	20, 21

Description	current track
L^{21}. Light for heater lever illumination	56
M^2. Tail/brake light, right	28, 43
M^4. Tail/brake light, left	23, 42
M^5. Turn signal and parking light front, left	24, 50
M^6. Turn signal, rear, left	51
M^7. Turn signal and parking light front, right	27, 53
M^8. Turn signal, rear, right	54
M^{11}. Side marker light, front left + right	25, 26
M^{16}. Backup light, left	59
M^{17}. Backup light, right	60
N. Ignition coil	62
N^1. Automatic choke	64
N^3. Electromagnetic pilot jet	65
O. Distributor	62, 63
P. Spark plug connectors	62, 63
Q. Spark plugs	62, 63
S^1. to Fuse box S^{12}.	11, 14, 16, 25, 28, 33, 40, 50, 51
S^{13}. Fuse for backup light (8 Amp)	59
S^{14}. Fuse for rear window defogger, (8 Amp)	4
T. Cable adapter, behind dashboard	
T^1. Wire connector, single	
a. below rear seat bench	
b. behind the dashboard	
c. behind the engine compartment insulation	
T^2. Wire connector, double	
a. below rear seat bench	
b. in the passenger seat	
T^3. Wire connector, triple	
a. in headlight housing, left	
b. in headlight, housing, right	
T^4. Wire connector, four connections, behind the dashboard	
T^7. Wire connector, double on passenger seat rail	
T^{20}. Test network, test socket	61
V. Windshield wiper motor	8, 9, 10
W. Interior light	32
X. license plate light	29, 30
Y. Clock	31
Z^1. Rear window defogger heating element	4

Current flow diagram—1973–74 Type 1 Karmann Ghia

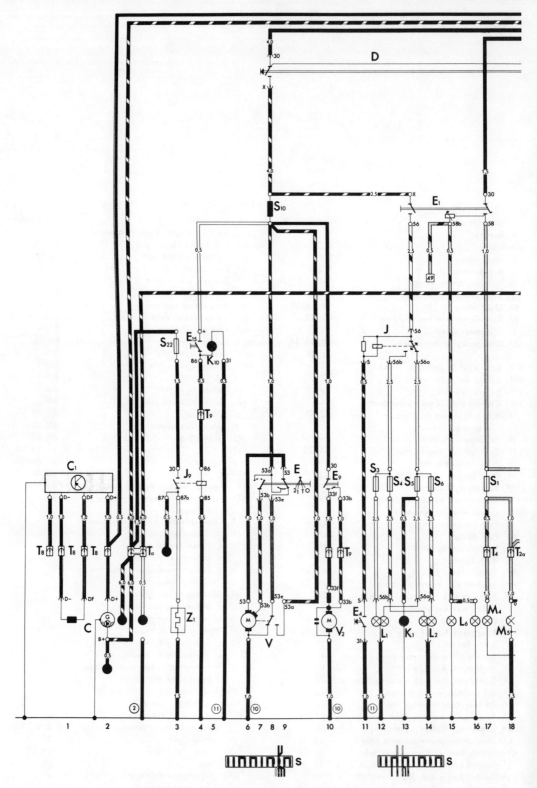

Current flow diagram—1974 Type 1 Super Beetle

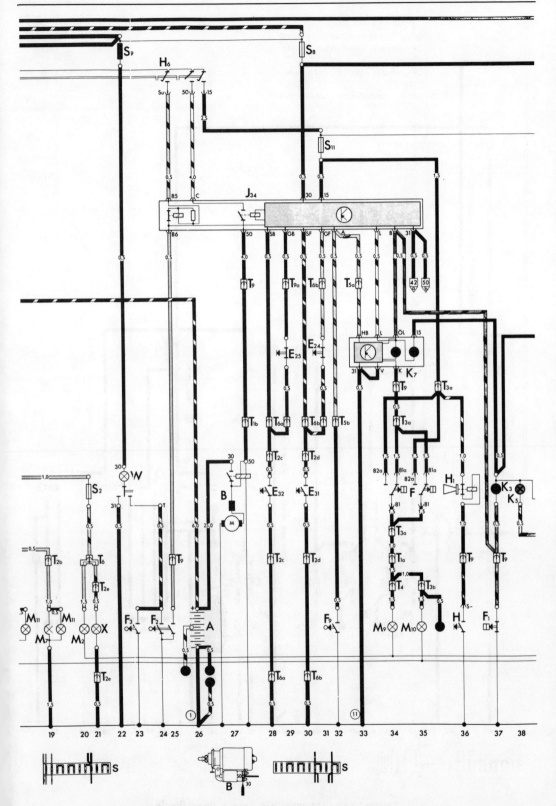

Current flow diagram—1974 Type 1 Super Beetle

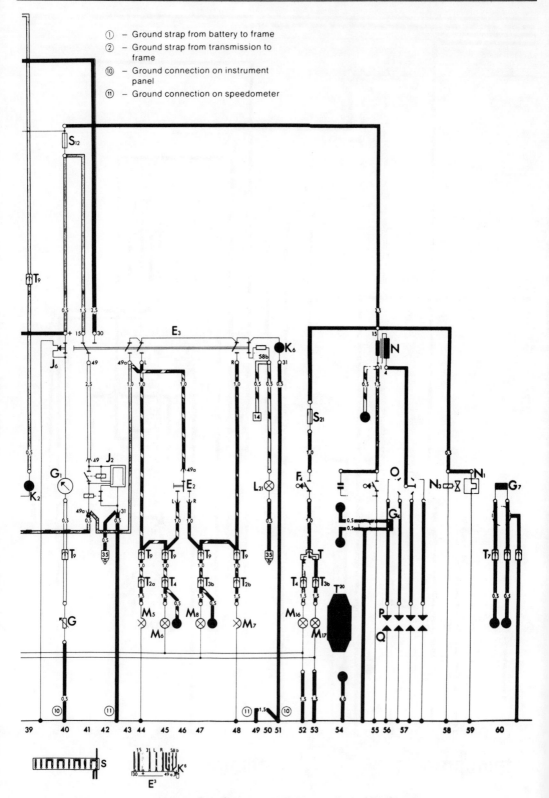

- ① – Ground strap from battery to frame
- ② – Ground strap from transmission to frame
- ⑩ – Ground connection on instrument panel
- ⑪ – Ground connection on speedometer

Current flow diagram—1974 Type 1 Super Beetle

Description	current track
A. Battery	26
B. Starter	27
C. Alternator	1, 2
C^1. Regulator	1, 2
D. Ignition/starter switch	8, 25, 26
E. Windshield wiper switch	7, 9
E^1. Light switch	13, 15, 17
E^2. Turn signal switch	46
E^3. Emergency flasher switch	41, 43, 44, 48, 50
E^4. Headlight dimmer switch	11
E^9. Fresh air fan motor switch	10
E^{15}. Rear window defogger switch	4, 5
E^{24}. Safety belt lock, left	31
E^{25}. Safety belt lock, right	29
E^{31}. Contact strip in drive seat	30
E^{32}. Contact strip in driver seat	28
F. Brake light switch	34, 35
F^1. Oil pressure switch	37
F^2. Door contact and buzzer alarm switch, left	24, 25
F^3. Door contact switch, right	23
F^4. Backup light switch	52
F^9. Parking brake control light switch	32
G. Fuel gauge sending unit	40
G^1. Fuel gauge	40
G^4. Ignition timing sensor	56
G^7. TDC marker unit	60
H. Horn button	36
H^1. Horn	36
H^6. Contact in ignition/starter switch for buzzer	25
J. Dimmer relay	11, 13, 14
J^2. Emergency flasher relay	41, 42
J^6. Voltage vibrator	40
J^9. Rear window defogger relay	3, 4
J^{34}. Safety belt warning system relay	25, 26, 27, 28, 29, 30, 31, 32, 33, 34, 35
K^1. High beam warning light	13
K^2. Alternator charging warning light	39
K^3. Oil pressure warning light	37
K^5. Turn signal warning light	38
K^6. Emergency flasher warning light	51
K^7. Dual circuit brake warning and safety belt interlock warning system	33, 34, 35
L^1. Sealed beam unit, left headlight	12
L^2. Sealed beam unit, right headlight	14
L^6. Speedometer light	15, 16
L^{21}. Light for heater lever illumination	50
M^2. Tail light, right	20
M^4. Tail light, left	17
M^5. Parking light front, left	18
M^5. Turn signal, front, left	44
M^6. Turn signal, rear, left	45
M^7. Parking light front, right	19

Description	current track
M^7. Turn signal, front right	48
M^8. Turn signal, rear, right	47
M^9. Brake light, left	34
M^{10}. Brake light, right	35
M^{11}. Side marker light front, left and right	18, 19
M^{16}. Backup light, left	52
M^{17}. Backup light, right	53
N. Ignition coil	55
N^1. Automatic choke	59
N^3. Electromagnetic cutoff valve	58
O. Ignition distributor	55, 57
P. Spark plug connectors	55, 56, 57
Q. Spark plugs	55, 56, 57
S^1. to Fuses in fuse box S^{12}.	8, 12, 14, 17, 20, 22, 30, 31, 40
S^{21}. Fuses for backup lights (8 Amp)	52
S^{22}. Fuses for rear window defogger (8 Amp)	3
T. Cable adapter, behind insulation in engine compartment	
a. under rear seat bench	
T^1. Wire connector, single	
a. behind instrument panel	
b. under rear seat bench	
T^2. Wire connector, double	
a. in luggage compartment, left	
b. in luggage compartment, right	
c. under passenger seat	
d. under driver's seat	
e. in hood of engine compartment	
T^3. Wire connector, 3 point	
a. in luggage compartment, left	
b. behind insulation in engine compartment, right	
T^4. Wire connector, 4 point behind insulation in engine compartment, left	
T^5. Wire connector, single	
a. behind instrument panel	
b. on passenger seat rail	
T^6. Wire connector, double	
a. under passenger seat	
b. under driver's seat	
T^7. Wire connector, 3 point, in engine compartment	
T^8. Wire connector, 4 point, under rear seat bench	
T^9. Wire connector, 8 point, behind instrument panel	
T^{20}. Test network, test socket	54
V. Windshield wiper motor	6, 7, 8
V^2. Fresh air motor	10
W. Interior light	22
X. License plate light	21
Z^1. Rear window defogger heating element	3

Current flow diagram—1974 Type 1 Super Beetle

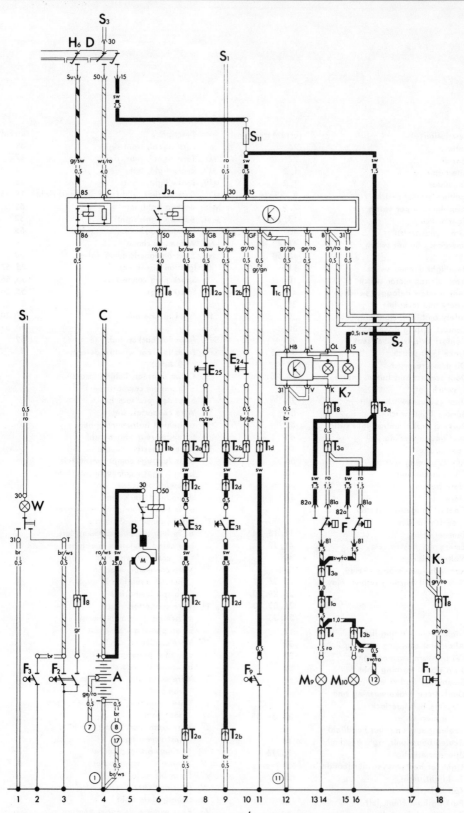

Supplemental current flow diagram—1974 Type 1, Type 4 seat belt/starter interlock wiring

	Description	current track
A.	Battery	4
B.	Starter	5
C.	to Alternator	4
D.	Ignition/starter switch	4
E^{24}.	Safety belt lock, with contact	10
E^{25}.	Safety belt lock, right contact	8
E^{31}.	Contact strip in driver's seat	9
E^{32}.	Contact strip in passenger seat	7
F.	Brake light switch	14, 16
F^1.	Oil pressure switch	18
F^2.	Door contact and buzzer alarm switch, front left	3
F^3.	Door contact switch, front right	2
F^9.	Parking brake control switch	11
H^6.	Contact in ignition/starter switch for ignition key warning system	3
J^{34}.	Relay for safety belt warning system	3, 6, 7, 9, 11, 14, 15
K^3.	to oil pressure warning light	18
K^7.	Warning light for dual circuit brake system and parking brake with warning light for safety belt warning system	12, 14
M^9.	Brake light bulb, left	14
M^{10}.	Brake light bulb, right	16
S^1.	to fuse box terminal 30 (closed side) to fuse box terminal 15 (closed side)	
S^3.	to fuse box terminal 30 (open side)	
S^{11}.	Fuse in fuse box	
T^{1a}.	Wire connector, single, behind the dashboard	
T^{1b}.	Wire connector, single, under rear seat	
T^{1c}.	Wire connector, single, behind the dashboard	
T^{1d}.	Wire connector, single, on central tunnel	
T^{2a}.	Wire connector, double, under passenger seat	
T^{2b}.	Wire connector, double, under driver's seat	
T^{2c}.	Wire connector, double, under passenger seat	
T^{2d}.	Wire connector, double, under driver's seat	
T^{3a}.	Wire connector, three-point, in luggage compartment, left	
T^{3b}.	Wire connector, three-point, behind engine compartment damping material, right	
T^4.	Wire connector, four-point, behind engine compartment damping material, left	
T^8.	Wire connector, eight-point, behind instrument panel	
W.	Interior light	1

Supplemental current flow diagram—1974 Type 1, Type 4 seat belt/starter interlock wiring

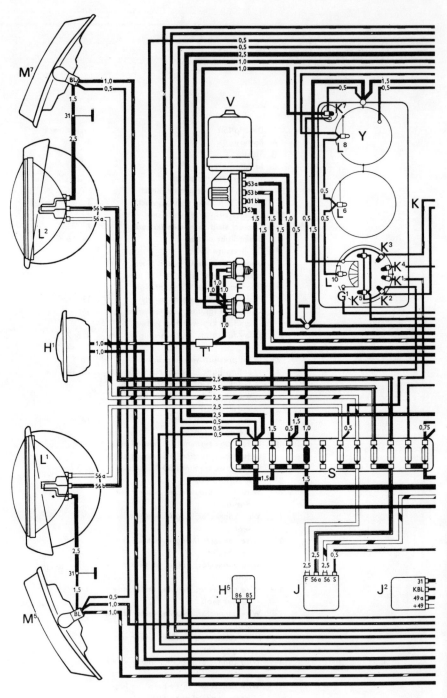

Wiring diagram—1970 Type 2

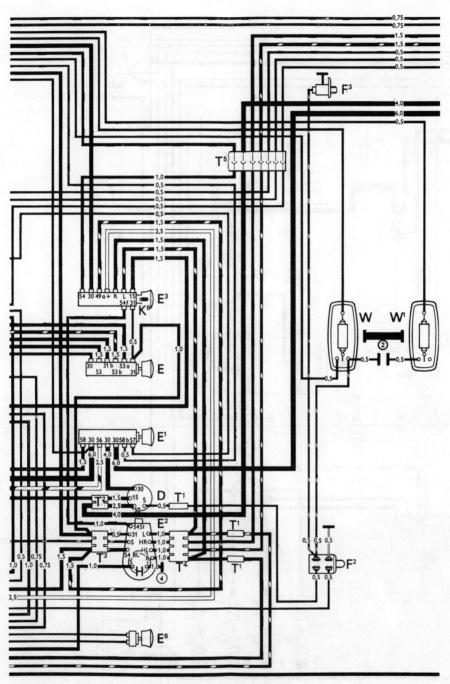

Wiring diagram—1970 Type 2

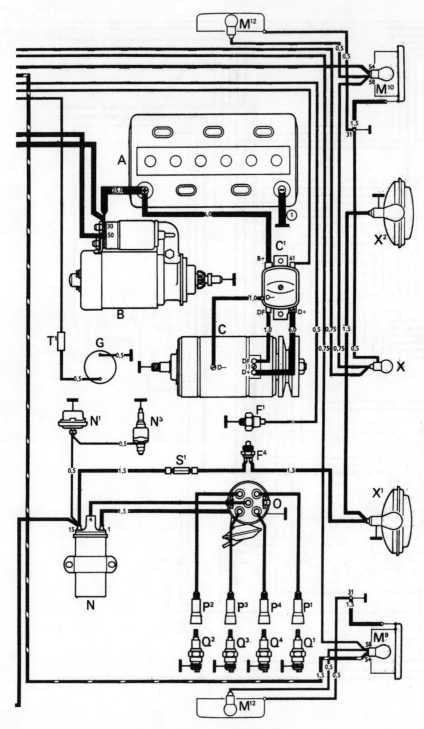

Wiring diagram—1970 Type 2

A. Battery
B. Starter
C. Generator
C^1. Regulator
D. Ignition/starter switch
E. Windshield wiper switch
E^1. Light switch
E^2. Turn signal and headlight dimmer switch
E^3. Emergency flasher switch
E^6. Switch for interior light, rear
F. Brake light switch
F^1. Oil pressure switch
F^2. Door contact switch, left
    with contact for buzzer H^5
F^3. Door contact switch, right
F^4. Switch for backup lights
G. Fuel gauge sending unit
G^1. Fuel gauge
H. Horn button
H^1. Horn
H^5. Ignition key warning buzzer
J. Dimmer relay
J^2. Emergency flasher relay
K. Instrument panel insert
K^1. High beam warning light
K^2. Generator charging warning light
K^3. Oil pressure warning light
K^4. Parking light warning light
K^5. Turn signal warning light
K^6. Emergency flasher warning light
K^7. Dual circuit brake system warning light
L^1. Sealed beam light, left headlight
L^2. Sealed beam light, right headlight
L^6. Speedometer light
L^8. Clock light

L^{10}. Instrument panel light
M^5. Turn signal and parking light, front, left
M^7. Turn signal and parking light, front, right
M^9. Tail/brake/turn signal light, left
M^{10}. Tail/brake/turn signal light, right
M^{12}. Side marker lights, rear
N. Ignition coil
N^1. Automatic choke
N^3. Electromagnetic pilot jet
O. Distributor
P^1. Spark plug connector, No. 1 cylinder
P^2. Spark plug connector, No. 2 cylinder
P^3. Spark plug connector, No. 3 cylinder
P^4. Spark plug connector, No. 4 cylinder
Q^1. Spark plug, No. 1 cylinder
Q^2. Spark plug, No. 2 cylinder
Q^3. Spark plug, No. 3 cylinder
Q^4. Spark plug, No. 4 cylinder
S. Fuse box
S^1. In-line fuse for backup lights
T^1. Cable connector, single
T^2. Cable connector, double
T^3. Cable connector, triple
T^4. Cable connector (four connections)
T^5. Push-on connector
V. Windshield wiper motor
W. Interior light, front
W^1. Interior light, rear
X. License plate light
X^1. Backup light, left
X^2. Backup light, right
Y. Clock
① Ground strap from battery to frame
② Ground strap from transmission to the frame
④ Ground cable from horn button

Wiring diagram—1970 Type 2

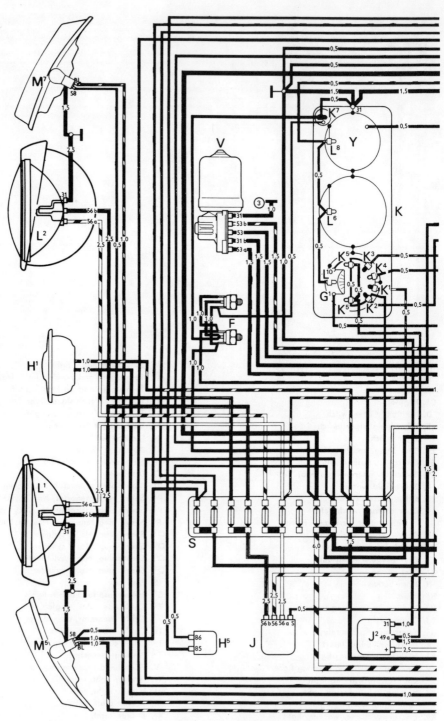

Wiring diagram—1971 Type 2

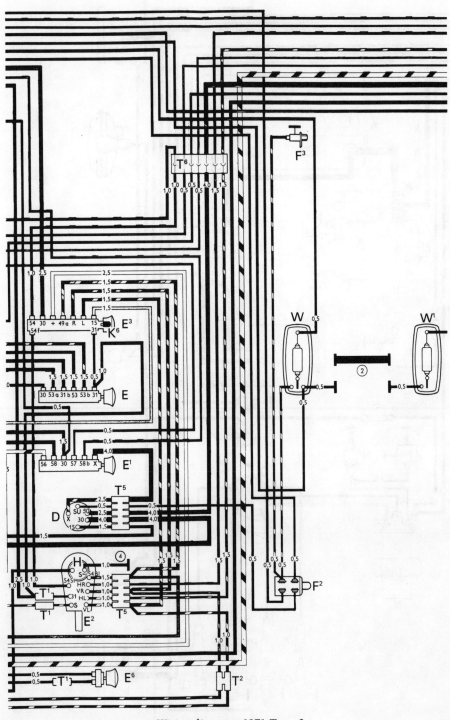

Wiring diagram—1971 Type 2

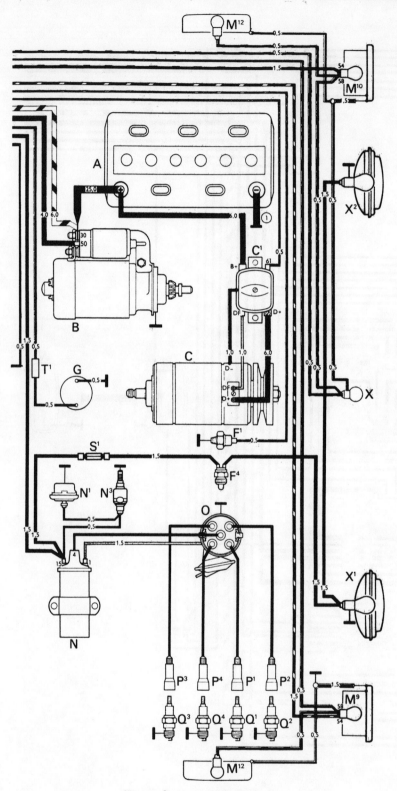

Wiring diagram—1971 Type 2

A. Battery
B. Starter
C. Generator
C^1. Regulator
D. Ignition/starter switch
E. Windshield wiper switch
E^1. Light switch
E^2. Turn signal and headlight dimmer switch
E^3. Emergency flasher switch
E^6. Interior light switch, rear
F. Brake light switch with warning switch
F^1. Oil pressure switch
F^2. Door contact, left,
    with contact for buzzer
F^3. Door contact switch, right
F^4. Backup light switch
G. Fuel gauge sending unit
G^1. Fuel gauge
H. Horn button
H^1. Horn
H^5. Ignition key warning buzzer
J. Dimmer relay
J^2. Emergency flasher relay
K. Instrument panel insert
K^1. High beam warning light
K^2. Generator charging warning light
K^3. Oil pressure warning light
K^4. Parking light warning light
K^5. Turn signal warning light
K^6. Emergency flasher warning light
K^7. Dual circuit brake system warning light
L^1. Sealed beam unit, left headlight
L^2. Sealed beam unit, right headlight
L^6. Speedometer light

L^8. Clock light
L^{10}. Instrument panel light
M^5. Turn signal and parking light, front, left
M^7. Turn signal and parking light, front, right
M^9. Tail/brake/turn signal light, left
M^{10}. Tail/brake/turn signal light, right
M^{12}. Side marker light, rear
N. Ignition coil
N^1. Automatic choke
O. Ignition distributor
P^1. Spark plug connector, No. 1 cylinder
P^2. Spark plug connector, No. 2 cylinder
P^3. Spark plug connector, No. 3 cylinder
P^4. Spark plug connector, No. 4 cylinder
Q^1. Spark plug, No. 1 cylinder
Q^2. Spark plug, No. 2 cylinder
Q^3. Spark plug, No. 3 cylinder
Q^4. Spark plug, No. 4 cylinder
S. Fuse box
S^1. Fuse for backup light
T^1. Cable connector, single
T^5. Cable connector, five connections
T^6. Cable connector, seven connections
V. Windshield wiper motor
W. Interior light, front
W^1. Interior light, rear
X. License plate light
X^1. Backup light, left
X^2. Backup light, right
Y. Clock
① Ground strap battery to frame
② Ground strap transmission to frame
③ Ground strap windshield wiper
④ Ground strap horn button to steering coupling

Wiring Diagram—1971 Type 2

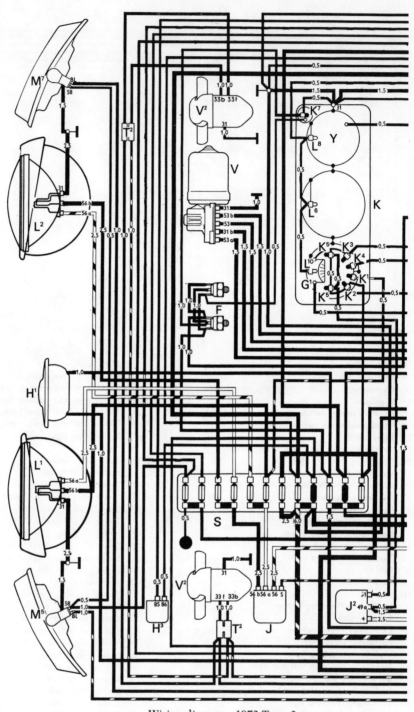

Wiring diagram—1972 Type 2

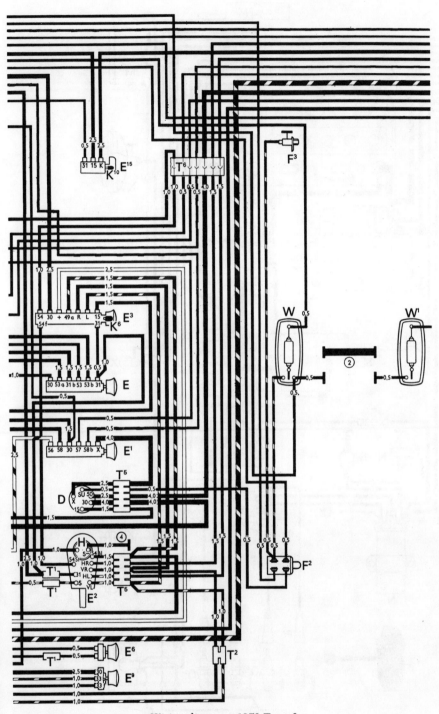

Wiring diagram—1972 Type 2

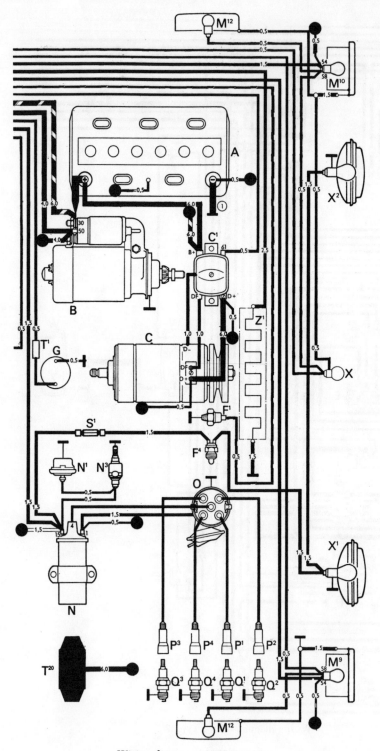

Wiring diagram—1972 Type 2

A. Battery
B. Starter
C. Generator
C^1. Regulator
D. Ignition/starter switch
E. Windshield wiper switch
E^1. Light switch
E^2. Turn signal and headlight dimmer switch
E^3. Emergency flasher switch
E^6. Interior light switch, rear
E^6. Switch for fan motors
E^{15}. Rear window defogger switch
F. Brake light switch with warning switch
F^1. Oil pressure switch
F^2. Door contact switch, left, with contact for buzzer
F^3. Door contact switch, right
F^4. Backup light switch
G. Fuel gauge sending unit
G^1. Fuel gauge
H. Horn button
H^1. Horn
H^3. Ignition key warning buzzer
J. Dimmer relay
J^2. Emergency flasher relay
K. Instrument panel insert
K^1. High beam warning light
K^2. Generator charging warning light
K^3. Oil pressure warning light
K^4. Parking light warning light
K^5. Turn signal warning light
K^6. Emergency flasher warning light
K^7. Dual circuit brake system warning light
K^{10}. Rear window defogger warning light
L^1. Sealed beam unit, left headlight
L^2. Sealed beam unit, right headlight
L^6. Speedometer light
L^8. Clock light

L^{10}. Instrument panel light
M^5. Turn signal and parking light, front, left
M^7. Turn signal and parking light, front, right
M^9. Tail/brake/turn signal light, left
M^{10}. Tail/brake/turn signal light, right
M^{12}. Side marker light, rear
N. Ignition coil
N^1. Automatic choke
N^3. Electromagnetic pilot jet
O. Ignition distributor
P^1. Spark plug connector, No. 1 cylinder
P^2. Spark plug connector, No. 2 cylinder
P^3. Spark plug connector, No. 3 cylinder
P^4. Spark plug connector, No. 4 cylinder
Q^1. Spark plug, No. 1 cylinder
Q^2. Spark plug, No. 2 cylinder
Q^3. Spark plug, No. 3 cylinder
Q^4. Spark plug, No. 4 cylinder
S. Fuse box
S^1. Fuse for backup light
T^1. Cable connector, single
T^2. Cable connector, double
T^5. Cable connectors, five connections
T^6. Cable connectors, eight connections
T^{20}. Test network, central plug
V. Windshield wiper motor
V^2. Fan motor, front
W. Interior light, front
W^1. Interior light, rear
X. License plate light
X^1. Backup light, left
X^2. Backup light, right
Y. Clock
Z^1. Rear window defogger heating element
① Ground strap from battery to frame
② Ground strap from transmission to the frame
④ Ground cable from horn button to steering coupling

Wiring diagram—1972 Type 2

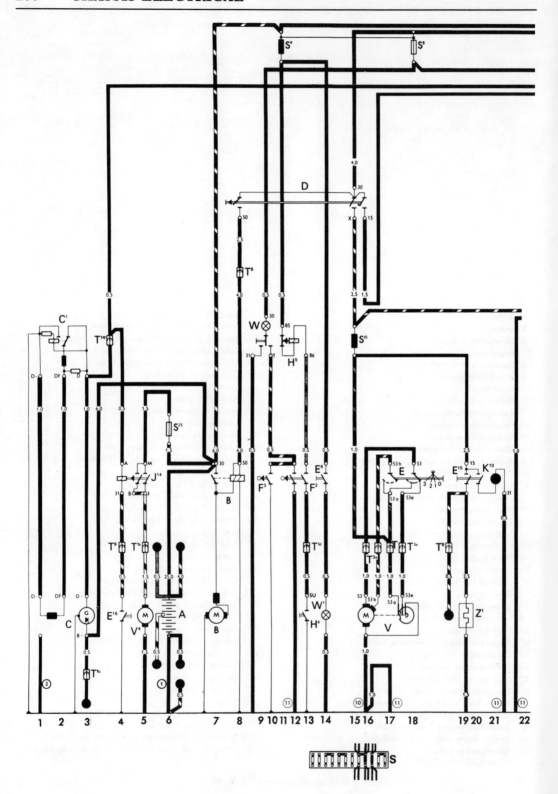

Current flow diagram—1973–74 Type 2

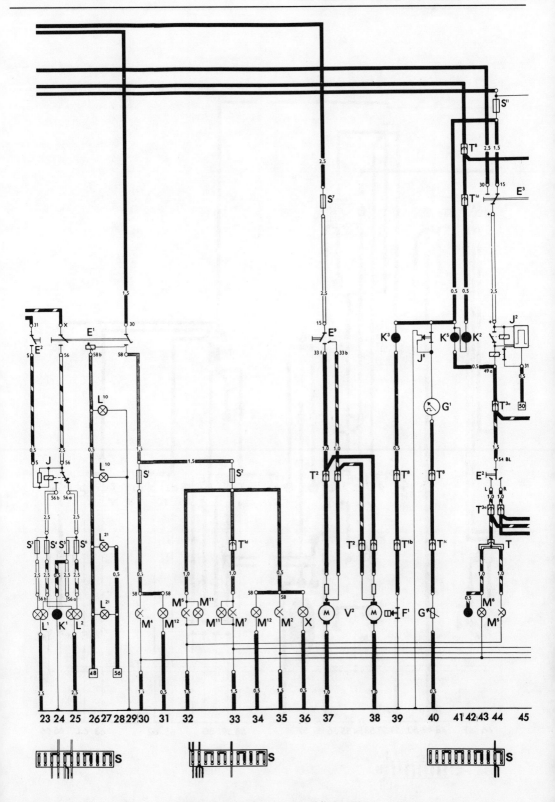

Current flow diagram—1973–74 Type 2

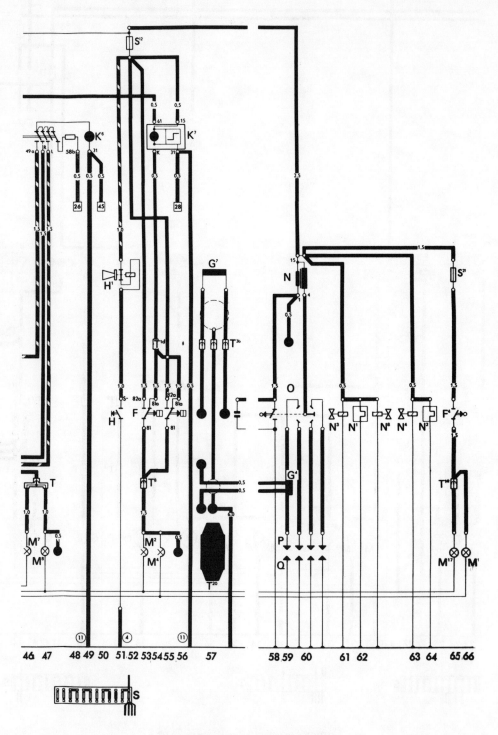

Current flow diagram—1973–74 Type 2

Description	current track	Description	current track
A. Battery	6	M^{12}. Side marker light, rear	31, 34
B. Starter	7, 8	M^{16}. Backup light, left	66
C. Alternator	1, 2, 3	M^{17}. Backup light, right	65
C^1. Regulator	1, 2, 3	N. Ignition coil	60
D. Ignition/starter switch	8, 15, 16	N^1. Automatic choke, left carburetor	62
E. Windshield wiper switch	17, 18	N^2. Automatic choke, right carburetor	64
E^1. Light switch	25, 26, 29	N^3. Electromagnetic pilot jet, left carburetor	61
E^2. Turn signal switch	44		
E^2. Headlight dimmer switch	22	N^4. Electromagnetic pilot jet, right carburetor	63
E^3. Emergency flasher switch	44, 46, 47, 48, 50		
		N^8. Cutoff valve for central idling system	62
E^6. Interior light switch, rear	14	O. Distributor	58, 60
E^9. Fresh air fan motor switch	37	P. Spark plug connectors	59, 60
E^{15}. Rear window defogger switch	19, 20	Q. Spark plugs	59, 60
E^{16}. Heater air blower switch	4	S^1. to S^{12}. Fuse box	11, 15, 18, 23, 25, 30, 33, 37, 44, 52
F. Brake light switch	53, 54, 55 56		
F^1. Oil pressure switch	39		
F^2. Door contact and buzzer alarm switch, left H^5	12, 13	S^{21}. Fuse for backup lights	65
		S^{25}. Fuse for heater air blower	6
F^3. Door contact switch, right	10	T. Cable adapter behind instrument panel	
F^4. Backup light switch	65		
G. Fuel gauge sending unit	40	T^1. Wire connector, single	
G^1. Fuel gauge	40	a. in engine compartment, right	
G^4. Ignition timing sensor	59	b. in engine compartment	
G^7. TDC marker unit	57	c. beside the fuel tank, right side	
H. Horn button	51	d. on the cluster of the instrument panel	
H^1. Horn	51		
H^5. Ignition key warning buzzer	12, 13	e. next to the tail/brake light, left	
H^6. Buzzer alarm contact in ignition/ starter switch	13	T^2. Wire connector, double point behind instrument panel	
J. Dimmer relay	22, 23, 24	T^{3a}. Wire connector, three point behind instrument panel	
J^2. Emergency flasher relay	44, 45		
J^6. Fuel gauge vibrator	40	T^{3b}. Wire connector, three point in engine compartment	
J^{14}. Heater air blower relay	4, 5		
K^1. High beam warning light	24	T^8. Wire connector, eight point behind instrument panel	
K^2. Alternator charging warning light	42		
K^3. Oil pressure warning light	39	T^{20}. Test network, test socket	57
K^5. Turn signal warning light	41	V. Windshield wiper motor	16, 18
K^6. Emergency flasher warning light	49	V^2. Fan motor	37, 38
K^7. Dual circuit brake warning light	54, 56	V^4. Heater air blower	5
K^{10}. Rear window defogger warning light	21	W. Interior light, front	10
L^1. Sealed beam unit, left headlight	23	W^1. Interior light, rear	14
L^2. Sealed beam unit, right headlight	25	X. License plate light	36
L^{10}. Instrument panel light	27	Z^1. Rear window defogger heating element	19
L^{21}. Light for heater lever illumination	27		
M^2. Tail/brake light, right	35, 53		
M^4. Tail/brake light, left	30, 54		
M^5. Turn signal and parking light front, left	32, 44		
M^6. Turn signal, rear, left	43	① Ground strap from battery to body	6
M^7. Turn signal and parking light front, right	33, 46	② Ground strap from transmission to frame	1
		④ Ground strap via steering coupling	52
M^8. Turn signal, rear, right	47	⑩ Ground connection, dashboard	
M^{11}. Side marker light, front	32, 33	⑪ Ground connection, speedometer	

Current flow diagram—1973–74 Type 2

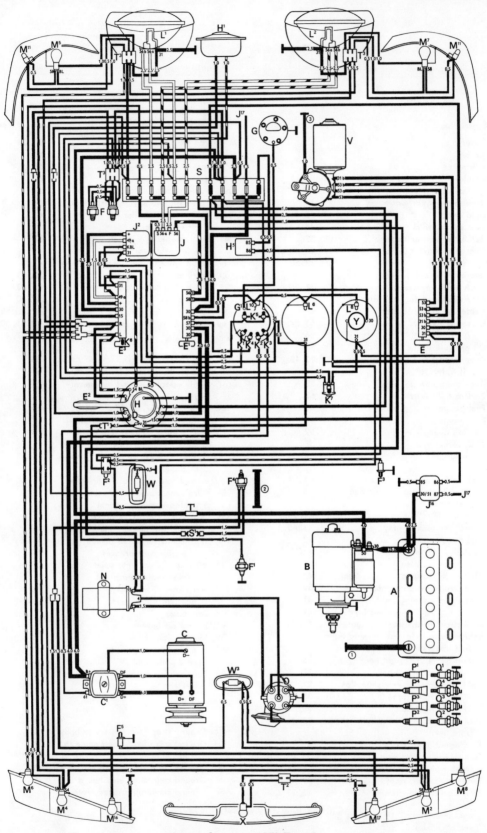

Wiring diagram—1970 Type 3

A. Battery
B. Starter
C. Generator
C^1. Regulator
D. Ignition/starter switch
E. Windshield wiper switch
E^1. Light switch
E^2. Turn signal and headlight dimmer switch
E^3. Emergency flasher switch
F. Brake light switch
F^1. Oil pressure switch
F^2. Door contact switch, left,
    with contact for buzzer
F^3. Door contact switch, right
F^4. Back-up light switch
F^5. Luggage compartment light switch
G. Fuel gauge sending unit
G^1. Fuel gauge
H. Horn button
H^1. Horn
H^5. Ignition key warning buzzer
J. Dimmer relay
J^2. Emergency flasher relay
J^{16}. Power supply relay for fuel injection
    system
J^{17}. To fuel pump relay
K^1. High beam warning light
K^2. Generator charging warning light
K^3. Oil pressure warning light
K^4. Parking light warning light
K^5. Turn signal warning lights
K^6. Hazard warning light
K^7. Dual circuit brake system warning light
L^1. Sealed beam unit, left
L^2. Sealed beam unit, right
L^6. Speedometer light

L^8. Clock light
L^{10}. Instrument panel light
M^3. Tail and brake light, right
M^4. Tail and brake light, left
M^5. Turn signal and parking light, front, left
M^6. Turn signal, rear, left
M^7. Turn signal and parking light, front, right
M^8. Turn signal, rear, right
M^{11}. Side marker light, front
^{14}. Back-up lght, left
M^{17}. Back-up light, right
N. Ignition coil
O. Distributor
P^1. Spark plug connector, No. 1 cylinder
P^2. Spark plug connector, No. 2 cylinder
P^3. Spark plug connector, No. 3 cylinder
P^4. Spark plug connector, No. 4 cylinder
Q^1. Spark plug, No. 1 cylinder
Q^2. Spark plug, No. 2 cylinder
Q^3. Spark plug, No. 3 cylinder
Q^4. Spark plug, No. 4 cylinder
S. Fuse box
S^1. Back-up light in-line fuse
T. Cable adapter
T^1. Cable connector, single
T^2. Cable connector, double
T^3. Cable connector, triple
V. Windshield wiper motor
W. Interior light
^{3}. Luggage compartment light
X. License plate light

① Battery to frame ground strap
② Transmission to frame ground strap
③ Windshield wiper motor to body ground
   strap

Wiring diagram—1970 Type 3

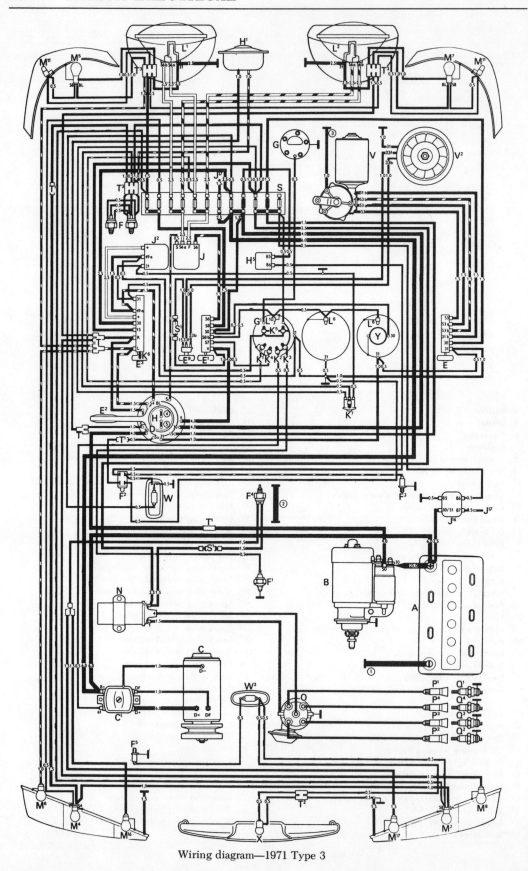

Wiring diagram—1971 Type 3

A. Battery
B. Starter
C. Generator
C^1. Regulator
D. Ignition/starter switch
E. Winshield wiper switch
E^1. Light switch
E^2. Turn signal and headlight dimmer switch
E^3. Emergency flasher switch
E^9. Fresh air fan motor switch
F. Brake light switch
F^1. Oil pressure switch
F^2. Door contact and buzzer alarm switch, left
F^3. Door contact switch, right
F^4. Back-up light switch
F^5. Luggage compartment light switch
G. Fuel tank sending unit
G^1. Fuel gauge
H. Horn button
H^1. Horn
H^5. Ignition key warning buzzer
J. Dimmer relay
J^2. Emergency flasher relay
J^{16}. Power supply relay for fuel injection
J^{17}. Connection to fuel pump relay
K^1. High beam warning light
K^2. Generator charging warning light
K^3. Oil pressure warning light
K^4. Parking light warning light
K^5. Turn signal warning light
K^6. Emergency flasher warning light
K^7. Dual brake circuit warning light
L^1. Sealed beam unit left headlight
L^2. Sealed beam unit right headlight
L^6. Speedometer light
L^8. Clock light
L^{10}. Instrument panel light

M^2. Tail/brake light, right
M^4. Tail/brake light, left
M^5. Turn signal and parking light, front, left
M^6. Turn signal, rear, left
M^7. Turn signal and parking light, front, right
M^8. Turn signal, rear, right
M^{11}. Side marker light, front
M^{16}. Back-up light, left
M^{17}. Back-up light, right
N. Ignition coil
O. Distributor
P^1. Spark plug connector, No. 1 cylinder
P^2. Spark plug connector, No. 2 cylinder
P^3. Spark plug connector, No. 3 cylinder
P^4. Spark plug connector, No. 4 cylinder
Q^1. Spark plug, No. 1 cylinder
Q^2. Spark plug, No. 2 cylinder
Q^3. Spark plug, No. 3 cylinder
Q^4. Spark plug, No. 4 cylinder
S. Fuse box
S^1. In-line fuse for back-up lights
    and fresh air fan motor
T. Cable adapter
T^1. Cable connector, single
T^2. Cable connector, double
T^3. Cable connector, triple
V. Windshield wiper motor
V^2. Fresh air motor front
W. Interior light
W^3. Luggage compartment light
X. License plate light
Y. Clock

① Ground strap from battery to frame
② Ground strap from transmission to frame
④ Ground cable from horn to steering coupling
⑤ Ground cable from front axle to frame

Wiring diagram—1971 Type 3

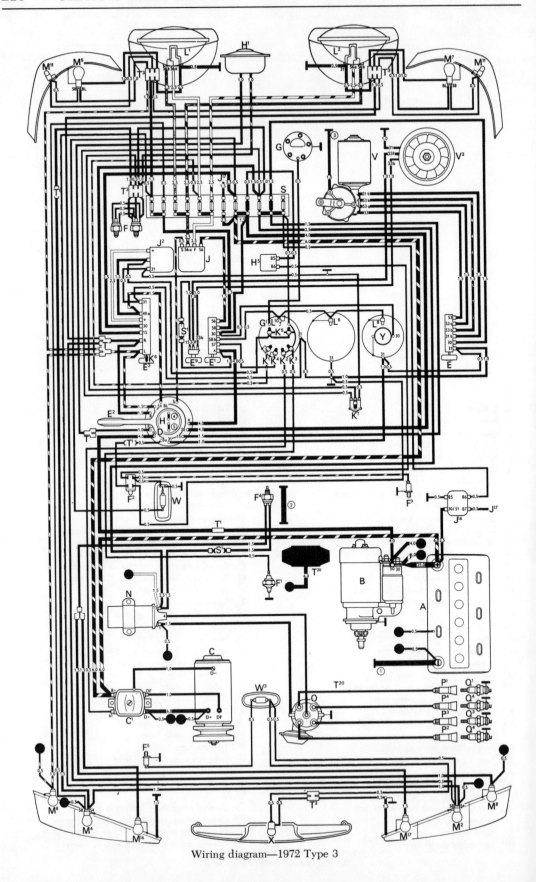

Wiring diagram—1972 Type 3

A. Battery
B. Starter
C. Generator
C^1. Regulator
D. Ignition/starter switch
E. Windshield wiper switch
E^1. Light switch
E^2. Turn signal and headlight dimmer switch
E^3. Emergency flasher switch
E^9. Fresh air fan motor switch
F. Brake light switch
F^1. Oil pressure switch
F^2. Door contact and buzzer alarm switch, left
F^3. Door contact switch, right
F^4. Back-up light switch
F^5. Luggage compartment light switch
G. Fuel gauge sending unit
G^1. Fuel gauge
H. Horn button
H^1. Horn
H^5. Ignition key warning buzzer
J. Dimmer relay
J^2. Emergency flasher relay
J^{16}. Power supply relay for fuel injection
J^{17}. Connection to fuel pump relay
K^1. High beam warning light
K^2. Generator charging warning light
K^3. Oil pressure warning light
K^4. Parking light warning light
K^5. Turn signal warning light
K^6. Emergency flasher warning light
K^7. Dual brake circuit warning light
L^1. Sealed beam unit left headlight
L^2. Sealed beam unit right headlight
L^6. Speedometer light
L^8. Clock light
L^{10}. Instrument panel light

M^2. Tail/brake light, right
M^4. Tail/brake light, left
M^5. Turn signal and parking light, front, left
M^6. Turn signal, rear, left
M^7. Turn signal and parking light, front, right
M^8. Turn signal, rear, right
M^{11}. Side marker light, front
M^{16}. Back-up light, left
M^{17}. Back-up light, right
N. Ignition coil
O. Distributor
P^1. Spark plug connector, No. 1 cylinder
P^2. Spark plug connector, No. 2 cylinder
P^3. Spark plug connector, No. 3 cylinder
P^4. Spark plug connector, No. 4 cylinder
Q^1. Spark plug, No. 1 cylnder
Q^2. Spark plug, No. 2 cylinder
Q^3. Spark plug, No. 3 cylinder
Q^4. Spark plug, No. 4 cylinder
S. Fuse box
S^1. In-line fuse for back-up lights
and fresh air fan motor
T. Cable adapter
T^1. Cable connector, single
T^2. Cable connector, double
T^3. Cable connector, triple
T^{20}. Test network, central plug
V. Windshield wiper motor
V^2. Fresh air motor front
W. Interior light
W^3. Luggage compartment light
X. License plate light
Y. Clock
① Ground strap from battery to frame
② Ground strap from transmission to frame
④ Ground cable from horn to steering coupling
⑤ Ground cable from front axle to frame

Wiring diagram—1972 Type 3

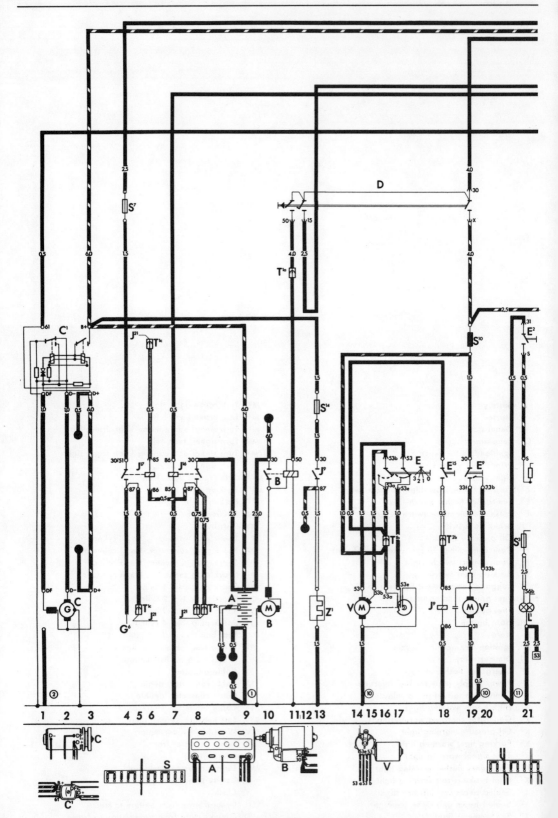

Current flow diagram—1973 Type 3

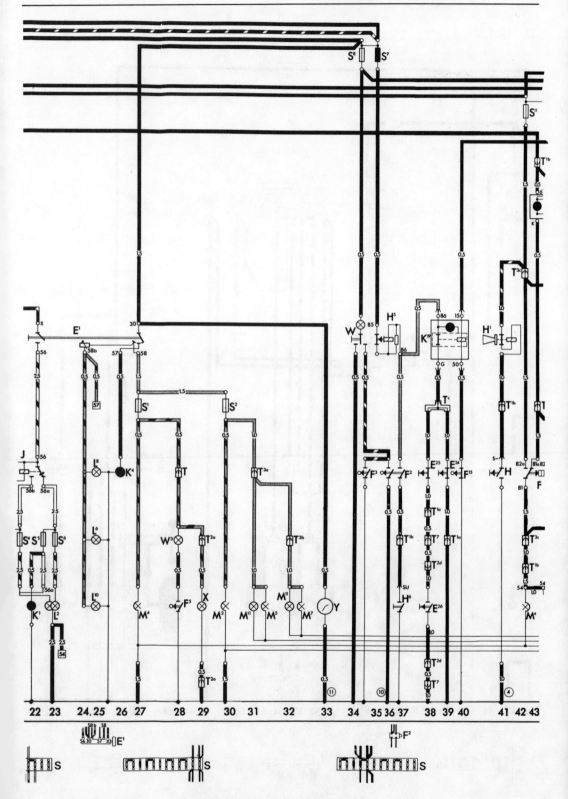

Current flow diagram—1973 Type 3

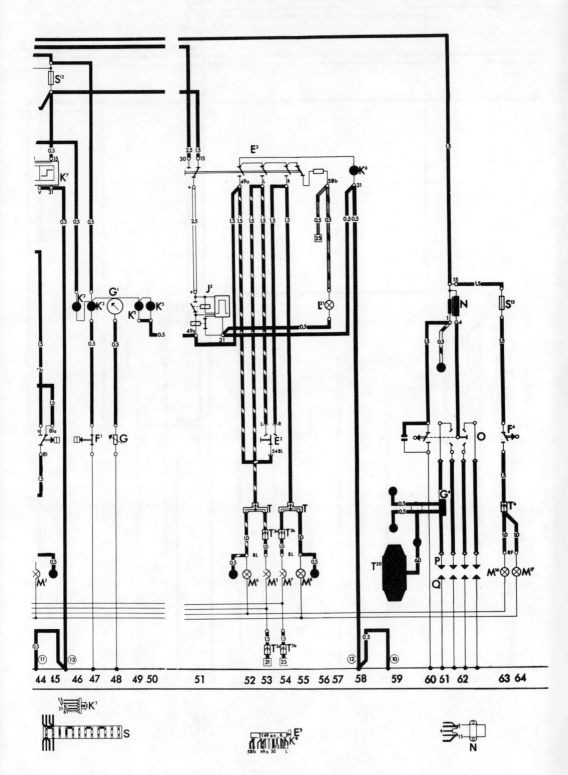

Current flow diagram—1973 Type 3

Description	current track
A. Battery	9
B. Starter	10, 11
C. Generator	1, 2, 3
C^1. Regulator	1, 2, 3
D. Ignition/starter switch	11, 12, 19 37
E. Windshield wiper switch	16, 17
E^1. Light switch	22, 24, 26, 27
E^2. Turn signal and headlight dimmer switch	21, 53, 54
E^3. Emergency flasher switch	51, 52, 53, 54, 57, 58
E^9. Fresh air fan motor switch	19, 20
E^{15}. Rear window defogger switch	18
E^{24}. Safety belt lock, left	39
E^{25}. Safety belt lock, right	38
E^{26}. Contact strip in passenger seat	38
F. Brake light switch	42, 43, 44, 45
F^1. Oil pressure switch	47
F^2. Door contact and buzzer alarm switch, left	36, 37
F^3. Door contact switch, right	34
F^4. Back-up light switch	63
F^5. Luggage compartment light switch	28
F^{15}. Transmission switch for safety belt warning system	40
G. Fuel gauge sending unit	48
G^1. Fuel gauge	48
G^4. Ignition timing sensor	61
G^6. to fuel pump	4
H. Horn button	41
H^1. Horn	41
H^5. Ignition key warning buzzer	35, 37
H^6. Contact in ignition/starter switch for buzzer	37
J. Dimmer relay	21, 23
J^2. Emergency flasher relay	51
J^9. Rear window defogger relay	13, 18
J^{16}. Power supply relay for fuel injection	7, 8
J^{17}. Fuel pump relay	4, 5, 6
J^{21}. to electronic control unit	5, 6, 8
K^1. High beam warning light	22
K^2. Generator charging warning light	46
K^3. Oil pressure warning light	47
K^4. Parking light warning light	26
K^5. Turn signal warning light	49, 50
K^6. Emergency flasher warning light	58
K^7. Dual brake circuit warning light	43, 45
K^{19}. Safety belt warning light system	38, 39, 40
L^1. Sealed beam unit, left headlight	21
L^2. Sealed beam unit, right headlight	23
L^6. Speedometer light	25
L^8. Clock light	25
L^{10}. Instrument panel light	25
L^{21}. Light for heater lever illumination	57
M^2. Tail/brake light, right	30, 44
M^4. Tail/brake light, left	27, 42
M^5. Turn signal and parking light, front, left	31, 53
M^6. Turn signal, rear, left	52
M^7. Turn signal and parking light, front, right	32, 54
M^8. Turn signal, rear, right	55
M^{11}. Side marker light, front	31, 32
M^{16}. Back-up light, left	63
M^{17}. Back-up light, right	64
N. Ignition coil	62
O. Distributor	60, 62
P. Spark plug connectors	61, 62
Q. Spark plugs	61, 62
S^1. to Fuse box	19, 21, 23, 27, 30, 34, 35, 42, 45
S^{12}.	
S^{13}. Fuse for back-up lights (8 Amp)	63
S^{14}. Fuse for rear window defogger (8 Amp)	13
T. Cable adapter	
a. below rear seat bench	
b. in engine compartment	
T^1. Wire connector, single	
a. under rear seat bench	
b. under instrument panel	
c. in engine compartment, left	
T^2. Wire connector, double	
a. on rear luggage compartment lid	
b. under instrument panel	
c. in engine compartment, left	
d. in passenger seat	
T^3. Wire connector, triple	
a. in headlight housing, left	
b. in headlight housing, right	
c. in front luggage compartment, left	
T^7. Wire connector, double on passenger seat rail	
T^{20}. Test network, test socket	59
V. Windshield wiper motor	14, 17
V^2. Fresh air motor	19
W. Interior light	34
W^3. Luggage compartment light	28
X. License plate light	29
Y. Clock	33
Z^1. Rear window defogger heating element	13
① Ground strap from battery to frame	9
② Ground strap from transmission to frame	1
④ Ground cable from horn to steering coupling	41
⑩ Ground connection on instrument panel	
⑪ Ground connection on speedometer	
⑫ Ground connection on fuel gauge	
⑬ Ground connection on clock	

Current flow Diagram—1973 Type 3

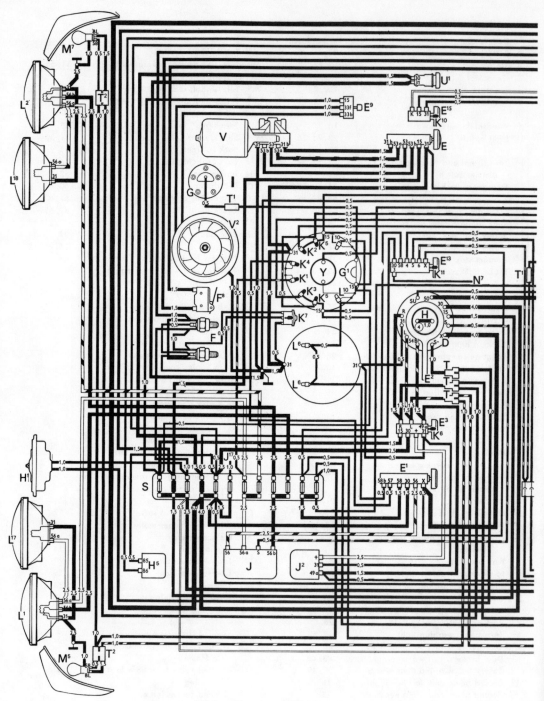

Wiring diagram—1971 Type 4

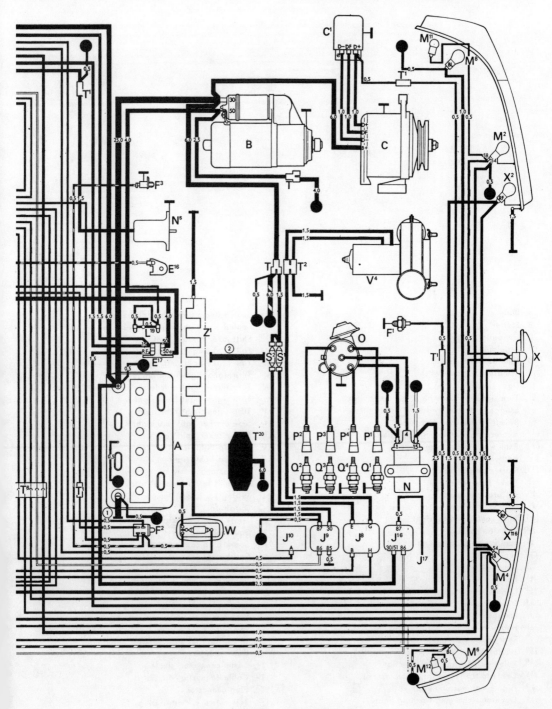

Wiring diagram—1971 Type 4

A. Battery
B. Starter
C. Generator
C^1. Regulator
D. Ignition/starter switch
E. Windshield wiper switch
E^1. Light switch
E^2. Turn signal and headlight dimmer switch
E^3. Emergency flasher switch
E^9. Switch for fresh air fan motor
E^{13}. Heater temperature regulating switch
E^{15}. Rear window defogger switch
E^{16}. Heater switch
E^{17}. Starter cut-out switch
F. Brake light switch
F^1. Oil pressure switch
F^2. Door contact and buzzer alarm switch, left
F^3. Door contact switch, right
F^8. Kick-down switch
G. Fuel gauge sending unit
G^1. Fuel gauge
H. Horn button
H^1. Horn
H^5. Ignition key warning buzzer
J. Dimmer relay
J^2. Emergency flasher relay
J^8. Heater relay
J^9. Rear window defogger relay
J^{10}. Heater safety switch
J^{16}. Relay of electronic fuel injection
J^{17}. Cable to fuel relay (injection system)
K^1. High beam warning light
K^2. Generator charging warning light
K^3. Oil pressure warning light
K^4. Parking light warning light
K^5. Turn signal warning light
K^6. Emergency flasher warning light
K^7. Dual circuit brake warning light
K^{10}. Rear window defogger warning light
K^{11}. Heater warning light
L^1. Sealed beam unit, left head light
L^2. Sealed beam unit, right head light
L^6. Speedometer illuminating light
L^{10}. Instrument panel light

L^{17}. Sealed beam unit left, high beam
L^{18}. Sealed beam unit right, high beam
L^{19}. Shift lever console light
M^2. Tail/brake light, right
M^4. Tail/brake light, left
M^5. Turn signal light front left
M^6. Turn signal light rear left
M^7. Turn signal light front right
M^8. Turn signal light rear right
M^{11}. Side marker light rear right
M^{12}. Side marker light rear left
M^{16}. Back-up light, left
M^{17}. Back-up light, right
N. Ignition coil
N^5. Solenoid for kick-down switch
N^7. Wiring for heater temperature sensor
O. Distributor
P^1. Spark plug connector, No. 1 cylinder
P^2. Spark plug connector, No. 2 cylinder
P^3. Spark plug connector, No. 3 cylinder
P^4. Spark plug connector, No. 4 cylinder
Q^1. Spark plug, No. 1 cylinder
Q^2. Spark plug, No. 2 cylinder
Q^3. Spark plug, No. 3 cylinder
Q^4. Spark plug, No. 4 cylinder
S. Fuse box
S^1. In-line fuse for heater
S^2. In-line fuse for rear window defogger
T. Cable adapter
T^1. Cable connector, single
T^2. Cable connector, double
T^5. Plug connector
T^{20}. Test network, central plug
V. Windshield wiper motor
V^2. Fresh air motor front
V^4. Heater motor
W. Interior light
X. License plate light
Y. Clock
Z^1. Rear window defogger heating element

① Ground strap from battery to frame
② Ground strap from transmission to frame
④ Ground cable for steering coupling

Wiring diagram—1971 Type 4

Light Bulb Specifications

Bulb	Type 1	Type 2	Type 3	Type 4
Sealed beam unit	12.8V; 50/40W	12.8V; 50/40W	12.8V; 50/40W	12.8V; 37.5/50W
Turn signal	12V; 21W	12V; 21W	12V; 21W	——
Stop/tail light	12V; 21/5W	12V; 21/5W	12V; 21/5W	12V; 32/4 cp
License plate	12V; 10W	12V; 10W	12V; 5W①	12V; 6 cp
Back-up light	12V; 25W	12V; 25W	12V; 25W	12V; 25W
Interior light	12V; 10W	12V; 10W	12V; 10W	10V; 10W
Parking light	12V; 4W	12V; 4W	12V; 4W	——
Warning light	12V; 2W	12V; 1.2W	12V; 2W	12V; 1.2W
Side marker light	12V; 2 cp	12V; 2 cp	12V; 2 cp	12V; 2 cp
Turn signal, parking light	——	——	——	32/4 cp

V—Volts   cp—Candle Power
W—Watts   ① Squareback Sedan—12V; 10W

Fuses

Type 1

Circuit	Fuse
Left parking, side marker, and tail lights	8 amps
Right parking, side marker, and tail lights	8 amps
Left low beam	8 amps
Right low beam	8 amps
Left high beam	8 amps
Right high beam, high beam indicator	8 amps
License plate light	8 amps
Emergency flasher system	8 amps
Interior lights	16 amps
Windshield wiper, rear window defogger, fresh air fan	16 amps
Horn, stop lights, ATF warning light	8 amps
Fuel gauge, turn signals, brake warning light, oil pressure, turn signal and generator warning lights	8 amps

Type 3

Circuit	Fuse
Right tail light, license plate light, parking and side marker light, luggage compartment light	8 amps
Left tail light	8 amps
Left low beam	8 amps
Right low beam	8 amps
Left high beam, high beam indicator	8 amps
Right high beam	8 amps
Electric fuel pump	8 amps
Emergency flasher, interior light	8 amps
Buzzer	16 amps
Windshield wipers, fresh air fan, rear window defogger	16 amps
Stop lights, turn signals, horn, brake warning light, back-up lights	8 amps
Accessories	8 amps

Type 2

Circuit	Fuse
Left tail and side marker lights	8 amps
Right tail and marker lights, license light, parking lights	8 amps
Left low beam	8 amps
Right low beam	8 amps
Left high beam, high beam indicator	8 amps
Right high beam	8 amps
Accessories	8 amps
Emergency flasher, front interior light	8 amps
Rear interior light, buzzer alarm, auxiliary heater	16 amps
Windshield wipers, rear window defogger	16 amps
Turn signals, warning lamps for alternator, oil pressure, fuel gauge, kickdown, and back-up lights	8 amps
Horn, stop lights, brake warning light	8 amps

Type 4

Circuit	Fuse
Parking lights, left tail and left rear side marker lights	8 amps
Right tail light, right rear side marker light, license plate light, selector lever console light	8 amps
Left low beam	8 amps
Right low beam	8 amps
Left high beam	8 amps
Right high beam, high beam indicator	8 amps
Fuel pump	8 amps
Interior light, emergency flasher, buzzer	8 amps
Cigarette lighter, heater	16 amps
Window wiper, fresh air fan, heater, rear window defogger	16 amps
Turn signals, back-up lights, warning lights for alternator, oil pressure, fuel gauge	8 amps
Horn, brake warning light, stop lights	8 amps

Chapter Six

Clutch and Transaxle

Transaxle

All transmissions are transaxles since the housing contains both transmission and final drive gears. Manual and automatic stick shift transaxles have a common sump and share the same hypoid gear lubricant. Automatic transaxles use ATF Dexron® in the transmission and hypoid gear lube in the final drive.

All transaxles are mounted in a yoke at the rear of the car and bolt up to the front of the engine. It is common practice when servicing the transaxle to remove the engine and transaxle as an assembly.

The transaxle case is a one piece unit and is constructed of aluminum alloy.

MANUAL TRANSAXLE

All manual transaxles employ four forward speeds and a reverse. All forward speeds have synchromesh engagement. The gears are helical and in constant mesh. Gear selection is accomplished by a floor-mounted lever working through a shift rod contained in the frame tunnel. The final drive pinion and ring gear are also helical cut.

Manual Transaxle Removal and Installation

1. Disconnect the negative battery cable.

2. Remove the engine.

3. Remove the socket head screws which secure the drive shafts to the transmission. Remove the bolts from the transmission end first and then remove the shafts.

NOTE: *It is not necessary to remove the drive shafts entirely from the car if the car does not have to be moved while the transaxle is out.*

4. Disconnect the clutch cable from the clutch lever and remove the clutch cable and its guide tube from the transaxle. Loosen the square head bolt at the shift linkage coupling located near the rear of the transaxle. Slide the coupling off the inner shift lever. There is an

Socket-head screws retaining driveshafts

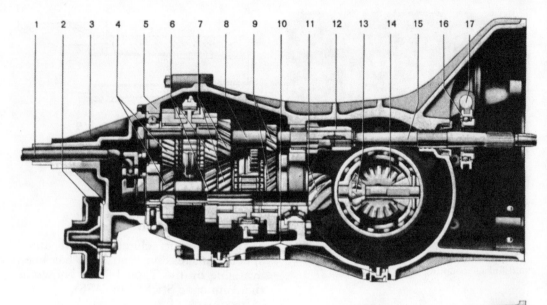

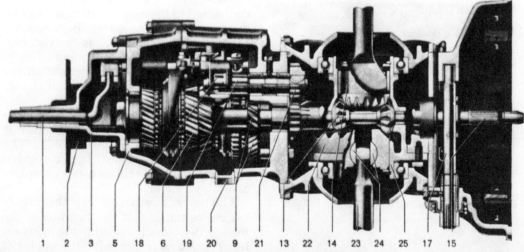

Cross-sectional view—manual transaxle

1. Transmission shift lever
2. Bonded rubber mounting
3. Gearshift housing
4. 4th speed
5. Gear carrier
6. 3rd speed
7. 2nd gear
8. Main driveshaft, front
9. 1st speed
10. Oil drain plugs
11. Drive pinion
12. Reverse gear
13. Differential pinion
14. Differential side gear
15. Main driveshaft, rear
16. Clutch release bearing
17. Clutch operating shaft
18. Reverse sliding gear
19. Reverse shaft
20. Oil filler plug
21. Reverse drive gear
22. Ring gear
23. Rear axle shaft
24. Fulcrum plate
25. Differential housing

access plate under the rear seat to reach the coupling on Type 1 and 3. It is necessary to work under the car to reach the coupling on Type 2 models.

5. Disconnect the starter wiring.

6. Disconnect the back-up light switch wiring.

7. Remove the front transaxle mounting bolts.

8. Support the transaxle with a jack

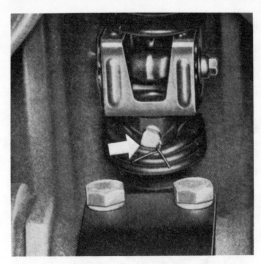

Shift linkage coupling

Front transaxle mounting bolts

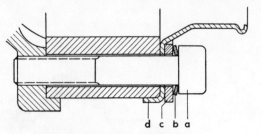

Drive axle bolt and washer positioning

a. Socket head screws   c. Spacer
b. Lockwasher   d. Protective cap

AUTOMATIC STICK SHIFT TRANSAXLE

An automatic clutch control three speed transmission (transaxle) has been available on the Type 1. It is known as the Automatic Stick Shift (ASS).

It consists of a three speed gear box connected to the engine through a hydrodynamic torque converter. Between the converter and gearbox is a vacuum-operated clutch, which automatically separates the power flow from the torque converter while in the process of changing gear ratios.

While the torque converter components are illustrated here, the picture is for familiarization purposes only. The unit cannot be serviced. It is a welded unit, and must be replaced as a complete assembly.

The power flow passes from the engine via converter, clutch and gearbox to the final drive, which, as with the conventional gearbox, is located in the center of the transmission housing.

The converter functions as a conventional clutch for starting and stopping. The shift clutch serves only for engaging and changing the speed ranges. Friction-wise, it is very lightly loaded.

There is an independent oil supply for the converter provided by an engine driven pump and a reservoir. The converter oil pump, driven off the engine oil pump, draws fluid from the reservoir and drives it around a circuit leading through the converter and back to the reservoir.

This circuit also furnishes cooling for the converter fluid.

Operation

The control valve is activated by a very light touch to the top of the shift selector

and remove the transmission carrier bolts.

9. Carefully lower the jack and remove the transaxle from the car.

10. To install, jack the transaxle into position and loosely install the bolts.

11. Tighten the transmission carrier bolts first, then tighten the front mounting nuts.

12. Install the drive shaft bolts with new lock washers. The lock washers should be positioned on the bolt with the convex side toward the screw head.

13. Reconnect the wiring, the clutch cable, and the shift linkage.

NOTE: *It may be necessary to align the transmission so that the drive shaft joints do not rub the frame.*

14. Install the engine.

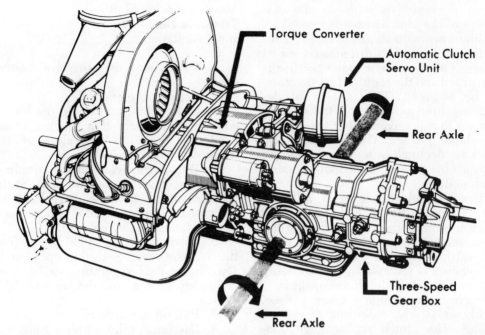

Basic components of automatic stick shift

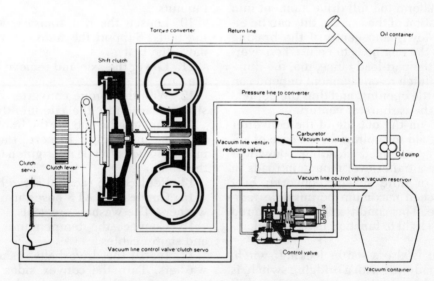

Automatic stick shift vacuum circuits

knob which, in turn, is connected to an electro-magnet. It has two functions.

At the beginning of the selection process, it has to conduct the vacuum promptly from the intake manifold to the clutch servo, so that the shift clutch disengages at once, and thus interrupts the power flow between converter and transmission. At the end of the selection process, it must, according to driving conditions, automatically ensure that the shift clutch engages at the proper speed. It may neither slip nor engage too harshly. The control valve can be adjusted for this purpose.

As soon as the selector lever is moved to the engaged position, the two contacts in the lever close the circuit. The electro-magnet is then under voltage and operates the main valve. By this means the clutch servo is connected to the engine intake manifold, and at the same time the connection to the atmosphere is closed. In the vacuum space of the servo system, a vacuum is built up, the diaphragm of the clutch servo is moved by the difference with atmospheric pressure and the shift clutch is disengaged via its linkage. The power flow to the gearbox is interrupted and the required speed range can be engaged. The process of declutching, from movement of the selector lever up to full separation of the clutch, lasts about 1/10 sec. The automatic can, therefore, declutch faster than would be possible by means of a foot-operated clutch pedal.

When the selector lever is released after changing the speed range, the switch interrupts the current flow to the electro-magnet, which then returns to its rest position and closes the main valve. The vacuum is reduced by the reducing valve and the shift clutch re-engages.

Clutch engagement takes place, quickly or slowly, according to engine loading. The clutch will engage suddenly, for example, at full throttle, and can transform the full drive moment into acceleration of the car. Or, this can be effected slowly and gently if the braking force of the engine is to be used on overrun. In the part-load range, too, the duration of clutch re-engagement depends on the throttle opening, and thus the depression in the carburetor venturi.

Vanes on the outside of the converter housing aid in cooling. In the case of abnormal prolonged loading, however (lugging a trailer over mountain roads in second or third speed), converter heat may exceed maximum permissible temperature. This condition will cause a red warning light to function in the speedometer.

There is also a starter locking switch. This, combined with a bridging switch, is operated by the inner transmission shift lever. It performs two functions:

1. With a speed range engaged, the electrical connection to the starter is interrupted. The engine, therefore, can only be started in neutral.

2. The contacts in the selector lever are not closed in the neutral position. Instead, the bridging switch transmits a voltage to the electromagnets of the control valve. This ensures that the separator clutch is also disengaged in the neutral shifter position.

Automatic Stick Shift Transaxle Removal and Installation

1. Disconnect the negative battery cable.
2. Remove the engine.
3. Make a bracket to hold the torque converter in place. If a bracket is not used, the converter will slide off the transmission input shaft.
4. Detach the gearshift rod coupling.
5. Disconnect the drive shafts at the transmission end. If the driveshafts are not going to be repaired, it is not necessary to detach the wheel end.
6. Disconnect the ATF hoses from the transmission. Seal the open ends. Disconnect the temperature switch, neutral safety switch, and the back-up light switch.
7. Pull off the vacuum servo hose.
8. Disconnect the starter wiring.
9. Remove the front transaxle mounting nuts.
10. Loosen the rear transaxle mounting bolts. Support the transaxle and remove the bolts.
11. Lower the axle and remove it from the car.
12. With the torque converter bracket still in place, raise the axle into the car.
13. Tighten the nuts for the front transmission mounting. Inseert the rear mounting bolts but do not tighten them at this time.
14. Replace the vacuum servo hose.
15. Connect the ATF hoses, using new washers. The washers are seals.
16. Connect the temperature switch and starter cables.
17. Install the driveshafts, using new washers. Turn the convex sides of the washers toward the screw head.
18. Align the transaxle so that the inner drive shaft joints do not rub on the frame fork and then tighten the rear mounting bolts.
19. Insert the shift rod coupling, tighten the screw, and secure it with wire.
20. Remove the torque converter bracket, and install the engine.
21. After installing the engine, bleed the ATF lines if return flow has not started after 2–3 minutes.

DRIVE SHAFT AND CONSTANT VELOCITY U-JOINT

Removal and Installation

1. Remove the bolts which secure the joints at each end of the shaft, tilt the shaft down, and remove the shaft.

2. Loosen the clamps which secure the rubber boot to the axle and slide the boot back on the axle.

3. Drive the stamped steel cover off of the joint with a drift.

NOTE: *After the cover is removed, do not tilt the ball hub as the balls will fall out of the hub.*

4. Remove the circlip from the end of the axle and press the axle out of the joint.

5. Reverse the above steps to install. The position of the dished washer is dependent on the type of transmission. On automatic transmissions, it is placed between the ball hub and the circlip. On manual transmissions, it is placed between the ball hub and the shoulder on the shaft. Be sure to pack the joint with grease.

NOTE: *The chamfer on the splined inside diameter of the ball hub faces the shoulder on the driveshaft.*

Shift Linkage Adjustment

The Volkswagen shift linkage is not adjustable. When shifting becomes difficult or there is an excessive amount of play in the linkage, check the shifting mechanism for worn parts. Make sure the shift linkage coupling is tightly connected to the inner shift lever located at the rear of the transaxle under the rear seat. Worn parts may be found in the shift lever mechanism and the supports for the linkage rod sometimes wear out.

The gear shift lever can be removed after the front floor mat has been lifted. After the two retaining screws have been removed from the gear shift lever ball housing, the gear shift lever, ball housing, rubber boot, and spring are removed as a unit.

CAUTION: *Carefully mark the position of the stop plate and note the position of the turned up ramp at the side of the stop plate. Normally the ramp is turned up and on the right hand side of the hole.*

Installation is the reverse of removal. Lubricate all moving parts with grease. Test the gear shift pattern. If there is difficulty in shifting, adjust the stop plate back and forth in its slotted holes.

Clutch

The clutch used in all models is a single dry disc mounted on the flywheel with a diaphragm spring type pressure plate. The release bearing is the ball bearing type and does not require lubrication. On Types 1, 2, and 3, the clutch is engaged mechanically via a cable which attaches to the clutch pedal. On the Type 4, the clutch is engaged hydraulically, using a clutch pedal operated master cylinder and a bell housing mounted slave cylinder.

Clutch Assembly Removal and Installation

MANUAL TRANSMISSION

1. Remove the engine.

2. Remove the pressure plate securing bolts one turn at a time until all spring pressure is released.

3. Remove the bolts and remove the clutch assembly.

NOTE: *Notice which side of the clutch disc faces the flywheel and install the new disc in the same direction.*

4. Before installing the new clutch, check the condition of the flywheel. It should not have excessive heat cracks and the friction surface should not be scored or warped. Check the condition of the throw out bearing. If the bearing is worn, replace it.

5. Lubricate the pilot bearing in the end of the crankshaft with grease.

6. Insert a pilot shaft, used for centering the clutch disc, through the clutch disc and place the disc against the flywheel. The pilot shaft will hold the disc in place.

7. Place the pressure plate over the disc and loosely install the bolts.

NOTE: *Make sure the correct side of the clutch disc is facing outward. The*

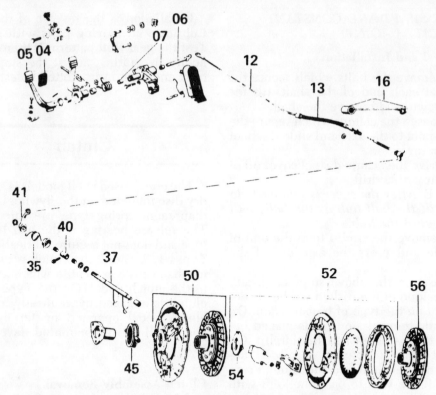

Exploded view of manual transaxle clutch system components—Types 1, 2, and 3

4. Clutch pedal pad
5. Clutch pedal
6. Clutch pedal shaft
7. Bushings for pedal cluster
12. Clutch cable
13. Clutch cable sleeve
16. Angle plate for clutch cable
35. Clutch return spring

37. Clutch cross-shaft
40. Bushing—operating shaft
41. Clutch operating lever
45. Clutch release bearing
50. Clutch
52. Pressure plate
54. Clutch release plate
56. Clutch disc

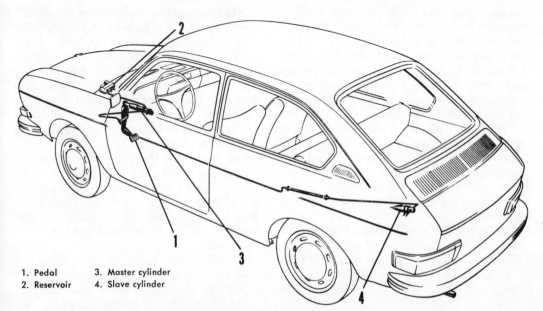

1. Pedal
2. Reservoir
3. Master cylinder
4. Slave cylinder

Clutch hydraulic system—Type 4

disc will rub the flywheel if it is incorrectly positioned.

8. After making sure that the pressure plate aligning dowels will fit into the pressure plate, gradually tighten the bolts.

9. Remove the pilot shaft and reinstall the engine.

10. Adjust the clutch pedal free-play.

AUTOMATIC STICK SHIFT

1. Disconnect the negative battery cable.

2. Remove the engine.

3. Remove the transaxle.

4. Remove the torque converter by sliding it off of the input shaft. Seal off the hub opening.

5. Mount the transaxle in a repair stand or on a suitable bench.

6. Loosen the clamp screw and pull off the clutch operating lever. Remove the transmission cover.

7. Remove the hex nuts between the clutch housing and the transmission case.

NOTE: *Two nuts are located inside the differential housing.*

8. The oil need not be drained if the clutch is removed with the cover opening up and the gearshift housing breather blocked.

9. Pull the transmission from the clutch housing studs.

10. Turn the clutch lever shaft to disengage the release bearing.

11. Remove both lower engine mounting bolts.

12. Loosen the clutch retaining bolts gradually and alternately to prevent distortion. Remove the bolts, pressure plate, clutch plate, and release bearing.

13. Do not wash the release bearing. Wipe it dry only.

14. Check the clutch plate, pressure plate, and release bearing for wear and damage. Check the clutch carrier plate, needle bearing, and seat for wear. Replace the necessary parts.

15. If the clutch is wet with ATF, replace the clutch carrier plate seal and the clutch disc. If the clutch is wet with transmission oil, replace the transmission case seal and clutch disc.

16. Coat the release bearing guide on the transmission case neck and both lugs on the release bearing with grease. Insert the bearing into the clutch.

17. Grease the carrier plate needle bearing. Install the clutch disc and pressure plate using a pilot shaft to center the disc on the flywheel.

18. Tighten the pressure plate retaining bolts evenly and alternately. Make sure that the release bearing is correctly located in the diaphragm spring.

19. Insert the lower engine mounting bolts from the front. Replace the sealing rings if necessary. Some units have aluminum sealing rings and cap nuts.

20. Push the transmission onto the

Exploded view of Type 1 automatic stick shift clutch assembly

1. Torque converter
2. One-way clutch support
3. Gasket
4. Circlip for carrier plate
5. Ball bearing
6. O-ring for stud
7. Converter housing
8. Spring washer
9. Socket head screw
10. Seal
11. Clutch carrier plate
12. Needle bearing
13. Seal/carrier plate
14. Clutch plate
15. Diaphragm clutch pressure plate
16. Spring washer
17. Socket head screw
18. Release bearing
19. Seal/converter
20. O-ring/one-way clutch support

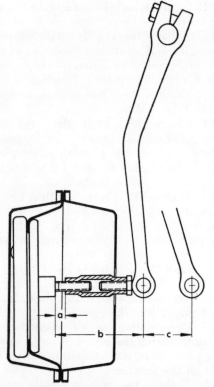

Automatic stick shift clutch basic adjusting dimensions

Wing nut for manual transaxle clutch cable adjustment

converter housing studs. Insert the clutch lever shaft behind the release bearing lugs. Push the release bearing onto the transmission case neck. Tighten the bolts which hold the clutch housing to the transmission case.

21. Install the clutch operating lever.

22. It is necessary to adjust the basic clutch setting. The clutch operating lever should contact the clutch housing. Tighten the lever clamp screw slightly.

23. First adjust dimension (a) to 0.335 in. Adjust dimension (b) to 3.03 in. Finally adjust dimension (c) to 1.6 in. by repositioning the clutch lever on the clutch shaft. Tighten the lever clamp screw.

24. Push the torque converter onto the support tube. Insert it into the turbine shaft by turning the converter.

25. Check the clutch play after installing the transaxle and engine.

Clutch Cable Adjustment

MANUAL TRANSMISSION— TYPES 1, 2, 3

1. Check the clutch pedal travel by measuring the distance the pedal travels toward the floor until pressure is exerted against the clutch. The distance is ⅜ to ¾ in.

2. To adjust the clutch, jack up the rear of the car and support it on jackstands.

3. Remove the left rear wheel.

4. Adjust the cable tension by turning the wing nut on the end of the clutch cable. Turning the wing nut counterclockwise decreases pedal free-play, turning it clockwise increases free-play.

5. When the adjustment is completed, the wings of the wing nut must be horizontal so that the lugs on the nut engage the recesses in the clutch lever.

6. Push on the clutch pedal several times and check the pedal free-play.

7. Install the wheel and lower the car.

AUTOMATIC STICK SHIFT— TYPE 1

The adjustment is made on the linkage between the clutch arm and the vacuum servo unit. To check the clutch play:

Clutch pedal free-play (travel) is distance "a"

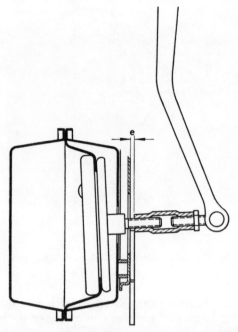

Adjusting automatic stick shift clutch—distance "d" is 0.25 in., measured between the locknut and the turnbuckle

Checking clutch adjustment—Automatic Stick Shift

1. Disconnect the servo vacuum hose.
2. Measure the clearance between the upper edge of the servo unit mounting bracket and the lower edge of the adjusting turn-buckle. If the clearance (e) is 0.16 in. or more, the clutch needs adjustment.
3. Reconnect the vacuum hose.

To adjust the clutch:
1. Disconnect the servo vacuum hose.
2. Loosen the turnbuckle locknut and back it off completely to the lever arm. Then turn the servo turnbuckle against the lock nut. Now back off the turnbuckle 5–5½ turns. The distance between the locknut and the turnbuckle should be 0.25 in.
3. Tighten the locknut against the adjusting sleeve.
4. Reconnect the vacuum hose and road test the vehicle. The clutch is properly adjusted when Reverse gear can be engaged silently and the clutch does not slip on acceleration. If the clutch arm contacts the clutch housing, there is no more adjustment possible and the clutch plate must be replaced.

The speed of engagement of the Automatic Stick Shift clutch is regulated by the vacuum operated valve rather than by the driver's foot. The adjusting screw is on top of the valve under a small protective cap. Adjust the valve as follows:

Speed of engagement adjusting screw (arrow)

1. Remove the cap.
2. To slow the engagement, turn the adjusting screw ¼–½ turn clockwise. To speed engagement, turn the screw counterclockwise.
3. Replace the cap.
4. Test operation by shifting from Second to First at 44 mph without depressing the accelerator. The shift should take exactly one second to occur.

Clutch Cable Replacement

TYPES 1, 2, AND 3

1. Jack up the car and remove the left rear wheel.

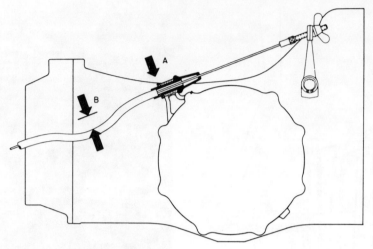

For smooth clutch action on Type 1 models, dimension "B" should be 1.0–1.7 in. Adjust cable to provide slight sag at point "B" by installing washers at point "A".

2. Disconnect the cable from the clutch operating lever.

3. Remove the rubber boot from the end of the guide tube and off the end of the cable.

4. On Type 1, unbolt the pedal cluster and remove it from the car. It will also be necessary to disconnect the brake master cylinder push rod and throttle cable from the pedal cluster. On Type 2, remove the cover under the pedal cluster, then remove the pin from the clevis on the end of the clutch cable. On Type 3, remove the frame head cover and remove the pin from the clevis on the end of the clutch cable.

5. Pull the cable out of its guide tube from the pedal cluster end.

6. Installation is the reverse of the above.

NOTE: *Grease the cable before installing it and readjust the clutch pedal free-play.*

CLUTCH MASTER CYLINDER

Removal and Installation

TYPE 4

1. Siphon the hydraulic fluid from the master cylinder (clutch) reservoir.

2. Pull back the carpeting from the pedal area and lay down some absorbent rags.

3. Pull the elbow connection from the top of the master cylinder.

4. Disconnect and plug the pressure line from the rear of the master cylinder.

5. Remove the master cylinder mounting bolts and remove the cylinder to the rear.

6. Reverse the above procedure to install, taking care to bleed the system and adjust pedal free-play.

CLUTCH SLAVE CYLINDER

Removal and Installation

TYPE 4

1. Locate the slave cylinder on the bell housing.

2. Disconnect and plug the pressure line from the slave cylinder.

3. Disconnect the return spring from the pushrod.

4. Remove the retaining circlip from the boot and remove the boot.

5. Remove the circlip and slide the slave cylinder rearwards from its mount.

6. Remove the spring clip from the mount.

7. Reverse the above procedure to install, taking care to bleed the system and adjust pedal free-play.

Clutch System Bleeding and Adjustment

TYPE 4

Whenever air enters the clutch hydraulic system due to leakage, or if any part of the system is removed for service, the system must be bled. The hydraulic system uses high quality brake fluid meeting SAE J1703 or DOT 3 or DOT 4 specifica-

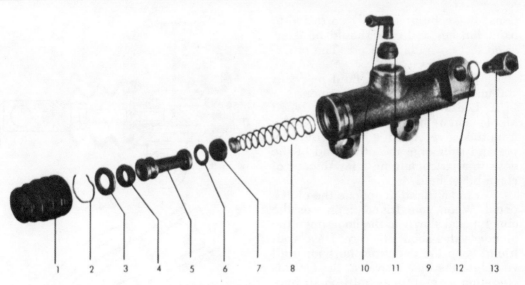

Exploded view of Type 4 master cylinder

1. Boot
2. Lockring
3. Stop ring
4. Secondary cup
5. Piston
6. Cup washer
7. Primary cup
8. Spring and spring plate
9. Cylinder
10. Elbow
11. Sealing plug
12. Seal
13. Residual pressure valve

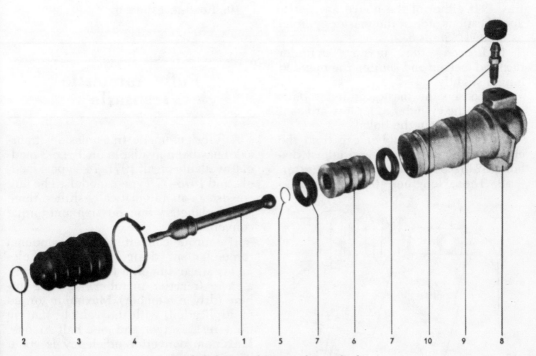

Exploded view of Type 4 slave cylinder

1. Pushrod
2. Retaining ring
3. Boot
4. Retaining ring
5. Lockspring
6. Piston
7. Cup
8. Cylinder
9. Bleeder valve
10. Cap

tions. Brake fluid is highly corrosive to paint finishes and care should be exercised that no spillage occurs. The procedure is as follows;

1. Top up the clutch fluid reservoir and make sure the cap vent is open.

2. Locate the slave cylinder bleed nipple and remove all dirt and grease from the valve. Attach a hose to the nipple and submerge the other end of the hose in a jar containing a few inches of clean brake fluid.

3. Find a friend to operate the clutch pedal. When your friend depresses the clutch pedal slowly to the floor, open the bleeder valve about one turn. Have your friend keep the pedal on the floor until you close the bleeder valve. Repeat this operation several times until no air bubbles are emitted from the tube.

NOTE: *Keep a close check on the fluid level in the fluid reservoir. Never let the level fall below the ½ full mark.*

4. After bleeding, discard the old fluid and top up the reservoir.

5. The clutch pedal should have a free-play of 0.20–0.28 in., and a 7 in. total travel. If either of the above are not to specifications, adjust the master cylinder as follows. (Steps 6–9).

6. Loosen the master cylinder pushrod locknut and shorten the pushrod length slightly.

7. Loosen the master cylinder bolts and push the cylinder as far forward as it will go. Retighten the bolts.

8. Remove the rubber cap from the clutch pedal stop screw and adjust distance S2 to 0.89 in. Install the rubber cap.

9. Then, lengthen the pushrod as

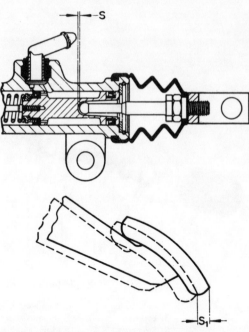

Adjusting clutch pedal free-play—Type 4

necessary to obtain a pedal free-play of 0.20–0.28 in. Tighten the pushrod locknut.

10. Road-test the car.

Fully Automatic Transaxle

A fully automatic transmission (transaxle) has been available on Type 3 models, available on all 1971–74 Type 4 models, and 1973–77 Type 2 models. The unit consists of an automatically shifted three speed planetary transmission and torque converter.

The torque converter is a conventional three-element design. The three elements are an impeller (driving member), a stator (reaction member), and the turbine (driven member). Maximum torque multiplication, with the vehicle starting from rest, is two and one-half to one. Maximum converter efficiency is about 96 percent.

The automatic transmission is a planetary unit with three forward speeds which engage automatically depending on engine loading and road speed. The converter, planetary unit, and control sys-

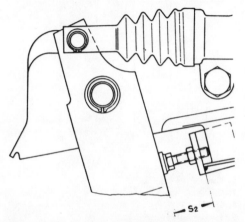

Adjusting clutch pedal stop screw—Type 4

tem are incorporated together with the final drive in a single housing. The final drive is located between the converter and the planetary gearbox.

The transmission control system includes a gear type oil pump, a centrifugal governor which regulates shift points, a throttle modulator valve which evaluates engine loading according to intake manifold pressure, and numerous other regulating components assembled in the transmission valve body.

Power flow passes through the torque converter to the turbine shaft, then to the clutch drum attached to the turbine shaft, through a clutch to a sungear. The output planet carrier then drives the rear axle shafts via the final drive.

Transmission ranges are Park, Reverse, Neutral, Drive (3), Second (2), and First (1).

Automatic Transmission Removal and Installation

NOTE: *The engine and transmission must be removed as an assembly on the Type 4 and Type 2/1700, 2/1800, 2/2000.*

1. Remove the battery ground cable.
2. On the sedan, remove the cooling air intake duct with the heating fan and hoses. Remove the cooling air intake connection and bellows, then detach the hoses to the air cleaner.
3. On the station wagons, remove the warm air hoses and air cleaner. Remove the boot between the dipstick tube and the body and the boot between the oil filler neck and the body. Disconnect the cooling air bellows at the body.
4. Disconnect the wires at the regulator and the alternator wires at the snap-connector located by the regulator. Disconnect the auxiliary air regulator and the oil pressure switch at the snap connectors located by the distributor.
5. Disconnect the fuel injection wiring on Type 3 and 4 models. There are 12 connections and they are listed as follows:
   a. Fuel injector cylinder 2, 2-pole, protective gray cap;
   b. Fuel injector cylinder 1, 2-pole, protective black cap;
   c. Starter, 1-pole, white;
   d. Throttle valve switch, 4-pole;
   e. Distributor, 3-pole;
   f. Thermo switch, 1-pole, white;
   g. Cold start valve, 3-pole;
   h. Temperature sensor crankcase, 2-pole;
   i. Ground connection, 3-pole, white wires;
   j. Temperature sensor for the cylinder head, 1-pole;
   k. Fuel injector cylinder 3, 2-pole, protective black cap;
   l. Fuel injector cylinder 4, 2-pole, protective gray cap.
6. Disconnect the accelerator cable.
7. Disconnect the right fuel return line.
8. Raise the car.
9. Disconnect the warm hoses from the heat exchangers.
10. Disconnect the starter wires and push the engine wiring harness through the engine cover plate.
11. Disconnect the fuel supply line and plug it.
12. Remove the heater booster exhaust pipe.
13. Remove the rear axles and cover the ends to protect them from dirt.
14. Remove the selector cable by unscrewing the cable sleeve.
15. Remove the wire from the kickdown switch.
16. Remove the bolts from the rubber transmission mountings, taking careful note of the position, number, and thickness of the spacers that are present.
CAUTION: *These spacers must be reinstalled exactly as they were removed. Do not detach the transmission carrier from the body.*
17. Support the engine and transmission assembly in such a way that it may be lowererd and moved rearward at the same time.
18. Remove the engine carrier bolts and the engine and transmission assembly from the car.
19. Matchmark the flywheel and the torque converter and remove the three attaching bolts.
20. Remove the engine-to-transmission bolts and separate the engine and transmission.
CAUTION: *Exercise care when separating the engine and transmission as the torque converter will easily slip off the input shaft if the transmission is tilted downward.*

21. Installation is as follows. Install and tighten the engine-to-transmission bolts after aligning the match marks on the flywheel and converter.

22. Making sure the match marks are aligned, install the converter-to-flywheel bolts.

23. Make sure the rubber buffer is in place and the two securing studs do not project more than 0.7 in. from the transmission case.

24. Tie a cord to the slot in the engine compartment seal. This will make positioning the seal easier.

25. Lift the assembly far enough to allow the accelerator cable to be pushed through the front engine cover.

26. Continue lifting the assembly into place. Slide the rubber buffer into the locating tube in the rear axle carrier.

27. Insert the engine carrier bolts and raise the engine until the bolts are at the top of their elongated slots. Tighten the bolts.

Type 2/1700, 2/1800, 2/2000, and Type 4 engine carrier bolts positioned at the tops of their elongated holes

NOTE: *A set of three gauges must be obtained to check the alignment of the rubber buffer in its locating tube. The dimensions are given in the illustration as is the measuring technique. The rubber buffer is centered horizontally when the 11 mm gauge can be inserted on both sides. The buffer is located vertically when the 10 mm gauge can be inserted on the bottom side and the 12 mm gauge can be inserted on the top side. See Steps 28 and 29 for adjustment procedure.*

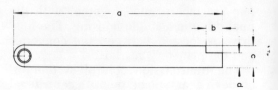

Buffer alignment gauges

a. 5.095 in.   c. 0.590 in.
b. 0.472 in.   d. 0.393, 0.433, and 0.472 in.

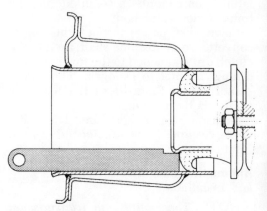

Measuring technique for centering the buffer

28. Install the rubber transmission mount bolts with spacers of the correct thickness. The purpose of the spacers is to center the rubber buffer vertically in its support tube. The buffer is not supposed to carry any weight; it absorbs torsional forces only.

29. To locate the buffer horizontally in its locating tube, the engine carrier must be vertical and parallel to the fan housing. It is adjusted by moving the engine carrier bolts in elongated slots. Further travel may be obtained by moving the brackets attached to the body. It may be necessary to adjust the two rear suspension wishbones with the center of the transmission after the rubber buffer is horizontally centered. Take the car to a dealer or alignment specialist to align the rear suspension.

30. Adjust the selector lever cable.

31. Connect the wire to the kickdown switch.

32. Install the rear axles. Make sure the lockwashers are placed with the convex side out.

33. Reconnect the fuel hoses and heat exchanger hoses. Install the pipe for the heater booster.

34. Lower the car and pull the engine

Checking position of engine carrier

compartment seal into place with the cord.

35. Reconnect the fuel injection and engine wiring. Push the starter wires through the engine cover plate and connect the wires to the starter.

36. Install the intake duct with the fan and hoses, also the cooling air intake.

Pan Removal and Installation

1. Some models have a drain plug in the pan. Remove the plug and drain the transmission oil. On models without the plug, loosen the pan bolts 2–3 turns and lower one corner of the pan to drain the oil.

2. Remove the pan bolts and remove the pan from the transmission.

NOTE: *It may be necessary to tap the pan with a rubber hammer to loosen it.*

3. Use a new gasket and install the pan. Tighten the bolts loosely until the pan is properly in place, then tighten the bolts fully, moving in a diagonal pattern.

NOTE: *Do not overtighten the bolts.*

4. Refill the transmission with ATF.

5. At 5 minute intervals, retighten the pan bolts two or three times.

Filter Service

The Volkswagen automatic transmission has a filter screen secured by a screw to the bottom of the valve body. Remove the pan and remove the filter screen from the valve body.

CAUTION: *Never use a cloth that will leave the slightest bit of lint in the transmission when cleaning transmission parts. The lint will expand when*

exposed to transmission fluid and clog the valve body and filter.

Clean the filter screen with compressed air.

Front (Second) Band Adjustment

Tighten the front band adjusting screw to 7 ft lbs. Then loosen the screw and tighten it to 3.5 ft lbs. From this position, loosen the screw exactly 1¾ to 2 turns and tighten the lock nut.

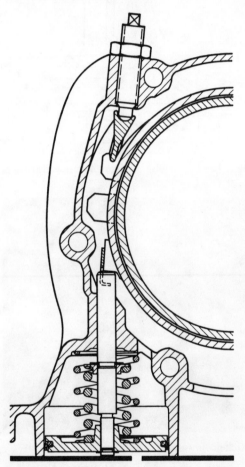

Front band assembly—adjustment screw at the top

Rear (First) Band Adjustment

Tighten the rear band adjusting screw to 7 ft lbs. Then loosen the screw and retighten it to 3.5 ft lbs. From this position, loosen the screw exactly 3¼ to 3½ turns and tighten the lock nut.

Kickdown Switch Adjustment

TYPE 3

1. Disconnect the accelerator cable return spring.

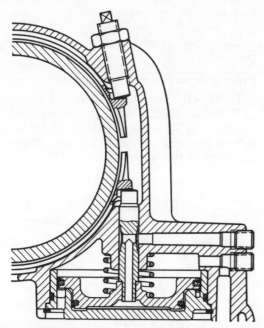

Rear band assembly—adjustment screw at the top

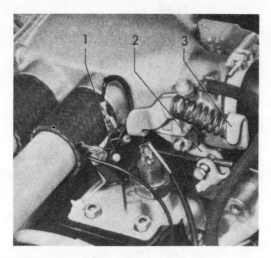

Kick-down switch

1. Kick-down switch 2. Accelerator cable lever
3. Throttle valve lever

2. Move the throttle to the fully open position. Adjust the accelerator cable to give 0.02–0.04 in. clearance between the stop and the end of the throttle valve lever.

3. When the accelerator cable is adjusted and the throttle is moved to the fully open position, the kickdown switch should click. The ignition switch must be ON for this test.

4. To adjust the switch, loosen the switch securing screws and slide the switch back and forth until the test in Step 3 is satisfied.

5. Reconnect the accelerator cable return spring.

TYPE 4

The Type 4 switch is not adjustable.

Shift Linkage Adjustment

Make sure the shifting cable is not kinked or bent and that the linkage and cable are properly lubricated.

1. Move the gear shift lever to the Park position.

2. Loosen the clamp which holds the

Clamp securing shift linkage rod halves

Pressing transmission lever rearward against its stop

front and rear halves of the shifting rod together. Loosen the clamping bolts on the transmission lever.

3. Press the lever on the transmission rearward as far as possible. Spring pressure will be felt. The manual valve must be on the stop in the valve body.

4. Holding the transmission lever against its stop, tighten the clamping bolt.

5. Holding the rear shifting rod half, push the front half forward to take up any clearance and tighten the clamp bolt.

6. Test the shift pattern.

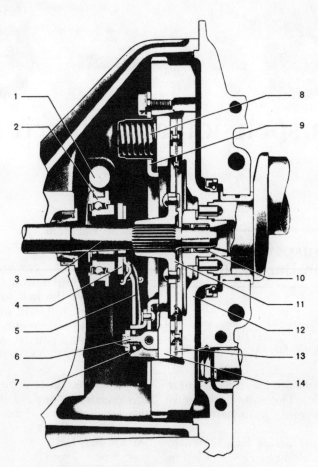

Cross-sectional view of clutch assembly

1. Operating shaft
2. Release bearing
3. Main driveshaft
4. Release plate
5. Release lever
6. Bolt and special nut
7. Release lever spring
8. Thrust spring
9. Cover
10. Needle bearing for gland nut
11. Driven plate
12. Flywheel
13. Lining
14. Pressure plate

Chapter Seven

Suspension and Steering

Front Suspension— Torsion Bar Type

TYPE 1 BEETLE,
1970 BEETLE CONVERTIBLE,
TYPE 1 KARMANN GHIA,
TYPE 2, TYPE 3

Each front wheel rotates on a ball joint mounted spindle. The spindle is suspended independently by a pair of torsion bars.

The principle of torsion bars is that of springing action taking place via twisting of the bars. When a front wheel goes up or down, the torsion bars are twisted, causing a downward or upward force in the opposite direction.

The supporting part of the Volkswagen front axle is the axle beam, which is two rigidly joined tubes attached to the frame with four screws. At each end of the tubes there is a side plate designed to provide additional strength and serve as the upper mounting point for the shock absorbers. Because the front axle is all-welded, it is replaced as a unit whenever damaged.

Torsion Bar Removal and Installation

1. Jack up the car and remove both wheels and brake drums.

2. Remove the ball joint nuts and remove the left and right steering knuckles. A forked ball joint removing tool is available at an auto parts store.

CAUTION: *Never strike the ball joint stud.*

3. Remove those arms attached to the torsion bars on one side only. To remove the arms, loosen and remove the arm set-screw and pull the arm off the end of the torsion bar.

4. Loosen and remove the set-screw which secures the torsion bar to the torsion bar housing.

5. Pull the torsion bar out of its housing.

6. To install, carefully note the number of leaves and the position of the countersink marks for the torsion bar and the torsion arm.

7. Align the countersink mark in the center of the bar with the hole for the set-screw and insert the torsion bar into its housing. Install the set-screw. Install the torsion arm.

8. Reverse Steps 1–3 to complete.

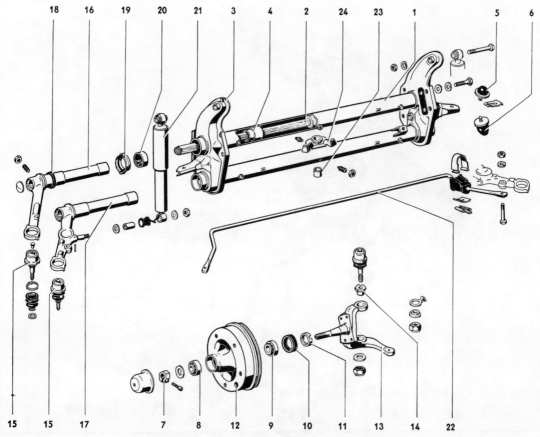

Exploded view of front torsion bar suspension—Type 2

1. Front axle beam
2. Torsion bar
3. Side plate
4. Torsion arm bush
5. Upper rubber buffer
6. Lower rubber buffer
7. Clamp nut for wheel bearing adjustment
8. Outer front wheel bearing
9. Inner front wheel bearing
10. Front wheel bearing seal
11. Spacer ring
12. Brake drum
13. Steering knuckle
14. Eccentric bush for camber adjustment
15. Ball joint
16. Upper torsion arm
17. Lower torsion arm
18. Seal for torsion arm
19. Seal retainer
20. Torsion arm needle bearing
21. Shock absorber
22. Stabilizer
23. Swing lever shaft bush
24. Swing lever stop

Torsion Arm Removal and Installation

1. Jack up the car and remove the wheel and tire.

2. Remove the brake drum and the steering knuckle.

3. If the lower torsion arm is being removed, disconnect the stabilizer bar. To remove the stabilizer bar clamp, tap the wedge shaped keeper toward the outside of the car or in the direction the narrow end of the keeper is pointing.

4. On Type 1 and 2, back off on the set-screw locknut and remove the set-screw. On Type 3, remove the bolt and keeper from the end of the torsion bar.

5. Slide the torsion arm off the end of the torsion bar.

6. Reverse the above steps to install. Check the camber and toe-in settings.

Shock Absorber Removal and Installation

1. Remove the wheel and tire.

2. Remove the nut from the torsion arm stud and slide the lower end of the shock off of the stud.

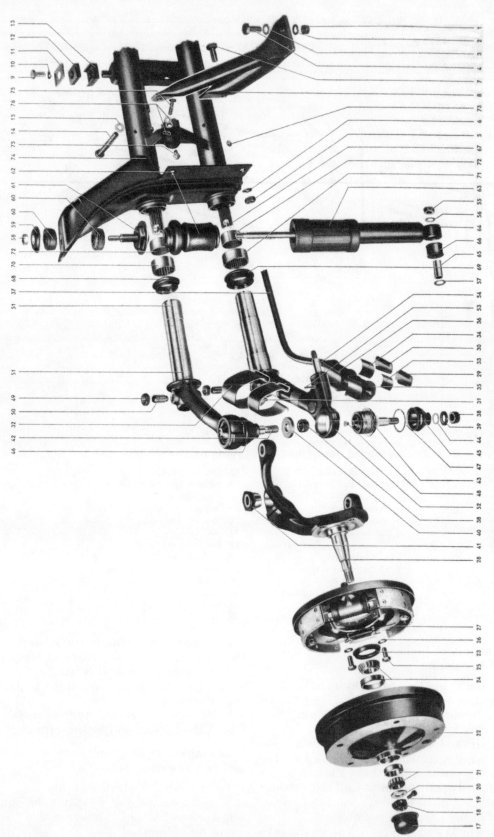

Exploded view of front torsion bar suspension—Type 1

3. Remove the nut from the shock absorber shaft at the upper mounting and remove the shock from the vehicle.

4. The shock is tested by operating it by hand. As the shock is extended and compressed, it should operate smoothly over its entire stroke with an even pressure. Its damping action should be clearly felt at the end of each stroke. If the shock is leaking slightly, the shock need not be replaced. A shock that has had an excessive loss of fluid will have flat spots in the stroke as the shock is compressed and extended. That is, the pressure will feel as though it has been suddenly released for a short distance during the stroke.

5. Installation is the reverse of Steps 1–3.

Ball Joint Inspection

A quick initial inspection can be made with the vehicle on the ground. Grasp the top of the tire and vigorously pull the top of the tire in and out. Test both sides in this manner. If the ball joints are excessively worn, there will be an audible tap as the ball moves around in its socket. Excess play can sometimes be felt through the tire.

A more rigorous test may be performed by jacking the car under the lower torsion arm and inserting a lever under the tire. Lift up gently on the lever so as to pry the tire upward. If the ball joints are worn, the tire will move upward ⅛–¼ in. or more. If the tire displays excessive movement, have an assistant inspect each joint, as the tire is pryed upward, to determine which ball joint is defective.

Ball Joint Replacement

1. Jack up the car and remove the wheel and tire.

2. Remove the brake drum and disconnect the brake line from the backing plate.

3. Remove the nut from each ball joint stud and remove the ball joint stud from the steering knuckle. Remove the steering knuckle from the car. A ball joint removal tool is available at an auto parts store. Do not strike the ball joint stud.

4. Remove the torsion arm from the torsion bar.

5. Remove the ball joint from the torsion arm by pressing it out.

6. Press a new ball joint in, making sure that the square notch in the joint is in line with the notch in the torsion arm eye.

NOTE: *Ball joints are supplied in different sizes designated by V-notches in the ring around the side of the joint. When replacing a ball joint, make sure that the new part has the same number of V-notches. If it has no notches, the*

1. Nut	26. Spring washer	50. Setscrew for torsion bar
2. Spring washer	27. Front wheel brake and	51. Torsion arm, upper
3. Washer	locking plate	52. Torsion arm, lower
4. Bolt	28. Steering knuckle	53. Pin
5. Nut	29. Retainer, small	54. Pin for shock absorber
6. Spring washer	30. Retainer, large	55. Nut
7. Bolt	31. Clip, small	56. Lockwasher
8. Support for axle	32. Clip, large	57. Lockwasher
9. Bolt	33. Plate, small	58. Nut
10. Spring washer	34. Plate, large	59. Plate for damper bushing
11. Plate	35. Rubber mounting, small	60. Damper bushing
12. Rubber packing, upper	36. Rubber mounting, large	61. Pin for buffer
13. Rubber packing, lower	37. Stabilizer bar	62. Buffer
14. Bolt	38. Self-locking nut	63. Tube
15. Spring washer	39. Washer, small	64. Shock absorber
16. Lockwasher	40. Washer, large	65. Sleeve for rubber bushing
17. Dust cap	41. Eccentric bushing for camber	66. Rubber bushing
18. Clamp nut for wheel bearing	adjustment	67. Torsion bar—10 leaf
19. Socket hd. screw for	42. Upper ball joint	68. Seal for upper torsion arm
clamp nut	43. Lower ball joint	69. Seal for lower torsion arm
20. Thrust washer	44. Ring for rubber boot	70. Needle bearing, upper
21. Outer tapered roller bearing	45. Boot for lower joint	71. Needle bearing, lower
22. Brake drum	46. Boot for upper joint	72. Metal bushing for torsion arms
23. Oil seal	47. Ring for rubber boot	73. Grease fitting
24. Inner tapered roller bearing	48. Plug	74. Axle beam
25. Bolt	49. Locknut	75. Bolt

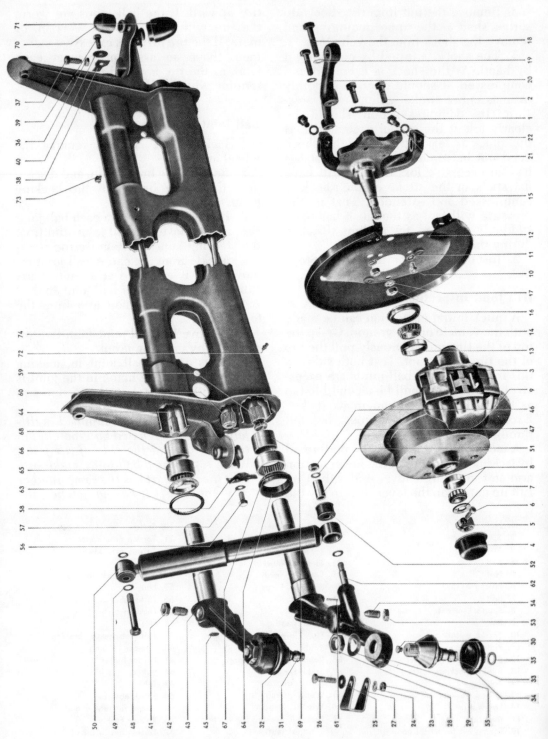

Exploded view of front torsion bar suspension—Type 3

Notch in ball joint indicating that it is oversized

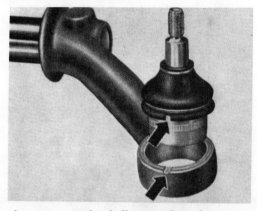

Align square notch in ball joint with notch in torsion arm upon installation

replacement joint should have no notches.

7. Reverse Steps 1–4 to complete the installation.

Front Suspension— Strut Type

TYPE 1 SUPER BEETLE, 1971–77 SUPER BEETLE CONVERTIBLE, AND TYPE 4

Each wheel is suspended independently on a shock absorber strut surrounded by a coil spring. The strut is located at the bottom by a track control arm and a ball joint, and at the top by a ball bearing which is rubber mounted to the body. The benefits of this type of suspension include a wider track, a very small amount of toe-in and camber change during suspension travel, and a reduced turning circle. The strut front suspension requires no lubrication. It is recommended, however, that the ball joint dust seals be checked every 6,000 miles and the ball joint play every 30,000 miles.

Suspension Strut Removal and Installation

1. Jack up the car and remove the wheel and tire.

2. If the left strut is to be removed, remove the speedometer cable from the steering knuckle.

3. Disconnect the brake line from the bracket on the strut.

4. At the base of the strut, bend down the locking tabs for the three bolts and remove the bolts.

1. Lockplate	20. Steering arm	39. Screw	57. Lockwasher
2. Screw	21. Screw	40. Washer	58. Retainer
3. Caliper	22. Lockwasher	41. Locknut	59. Torsion arm, left
4. Dust cap	23. Nut	42. Set screw	60. Torsion arm, right
5. Clamp nut	24. Lockwasher	43. Upper torsion arm	61. Dowel pin
6. Screw	25. Washer	44. Stabilizer	62. Pin
7. Thrust washer	26. Screw	45. Sealing washer	63. Seal
8. Bearing	27. Stop	46. Nut	64. Seal
9. Brake disc	28. Nut	47. Lockwasher	65. Axial ring
10. Screw	29. Lockwasher	48. Screw	66. Needle bearing
11. Lockwasher	30. Plug	49. Lockwasher	67. Needle bearing
12. Backing plate	31. Upper ball joint	50. Shock absorber	68. Bushing
13. Bearing	32. Seal	51. Sleeve	69. Bushing
14. Oil seal	33. Lower ball joint	52. Bushing	70. Buffer
15. Steering knuckle	34. Seal	53. Nut	71. Buffer
16. Nut	35. Retaining ring	54. Set screw	72. Grease fitting
17. Lockwasher	36. Nut	55. Lower torsion arm	73. Grease fitting
18. Screw	37. Screw	56. Screw	74. Front axle beam
19. Lockwasher	38. Lockplate		

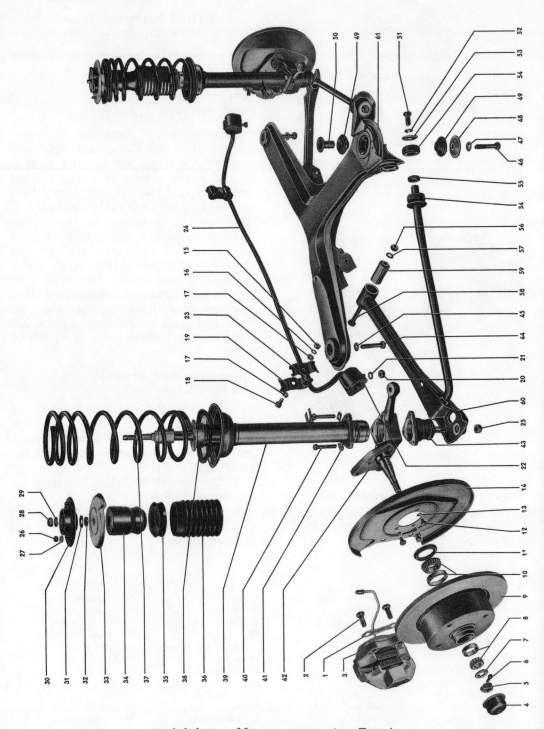

Exploded view of front strut suspension—Type 4

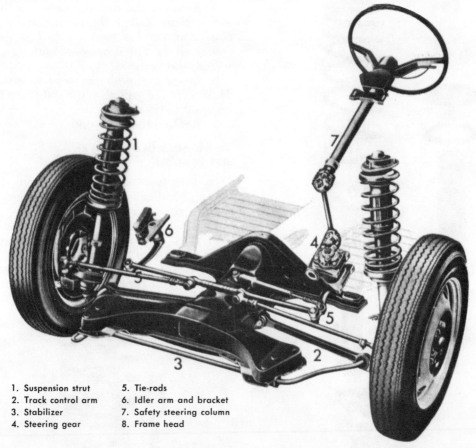

1. Suspension strut
2. Track control arm
3. Stabilizer
4. Steering gear
5. Tie-rods
6. Idler arm and bracket
7. Safety steering column
8. Frame head

1971–77 Type 1 Super Beetle and Convertible, front suspension and steering

1. Lockplate
2. Bolt
3. Caliper
4. Hub cap
5. Wheel bearing locknut
6. Allen screw for locknut
7. Thrust washer
8. Outer taper roller bearing
9. Brake disc
10. Inner taper roller bearing
11. Oil seal
12. Bolt
13. Spring washer
14. Splash sheld for disc
15. Nut
16. Spring washer
17. Washer
18. Bolt
19. Clamp for stabilizer bar
20. Nut
21. Spring washer
22. Stabilizer mounting for control arm

23. Rubber bushing for clamp
24. Stabilizer bar
25. Self-locking nut
26. Self-locking nut
27. Washer
28. Self-locking nut
29. Washer, small
30. Suspension strut bearing
31. Sealing plate
32. Spacer ring
33. Spring plate
34. Rubber stop for shock absorber
35. Retaining ring for protective tube
36. Protective tube for shock absorber
37. Coil spring
38. Damping ring, coil spring
39. Shock absorber
40. Bolt
41. Lockwasher
42. Steering knuckle

43. Ball joint
44. Bolt
45. Lockwasher
46. Bolt
47. Lockwasher
48. Seat for damping ring
49. Damping ring for front axle carrier
50. Spacer sleeve
51. Bolt
52. Spring washer
53. Plate for damping ring
54. Damping ring for radius rod
55. Locating ring for radius rod
56. Nut
57. Spring washer
58. Bolt
59. Bushing for track control arm
60. Track control arm
61. Front axle carrier

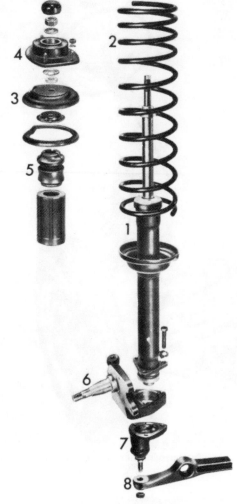

Type 1 Super Beetle and Convertible front strut details

1. Shock absorber
2. Coil spring
3. Spring plate
4. Strut bearing
5. Hollow rubber spring
6. Steering knuckle
7. Ball joint
8. Track control arm

3. Remove the nut and eccentric bolt at the frame. This is the pivot bolt for the control arm and is used to adjust camber.

4. Pull the arm downward and remove it from the vehicle.

5. Reverse the above steps to install. Make sure the groove in the stabilizer bar bushing is horizontal.

6. Realign the front end.

Shock Absorber Removal and Installation

In this type suspension system, the shock absorber is actually the supporting vertical member.

1. Remove the strut as outlined above.

2. It is necessary to disassemble the strut to replace the shock absorber. To remove the spring, it must be compressed. The proper type compressor is available at an auto parts store.

Compressing coil spring of strut suspension

5. Push down on the steering knuckle and pull the strut out of the knuckle.

6. Remove the three nuts which secure the top of the strut to the body. Before removing the last nut, support the strut so that it does not fall out of the car.

7. Reverse the above steps to install the strut. Always use new nuts and locking tabs during installation.

Track Control Arm Removal and Installation

1. Remove the ball joint stud nut and remove the stud from the control arm.

2. Disconnect the stabilizer bar from the control arm.

3. Remove the nut from the end of the shock absorber shaft and slowly release the spring. The strut can now be disassembled. Testing is the same as the torsion bar shock absorber.

4. Reverse the above steps to install.

Ball Joint Inspection

Vehicles with strut suspension have only one ball joint on each side located at the base of the strut in the track control arm.

Raise the car and support it under the frame. The wheel must be clear of the ground.

With a lever, apply upward pressure to the track control arm. Apply the pressure gently and slowly; it is important that only enough pressure is exerted to check the play in the ball joint and not compress the suspension.

Using a vernier caliper, measure the distance between the control arm and the lower edge of the ball joint flange. Record the reading. Release the pressure on the track control arm and again measure the distance between the control arm and the lower edge of the ball joint flange. Record the reading. Subtract the higher reading from the lower reading. If the difference is more than 0.10 in., the ball joint should be replaced.

NOTE: *Remember that even in a new joint there will be measurable play because the ball in the ball joint is spring loaded.*

Ball Joint Replacement

1. Jack up the car and remove the wheel and tire.
2. Remove the nut from the ball joint stud and remove the stud from the track control arm.
3. Bend back the locking tab and remove the three ball joint securing screws.
4. Pull the track control arm downward and remove the ball joint from the strut.
5. Reverse the above steps to install.

FRONT END ALIGNMENT—
ALL TYPES

Caster Adjustment

Caster is the forward or backward tilt of the spindle. Forward tilt is negative caster and backward tilt is positive caster. Caster is not adjustable on either the torsion bar or the strut suspensions.

Camber Adjustment

Camber is the tilt of the top of the wheel, inward or outward, from true vertical. Outward tilt is positive, inward tilt is negative.

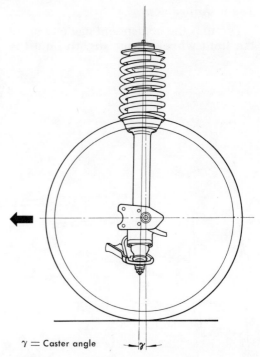

$\gamma = $ Caster angle

Caster angle—strut suspension shown

Torsion Bar Suspension

The upper ball joint on each side is mounted in an eccentric bushing. The bushing has a hex head and it may be rotated in either direction using a wrench.

Strut Suspension

The track control arm pivots on an eccentric bolt. Camber is adjusted by loosening the nut and rotating the bolt.

Unloaded Rear Torsion Bar Settings

Type	Model	Transmission	Setting	Range
1	all	all	20° 30'	+ 50'
2	221, 223, 226	Manual	21° 10'	+ 50'
2	222	Manual	23°	+ 50'
2③	221, 223	all	20°	+ 50'
2④	222	all	23°	+ 50'
3	311	Manual	23°	+ 50'
3	311	Automatic	24°	+ 50'
3	361	all	21° 30'	+ 50'

③ From chassis 212 2 000 001 (1972-up)
④ From chassis 212 2 000 001 (1972-up)

Toe-in Adjustment

Toe-in is the adjustment made to make the front wheels point slightly into the front. Toe-in is adjusted on both types of front suspensions by adjusting the length of the tie-rod sleeves.

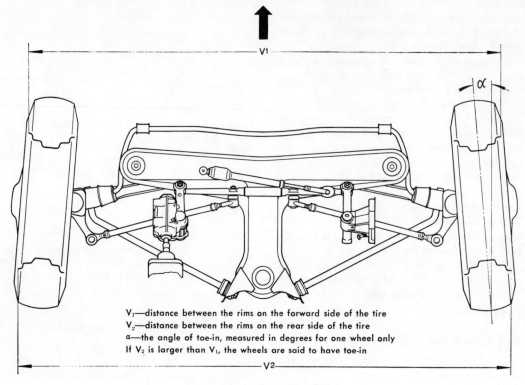

V_1—distance between the rims on the forward side of the tire
V_2—distance between the rims on the rear side of the tire
α—the angle of toe-in, measured in degrees for one wheel only
If V_2 is larger than V_1, the wheels are said to have toe-in

Toe-in—strut suspension shown

Wheel Alignment Specifications

| Year | Model | FRONT AXLE | | | | | REAR AXLE | | |
| | | CASTER | | CAMBER | | | CAMBER | | |
		Range (deg)	Pref Setting (deg)	Range (deg)	Pref Setting (deg)	Toe-in (in.)	Range (deg)	Pref Setting (deg)	Toe-in (deg)
1970–77	Type 1	± 1°	+ 3° 20′	± 20′	+ 30′	+ 0.071– + 0.213	± 40′	− 1°	0′ ± 15′
1971–77	Type 1①	± 35′	+ 2°	+ 20′ − 40′	+ 1°	+ 0.071– + 0.213	± 40′	− 1°	0′ ± 15′
1970–77	Type 2	± 40′	+ 3°	± 20′	+ 40′	0.0– + 0.136	± 30′	− 50′	+ 10′ ± 20′
1970–73	Type 3	± 40′	+ 4°	± 20′	+ 1° 20′	+ 0.118	± 40′	− 1° 20′	0′ ± 15′②
1971–74	Type 4	± 35′	+ 1° 45′	+ 25′ − 30′	+ 1° 10′	+ 0.024– + 0.165	± 30′	− 1°	+ 10′ ± 15′

① Super Beetle and Convertible
② Squareback given; Sedan 5′ ± 15′

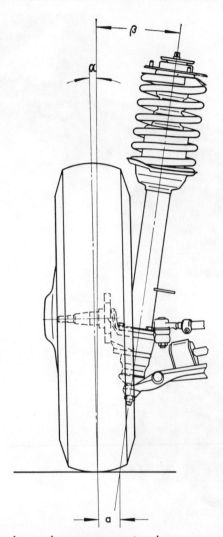

Camber angle—strut suspension shown

Angle α = camber
Angle β = steering pivot angle
a = steering roll radius

Rear Suspension—
Diagonal Arm Type

TYPES 1, 2, AND 3

The rear wheels of Types 1, 2, and 3 models are independently sprung by means of torsion bars. The inside ends of the torsion bars are anchored to a body crossmember via a splined tube which is welded to the frame. The torsion bar at each side of the rear suspension has a different number of splines at each end.

This makes possible the adjustment of the rear suspension.

On Type 3 models, an equalizer bar, located above the rear axle, is used to aid the handling qualities and lateral stability of the rear axle. This bar also acts progressively to soften bumps in proportion to their size.

Shock Absorber Removal
and Installation

The shock absorber is secured at the top and bottom by a through bolt. Raise the car and remove the bolts. Remove the shock absorber from the car.

Diagonal Arm Removal
and Installation

1. Remove the wheel shaft nuts. CAUTION: *Do not raise the car to remove the nuts. They can be safely removed only if the weight of the car is on its wheels.*

2. Disconnect the driveshaft of the side to be removed.

3. Remove the lower shock absorber mount. Raise the car and remove the wheel and tire.

4. Remove the brake drum, disconnect the brake lines and emergency brake cable, and remove the backing plate.

5. Matchmark the torsion bar plate and the diagonal arm with a cold chisel.

6. Remove the four bolts and nuts which secure the plate to the diagonal arm.

7. Remove the pivot bolts for the di-

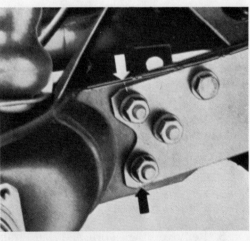

Marking diagonal arm and torsion bar for alignment

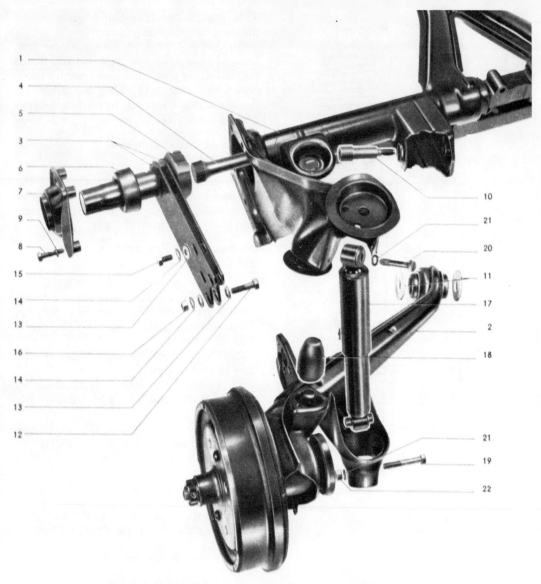

Exploded view of diagonal arm rear suspension—Type 1 shown

1. Frame or sub-frame	9. Lockwasher	17. Shock absorber
2. Diagonal arm (complete)	10. Fitted bolt	18. Rubber stop
3. Double spring plate	11. Spacer	19. Bolt
4. Torsion bar	12. Bolt	20. Bolt
5. Rubber bushing, inner left	13. Washer	21. Lockwasher
6. Rubber bushing, outer	14. Lockwasher	22. Nut
7. Cover for spring plate hub	15. Bolt	
8. Bolt	16. Nut	

agonal arm and remove the arm from the car.

NOTE: *Take careful note of the washers at the pivot bolts. These washers are used to determine alignment and they must be put back in the same place.*

8. Remove the spring plate hub cover.

9. Using a steel bar, lift the spring plate off of the lower suspension stop.

10. On Type 1, remove the five bolts at the front of the fender. On all others, remove the cover in the side of the fender.

11. Remove the spring plate and pull the torsion bar out of its housing.

NOTE: *There are left and right torsion*

bars designated by an (L) or (R) on the end face. (Coat any rubber bushings with talcum powder upon installation. Do not use graphite, silicon, or grease.

12. To install, insert the torsion bar, outer bushing, and spring plate. The torsion bar is properly adjusted when the spring plate, with no load, is the specified number of degrees below a horizontal position.

13. Using two bolts, loosely secure the spring plate hub cover. Place a thick nut between the leaves of the spring plate.

14. Lift the spring plate up to the lower suspension stop and install the remaining bolts into the hub cover. Tighten the hub cover bolts.

15. Install the diagonal arm pivot bolt and washers and peen it with a chisel. There must always be at least one washer on the outside end of the bolt.

16. Align the chisel marks and attach the diagonal arm to the spring plate.

17. Install the backing plate, parking brake cable, and brake lines.

18. Reconnect the shock absorber. Install the brake drum and wheel shaft nuts.

19. Reconnect the driveshaft. Bleed the brakes.

20. Install the wheel and tire.

21. Check the suspension alignment.

Diagonal arm pivot bolt—both spacer washers on the outside

Rear Suspension— Coil Spring and Trailing Arm Type

TYPE 4

The rear wheels of Type 4 models are independently sprung by means of coil springs and trailing arms. The shock absorbers mount inside the coil springs. Each coil spring and shock absorber mounts between the trailing arm and a sheet metal shock tower. Each trailing arm pivots on a body crossmember.

Shock Absorber Removal and Installation

The shock absorber is the lower stop for the suspension.

CAUTION: *The A-arm must be se-*

curely supported when the shock absorber is disconnected to prevent the spring tension from being released suddenly.

Leaving the car on the ground or raising the car and securely supporting the A-arm, remove the lower shock absorber through bolt. To gain access to the upper shock mounting, remove the access panel for each shock located at the sides of the rear luggage shelf. Remove the self locking nut from the shock absorber shaft and remove the shock. Installation is the reverse of removal.

Trailing Arm Removal and Installation

1. Raise the car and place it on jackstands. Securely block up the A-arm.

CAUTION: *The A-arm must be securely supported when the shock absorber is disconnected to prevent the spring tension from being released suddenly. The shock absorber is the lower stop for the suspension.*

2. Disconnect the driveshaft.

3. Disconnect the handbrake cable at the brake lever and remove it.

4. Disconnect the brake lines and the stabilizer bar if equipped.

5. With the vehicle on the ground or the A-arm securely supported, remove the lower shock absorber mounting bolt.

6. Slowly release the A-arm and remove the coil springs.

7. Mark the position of the brackets or the eccentric bolts, whichever are removed, with a chisel. Remove the nuts

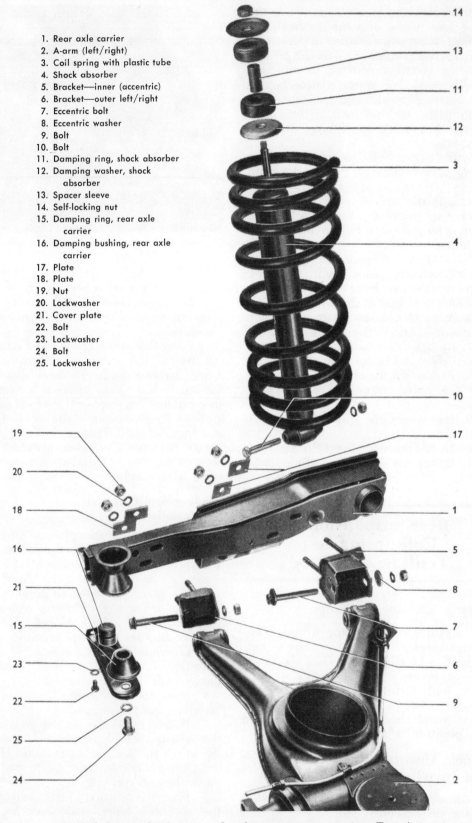

1. Rear axle carrier
2. A-arm (left/right)
3. Coil spring with plastic tube
4. Shock absorber
5. Bracket—inner (accentric)
6. Bracket—outer left/right
7. Eccentric bolt
8. Eccentric washer
9. Bolt
10. Bolt
11. Damping ring, shock absorber
12. Damping washer, shock absorber
13. Spacer sleeve
14. Self-locking nut
15. Damping ring, rear axle carrier
16. Damping bushing, rear axle carrier
17. Plate
18. Plate
19. Nut
20. Lockwasher
21. Cover plate
22. Bolt
23. Lockwasher
24. Bolt
25. Lockwasher

Exploded view of coil spring and trailing arm rear suspension—Type 4

which secure the brackets in the rear axle carrier, or the pivot bolts in the bonded rubber bushings, and remove the A-arm.

8. Loosely install the A-arm. If the pivot bolts were removed, install them loosely. If the eccentric bolts and brackets were removed, install them, aligning the chisel marks, and then tighten them.

9. Insert the coil spring and slowly compress it into place. Install the lower shock absorber mount.

REAR SUSPENSION ADJUSTMENTS

TYPE 1, DIAGONAL ARM SUSPENSION

The only adjustment is the toe-in adjustment. The adjustment is performed by varying the number of washers at the diagonal arm pivot. There must always be one washer located on the outboard side of the pivot.

TYPE 2, 3, DIAGONAL ARM SUSPENSION

The transmission and engine assembly position in the vehicle is adjustable. It is necessary that the assembly be correctly centered before the suspension is aligned. It may be adjusted by moving the engine and transmission brackets in their elongated slots.

The distance between the diagonal arms may be adjusted by moving the washers at the A-arm pivots. The washers may be positioned only two ways. Either both washers on the outboard side of the pivot or a single washer on each side of the pivot. To adjust the distance, position the diagonal arms and move the washers in the same manner at both pivots.

The wheel track angle may be adjusted by moving the diagonal arm flange in the elongated slot in the spring plate.

The toe-in is adjusted by positioning the washers and the diagonal arm pivot.

TYPE 4, A-ARM SUSPENSION

The toe-in is adjusted by the eccentric A-arm pivot bolts.

The rubber buffer centralization procedure is given in the "Type 4 Transaxle (Automatic) Removal and Installation" procedure.

The track width can be adjusted by

Type 4 Engine and Transmission Assembly Centering Specifications

Offset between vehicle center and engine/transmission unit center	1.0 in.
Center of left measuring hole to center of right measuring hole	44.3 ± 0.04 in.
Center of left measuring hole to center of rib on transmission	23.1 ± 0.02 in.
Center of right measuring hole to center of rib on transmission	21.2 ± 0.02 in.

loosening the A-arm mounting bracket bolts and moving the brackets in or out to the proper position.

Steering

Steering Wheel Removal and Installation

1. Disconnect the negative battery cable.

2. Remove the center emblem. This emblem will gently pry off the wheel, or is attached by screws from the back of the steering wheeel.

3. Remove the nut from the steering shaft. This is a right-hand thread.

NOTE: *Mark the steering shaft and steering wheel so that the wheel may be installed in the same position on the shaft.*

4. Using a steering wheel puller, remove the wheel from the splined steer-

Steering wheel removal—Type 2 shown

ing shaft. Do not strike the end of the steering shaft.

5. Reverse the above steps to install. Make sure to align the match marks made on the steering wheel and steering shaft. The gap between the turn signal switch housing and the back of the wheel is 0.08–0.12 in. (distance "a").

Turn Signal Switch Removal and Installation

1. Disconnect the negative battery cable.

2. Remove the steering wheel.

3. Remove the four turn signal switch securing screws.

4. Disconnect the turn signal switch wiring plug under the steering column.

5. Pull the switch and wiring guide rail up and out of the steering column.

6. Reverse the above steps to install. Make sure the spacers located behind the switch, if installed originally, are in position. The distance between the steering wheel and the steering column housing is (distance "a") 0.08–0.12 in. Install the switch with the lever in the central position.

Steering Linkage Removal and Installation

All tie-rod ends are secured by a nut which holds the tapered tie-rod end stud into a matching tapered hole. There are several ways to remove the tapered stud from its hole after the nut has been removed.

First, there are several types of removal tools available from auto parts stores. These tools include directions for

Removing tie-rod end stud with ball joint puller

their use. One of the most commonly available tools is the fork shaped tool which is a wedge that is forced under the tie-rod end. This tool should be used with caution because instead of removing the tie-rod end from its hole it may pull the ball out of its socket, ruining the tie-rod end.

It is also possible to remove the tie-rod end by holding a heavy hammer on one side of the tapered hole and striking the opposite side of the hole sharply with another hammer. The stud will pop out of its hole.

CAUTION: *Never strike the end of the tie-rod end stud. It is impossible to remove the tie-rod end in this manner.*

Once the tie-rod end stud has been removed, turn the tie-rod end out of the adjusting sleeve. On the pieces of the steering linkage that are not used to adjust the toe-in, the tie-rod end is welded in place and it will be necessary to replace the whole assembly.

When reassembling the steering linkage, never put lubricant in the tapered hole.

Manual Steering Gear Adjustment

There are three types of steering gear types. The first type is the roller type, identified by the square housing cover secured by four screws, one at each corner. The second type is the worm and peg type, identfied by an assymetric housing cover with the adjusting screw located at one side of the housing cover. The third type is the rack and pinion type used on 1975 Super Beetles, and 1975–77 Convertibles.

WORM AND ROLLER TYPE—
TYPES 1, 3, 4 AND
1973–77 TYPE 2 MODELS

Disconnect the steering linkage from the pitman arm and make sure the gearbox mounting bolts are tight. Have an assistant rotate the steering wheel so that the pitman arm moves alternately 10° to the left and then 10° to the right of the straight ahead position. Turn the adjusting screw in until no further play can be felt while moving the pitman arm. Tighten the adjusting screw locknut and recheck the adjustment.

Adjusting worm and peg steering gear—worm and roller type similar

WORM AND PEG TYPE—1970–72 TYPE 2 MODELS

Have an assistant turn the steering wheel back and forth through the center position several times. The steering wheel should turn through the center position without any noticeable binding.

To adjust, turn the adjusting screw inward while the assistant is turning the steering wheel. Turn the screw in until the steering begins to tighten up. Back out the adjusting screw until the steering no longer binds while turning through the center point and tighten the adjusting screw locknut.

The adjustment is correct when there is no binding and no perceptible play.

RACK AND PINION TYPE— 1975 TYPE 1 SUPER BEETLE AND 1975–77 CONVERTIBLE

The steering gear requires adjustment if it begins to rattle noticeably. First, remove the access cover in the spare tire well. Then, with the car standing on all four wheels, turn the adjusting screw in by hand until it contacts the thrust washer. While holding the screw in this position, tighten the locknut.

The adjustment is correct when there is no binding and the steering self-centers properly.

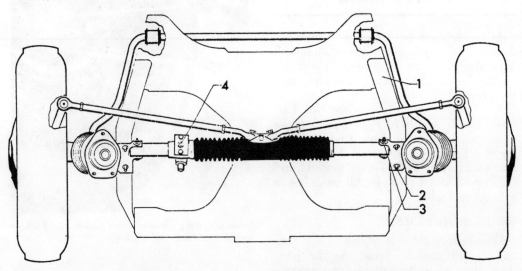

Type 1 rack and pinion steering details—1975 La Grande Bug (Super Beetle) and 1975–76 Convertible

1. Side member
2. Bracket-to-side member bolts 4.5 mkg (32 ft lbs)
3. Steering gear-to-bracket bolts 2.5 mkg (18 ft lbs)
4. Adjusting screw

Chapter Eight

Brakes

Brake System

All models are equipped with dual hydraulic brake systems in accordance with federal regulations. In case of a hydraulic system failure, ½ braking efficiency will be retained.

All Type 1 models (except the Karmann Ghia), and 1970 Type 2 models are equipped with front drum brakes. Discs are used at the front of all Type 1 Karmann Ghias, 1971–77 Type 2 models, and all Type 3 and 4 models. All models use rear drum brakes.

BRAKE ADJUSTMENT

Disc brakes are self adjusting and cannot be adjusted by hand. As the pads wear, they will automatically compensate for the wear by moving closer to the disc, maintaining the proper operating clearance.

Drum brakes, however, must be manually adjusted to take up excess clearance as the shoes wear. To adjust drum brakes, both front and rear, it is necessary to jack up the car and support it on a jackstand. The wheel must spin freely. On the backing plate there are four inspection holes with a rubber plug in each hole. Two of

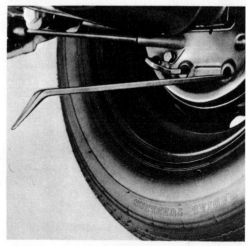

Brake adjusting spoon inserted into hole in backing plate—rear drum brake shown

the holes are for checking the thickness of the brake lining and the other two are used for adjustment.

NOTE: *There is an adjustment for each brake shoe. That means that on each wheel it is necessary to make two adjustments, one for each shoe on that wheel.*

Remove the adjustment hole plugs and, using a screwdriver or brake adjusting tool, insert the tool into the hole.

Turn the star wheel until a slight drag is noticed as the wheel is rotated by hand. Back off on the star wheel 3–4 notches so that the wheel turns freely. Perform the same adjustment on the other shoe.

NOTE: *One of the star wheels in each wheel has left-hand threads and the other star wheel has right-hand threads.*

Repeat the above procedure on each wheel with drum brakes.

Hydraulic System

MASTER CYLINDER

Removal and Installation

1. Drain the brake fluid from the master cylinder reservoir.

CAUTION: *Do not get any brake fluid on the paint, as it will dissolve the paint.*

2. On Type 3, remove the master cylinder cover plate.

3. Pull the plastic elbows out of the rubber sealing rings on the top of the master cylinder.

4. Remove the two bolts which secure the master cylinder to the frame and remove the cylinder. Note the spacers on the Type 1 between the frame and the master cylinder.

5. To install, bolt the master cylinder to the frame. Do not forget the spacers on the Type 1.

6. Lubricate the elbows with brake fluid and insert them into the rubber seals.

7. If necessary, adjust the brake pedal free travel. On Type 1, 3, and 4, adjust the length of the master cylinder pushrod so that there is 5–7 mm of brake pedal free-play before the pushrod contacts the master cylinder piston. On Type 2, the free-play is properly adjusted when the length of the pushrod, measured between the ball end and the center of the clevis pin hole, is 4.17 in.

8. Refill the master cylinder reservoir and bleed the brakes.

Master Cylinder Overhaul

1. Remove the master cylinder from the car.

2. Remove the rubber sealing boot.

3. Remove the stop screw and sealing ring on the top of the unit.

4. Insert a screwdriver in the master cylinder piston, exert inward pressure, and remove the snap-ring from its groove in the end of the unit. The internal parts are spring loaded and must be kept from flying out when the snap-ring is removed.

5. Carefully remove the internal parts of the unit and make note of their order and the orientation of the internal parts. If parts remain in the cylinder bore, they may be removed with a wire hook or very gentle application of low pressure air to the stop screw hole. Cover the end of the cylinder bore with a rag and stand away from the open end of the bore when using compressed air.

6. Use alcohol or brake fluid to clean the master cylinder and its parts.

7. It may be necessary to hone the cylinder bore, or clean it by lightly sanding it with emery cloth. Clean thoroughly after honing or sanding. Lubricate the bore with brake fluid before reassembly.

8. Holding the master cylinder with the open end downward, place the cup washer, primary cup, support washer, spring retainer, and spring onto the front brake circuit piston and insert the piston vertically into the master cylinder bore.

9. Assemble the rear brake circuit piston, cup washer, primary cup, support washer, spring retainer, stop sleeve, spring, and stroke limiting screw and insert the assembly into the master cylinder.

10. Install the stop washer and snap-ring.

11. Install the stop screw and seal, making sure the hole for the screw is not blocked by the piston. If the hole is blocked, it will be necessary to push the piston further in until the screw can be turned in.

NOTE: *1971–77 Type 2 vehicles have a brake servo and the order of assembly of the additional seals is illustrated.*

12. Install the master cylinder and bleed the brakes.

HYDRAULIC SYSTEM BLEEDING

The hydraulic brake system must be bled any time one of the lines is disconnected or air enters the system. This may

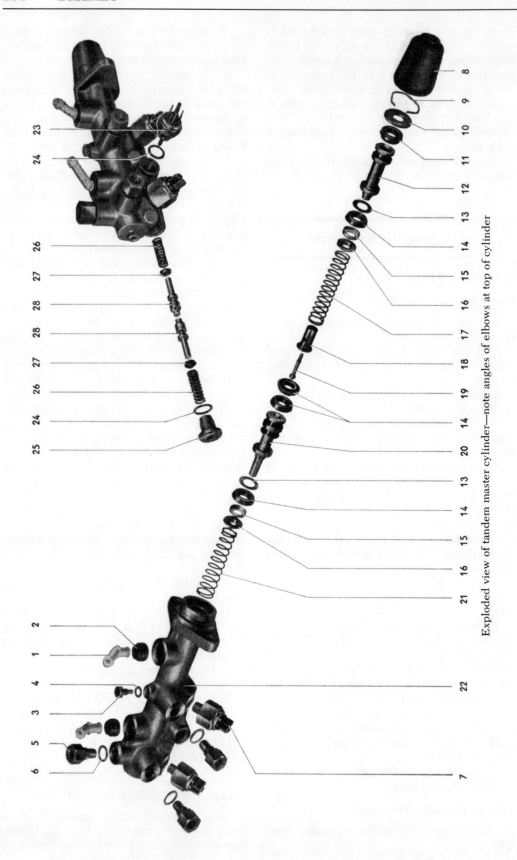

Exploded view of tandem master cylinder—note angles of elbows at top of cylinder

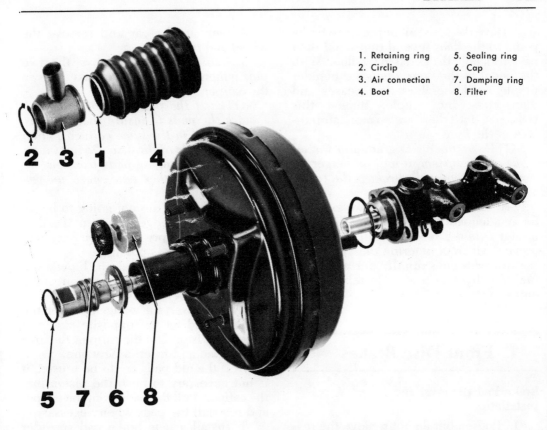

1. Retaining ring   5. Sealing ring
2. Circlip   6. Cap
3. Air connection   7. Damping ring
4. Boot   8. Filter

Exploded view of 1971–77 Type 2 brake servo

be done manually or by the pressure method.

Pressure Bleeding

1. Clean the top of the master cylinder, remove the caps, and attach the pressure bleeding adapter.

2. Check the pressure bleeder reservoir for correct pressure and fluid level, then open the release valve.

3. Fasten a bleeder hose to the wheel cylinder bleeder nipple and submerge the free end of the hose in a transparent receptacle. The receptacle should contain enough brake fluid to cover the open end of the hose.

4. Open the wheel cylinder bleeder nipple and allow the fluid to flow until all bubbles disappear and an uncontaminated flow of fluid exists.

5. Close the nipple, remove the bleeder hose, and repeat the procedure on the other wheel cylinders or brake calipers as equipped.

Manual Bleeding

This method requires two people: one to depress the brake pedal and the other to open the bleeder nipples.

1. Remove the reservoir caps and fill the reservoir.

2. Attach a bleeder hose and a clear container as outlined in the pressure bleeding procedure.

1. Elbow	11. Secondary cup	21. Front brake circuit spring
2. Sealing plug	12. Rear brake circuit piston	22. Master cylinder housing
3. Stop screw	13. Cup washer	23. Warning light switch
4. Seal	14. Cup	24. Seal
5. Residual pressure valve	15. Support washer	25. Plug
6. Sealing ring	16. Spring retainer	26. Spring
7. Brake light switch	17. Rear brake circuit spring	27. Cup
8. Rubber boot	18. Stop sleeve	28. Piston
9. Lockring	19. Stroke limiting screw	
10. Stop washer	20. Front brake circuit piston	

3. Have the assistant depress the brake pedal to the floor several times and then have him hold the pedal to the floor. With the pedal to the floor, open the bleeder nipple until the fluid flow ceases and then close the nipple. Repeat this sequence until there are no more air bubbles in the fluid.

NOTE: *As the air is gradually forced out of the system, it will no longer be possible to force the brake pedal to the floor.*

Periodically check the master cylinder for an adequate supply of fluid. Keep the master cylinder reservoir full of fluid to prevent air from entering the system. If the reservoir does run dry during bleeding, it will be necessary to rebleed the entire system.

Front Disc Brakes

Brake Pad Removal and Installation

1. Loosen but do not remove the reservoir cover.

2. Jack up the car and remove the wheel and tire.

3. Using a punch, remove the two pins which retain the disc brake pads in the caliper.

NOTE: *If the pads are to be reused, mark the pads to insure that they are reinstalled in the same caliper and on the same side of the disc. Do not invert the pads. Changing pads from one location to another can cause uneven braking.*

4. If the pads are not going to be reused, force a wedge between the disc and the pad and pry the piston back into the caliper as far as possible.

5. Using compressed air, blow away the brake dust. Pull the old pad out of the caliper and insert a new one.

6. Now insert the wedge between the disc and pad on the opposite side and force that piston into the caliper. Remove the old pad and insert a new one.

7. If the old pads are to be reused, it is not necessary to push the piston into the caliper. Pull the pads from the caliper and reinstall the pads when necessary.

8. Install a new brake pad spreader spring and insert the retaining pins. Be

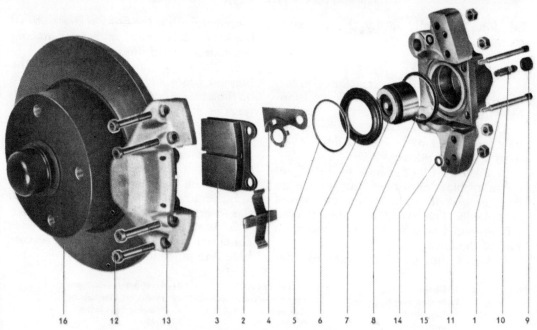

16   12   13   3   2   4   5   6   7   8   14   15   11   1   10   9

Exploded view of ATE disc brake components—1971–77 Type 2 shown

1. Friction pad retaining pin
2. Spreader spring
3. Friction pad
4. Piston retaining plate
5. Clamp ring
6. Seal
7. Piston
8. Rubber seal
9. Dust cap
10. Bleeder valve
11. Nut
12. Cheese head screw
13. Caliper outer housing
14. Seal
15. Caliper inner housing
16. Brake disc

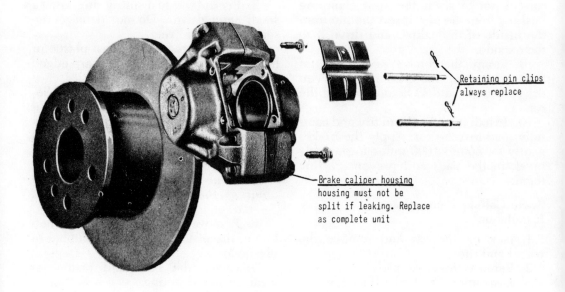

Retaining pin clips
always replace

Brake caliper housing
housing must not be
split if leaking. Replace
as complete unit

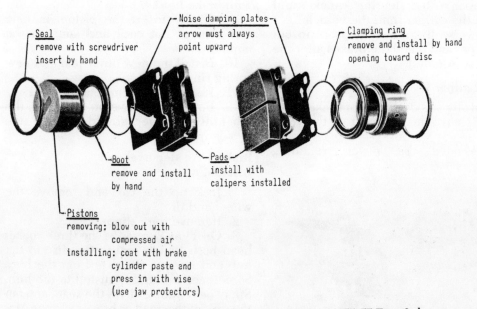

Seal
remove with screwdriver
insert by hand

Noise damping plates
arrow must always
point upward

Clamping ring
remove and install by hand
opening toward disc

Boot
remove and install
by hand

Pads
install with
calipers installed

Pistons
removing: blow out with
compressed air
installing: coat with brake
cylinder paste and
press in with vise
(use jaw protectors)

Exploded view of Girling disc brake components—1975–77 Type 2 shown

careful not to shear the split clamping bushing from the pin. Insert the pin from the inside of the caliper and drive it to the outside.

9. Pump the brake pedal several times to take up the clearance between the pads and the disc before driving the car.

10. Install the wheel and tire and carefully road test the car. Apply the brakes gently for 500 to 1000 miles to properly break in the pads and prevent glazing them.

Brake Caliper Removal and Installation

1. Jack up the car and remove the wheel and tire.

2. Remove the brake pads.

3. Disconnect the brake line from the caliper.

4. Remove the two bolts which secure the caliper to the steering knuckle and remove the caliper from the vehicle.

5. Reverse the above steps to install the caliper and bleed the brakes after the caliper is installed.

Brake Caliper Overhaul

Clean all parts in alcohol or brake fluid.

1. Remove the caliper from the vehicle.

2. Remove the piston retaining plates.

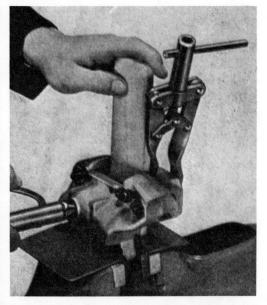

Clamping a piston in place and applying compressed air to the brake hose port

3. Pry out the seal spring ring using a small screwdriver. Do not damage the seal beneath the ring.

4. Remove the seal with a plastic or hard rubber rod. Do not use sharp edged or metal tools.

5. Rebuild one piston at a time. Securely clamp one piston in place so that it cannot come out of its bore. Place a block of wood between the two pistons and apply air pressure to the brake fluid port.

CAUTION: *Use extreme care with this technique because the piston can fly out of the caliper with tremendous force.*

6. Remove the rubber seal at the bottom of the piston bore using a rubber or plastic tool.

7. Check the bore and piston for wear, rust, and pitting.

8. Install a new seal in the bottom of the bore and lubricate the bore and seal with brake fluid.

9. Gently insert the piston, making sure it does not cock and jamb in the bore.

10. Install the new outer seal and new spring ring.

11. Install the piston retaining plate.

12. Repeat the above procedure on the other piston. Never rebuild only one side of a caliper.

Brake Disc Removal and Installation

1. Jack up the car and remove the wheel and tire.

2. Remove the caliper.

3. On Type 2, remove the three socket head bolts which secure the disc to the hub and remove the disc from the hub. Sometimes the disc is rusted to the hub. Spray penetrating oil on the seam and tap the disc with a lead or brass hammer. If it still does not come off, screw three 8 mm by 40 screws into the socket head holes. Tighten the screws evenly and pull the disc from the hub.

4. On Type 1, 3, and 4, remove the wheel bearing cover. On the left side it will be necessary to remove the small clip which secures the end of the speedometer cable to the cover.

5. Unscrew the wheel bearing nut and remove the nut and outer wheel bearing.

6. Pull the disc off of the spindle.

7. To remove the wheel bearing races,

see the "Wheel Bearing Removal and Installation" procedure.

8. Installation is the reverse of the above. Make sure the wheel bearing is properly adjusted.

Brake Disc Inspection

Visually check the rotor for excessive scoring. Minor scores will not affect the performance; however, if the scores are over $1/32$ in., it is necessary to replace the disc or have it resurfaced. The disc must be 0.02 in. over the wear limit to be resurfaced. The disc must be free of surface cracks and discoloration (heat bluing). Hand spin the disc and make sure that it does not wobble from side to side.

FRONT WHEEL BEARINGS

Removal and Installation

1. Jack up the car and remove the wheel and tire.

2. Remove the caliper and disc (if equipped with disc brakes) or brake drum.

3. To remove the inside wheel bearing, pry the dust seal out of the hub with a screwdriver. Lift out the bearing and its inner race.

4. To remove the outer race for either the inner or outer wheel bearing, insert a long punch into the hub opposite the end from which the race is to be removed. The race rests against a shoulder in the hub. The shoulder has two notches cut into it so that it is possible to place the end of the punch directly against the back side of the race and drive it out of the hub.

5. Carefully clean the hub.

6. Install new races in the hub. Drive them in with a soft faced hammer or a large piece of pipe of the proper diameter. Lubricate the races with a light coating of wheel bearing grease.

7. Force wheel bearing grease into the sides of the tapered roller bearings so that all the spaces are filled.

8. Place a small amount of grease inside the hub.

9. Place the inner wheel bearing into its race in the hub and tap a new seal into the hub. Lubricate the sealing surface of the seal with grease.

10. Install the hub on the spindle and install the outer wheel bearing.

Exploded view of Type 1 front wheel roller bearings

1. Speedometer cable circlip
2. Hub cap dust cover
3. Clamp nut allen screw
4. Wheel bearing clamp nut
5. Thrust washer
6. Outer taper roller bearing
7. Brake drum
8. Drum seal (grease)
9. Inner taper roller bearing
10. Bolt
11. Spring washer
12. Front brake unit
13. Steering knuckle

11. Adjust the wheel bearing and install the dust cover.

12. Install the caliper (if equipped with disc brakes).

Adjustment

The bearing may be adjusted by feel or by a dial indicator.

To adjust the bearing by feel, tighten the adjusting nut so that all the play is taken up in the bearing. There will be a slight amount of drag on the wheel if it is hand spun. Back off fully on the adjusting nut and retighten very lightly. There should be no drag when the wheel is hand spun and there should be no perceptible play in the bearing when the wheel is grasped and wiggled from side to side.

To use a dial indicator, remove the dust cover and mount a dial indicator against the hub. Grasp the wheel at the side and pull the wheel in and out along the axis of the spindle. Read the axial play on the dial indicator. Screw the adjusting nut in or out to obtain 0.001–0.005 in. of axial play. Secure the adjusting nut and recheck the axial play.

Front Drum Brakes

Brake Drum Removal and Installation

1. Jack up the car and remove the wheel and tire.

2. On the left side, remove the clip which secures the speedometer cable to the wheel bearing dust cover. Remove the dust cover.

3. Remove the wheel bearing adjusting nut and slide the brake drum off of the spindle. It may be necessary to back off on the brake shoe star wheels so that there is enough clearance to remove the drum.

4. Installation is the reverse of removal. Adjust the wheel bearings after installing the drum.

CAUTION: *Do not forget to readjust the brake shoes if they were disturbed during removal.*

Brake Drum Inspection

If the brake drums are scored or cracked, they must be replaced or machined. If the vehicle pulls to one side or

Front wheel brake   **Rear wheel brake**

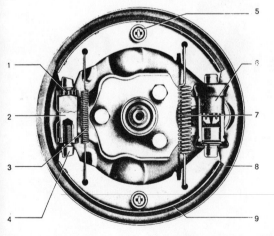 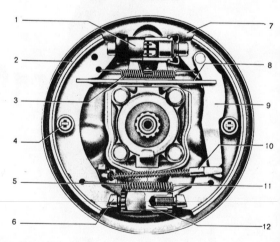

Front and rear drum brakes—Type 1

FRONT
1. Adjusting screw
2. Anchor block
3. Front return spring
4. Adjusting nut
5. Guide spring with cup and pin
6. Cylinder
7. Rear return spring

8. Back plate
9. Brake shoe with lining

REAR
1. Cylinder
2. Brake shoe with lining
3. Upper return spring
4. Spring with cup and pin

5. Lower return spring
6. Adjusting screw
7. Back plate
8. Connecting link
9. Lever
10. Brake cable
11. Adjusting nut
12. Anchor block

exhibits a pulsating braking action, the drum is probably out of round and should be checked at a machine shop. The drum may have a smooth even surface and still be out of round. The drum should be free of surface cracks and dark spots.

Brake Linings Removal and Installation

TYPE 1

1. Jack up the car and remove the wheel and tire.
2. Remove the brake drum.
3. Remove the small disc and spring which secure each shoe to the backing plate.
4. Remove the two long springs between the two shoes.
5. Remove the shoes from the backing plate.
6. If new shoes are being installed, remove the adjusters in the end of each wheel cylinder and screw the star wheel up against the head of the adjuster. When inserting the adjusters back in the wheel cylinders, notice that the slot in the adjuster is angled and must be positioned as illustrated.

The notched adjusters must be positioned as shown

7. Position new shoes on the backing plate. The slot in the shoes and the stronger return spring must be at the wheel cylinder end.
8. Install the disc and spring which secure the shoe to the backing plate.
9. Install the brake drum and adjust the wheel bearing.

TYPE 2

1. Remove the brake drum.
2. Pry the rear brake shoe out of the adjuster, as illustrated, and detach the return springs. Remove the forward shoe.
3. If new shoes are to be installed, screw the star wheel up against the head of the adjuster.
4. Install the rear brake shoe.
5. Attach the return spring to the front brake shoe and then to the rear shoe.
6. Position the front brake shoe in the slot of the adjusting screw and lever it into position in the same manner as it was removed. Make sure that the return springs do not touch the brake line between the upper and lower wheel cylinders.
7. Install the brake-drum and adjust the wheel bearings.

Wheel Cylinder Removal and Installation

1. Remove the brake shoes.
2. On Type 1, disconnect the brake line from the rear of the cylinder. On Type 2, disconnect the brake line from the rear of the cylinder and transfer line from the front of the cylinder.
3. Remove the bolts which secure the cylinder to the backing plate and remove the cylinder from the vehicle.
4. Reverse the above steps to install and bleed the brakes.

Wheel Cylinder Overhaul

1. Remove the wheel cylinder.
2. Remove the brake adjusters and remove the rubber boot from each end.
NOTE: *The Type 2 cylinder has only one rubber boot, piston, and cup. The rebuilding procedures are the same.*
3. On Type 1, push in on one of the pistons to force out the opposite piston and rubber cup. On Type 2, remove the piston and cup by blowing compressed air into the brake hose hole.
4. Wash the pistons and cylinder in clean brake fluid or alcohol.
5. Inspect the cylinder bore for signs of pitting, scoring, and excessive wear. If it is badly scored or pitted, the whole cylinder should be replaced. It is possible to remove the glaze and light scores with crocus cloth or a brake cylinder hone. Before rebuilding the cylinder, make

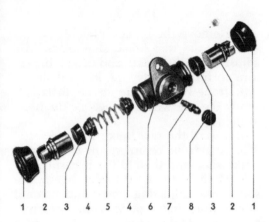

Front wheel cylinders disassembled—Type 1 (left) and Type 2 (right)

1. Boot	3. Cup	5. Spring	7. Bleeder valve	9. Adjusting nut
2. Piston	4. Cup expander	6. Housing	8. Dust cap	10. Adjusting screw

sure the bleeder screw is free. If the bleeder is rusted shut or broken off, replace the entire cylinder.

6. Dip the new pistons and rubber cups in brake fluid. Place the spring in the bore and insert the rubber cups into the bore against the spring. The concave side of the rubber cup should face inward.

7. Place the pistons in the bore and install the rubber boot.

8. Install the cylinder and bleed the brakes after the shoes and drum are in place. Make sure that the brakes are adjusted.

Rear Drum Brakes

Brake Drum Removal and Installation

TYPE 1, 2, 3

1. With the wheels still on the ground, remove the cotter pin from the slotted nut on the rear axle and remove the nut from the axle.

CAUTION: *Make sure the emergency brake is now released.*

2. Jack up the car and remove the wheel and tire.

3. The brake drum is splined to the rear axle and the drum should slip off the axle. However, the drum sometimes rusts on the splines and it is necessary to remove the drum using a puller.

Removing rear drum with puller—Types 1, 2, and 3

Tightening rear axle nut (36 mm or 1 7/16 in.) to 217 ft lbs using 0–150 ft lb torque wrench and half-length adaptor (a 3 or 4 foot metal pipe will do nicely)

4. Before installing the drum, lubricate the splines. Install the drum on the axle and tighten the nut on the axle to 217 ft lbs. Line up a slot in the nut with a hole in the axle and insert a cotter pin. Never loosen the nut to align the slot and hole.

TYPE 4

The drum is held in place by the wheel lugs. Jack up the car and remove the wheel and tire. After the wheel is removed, there are two small screws that secure the drum to the hub and they must be removed before the drum will slip off the hub.

Inspection

Inspection is the same as given in the "Front Drum Brake" section.

Brake Lining Removal and Installation

1. Remove the brake drum.
2. Remove both shoe retaining springs.
3. Disconnect the lower return spring.
4. Disconnect the hand brake cable from the lever attached to the rear shoe.
5. Remove the upper return spring and clip.
6. Remove the brake shoes and connecting link.
7. Remove the emergency brake lever from the rear shoe.

Parking brake lever attachment

Details of parking brake lever attachment to rear shoe

1. Pin	4. Shoe
2. Spring washer	5. Clip
3. Lever	

8. Lubricate the adjusting screws and the star wheel against the head of the adjusting screw.
9. Reverse Steps 1–7 to install the shoes.
10. Adjust the brakes.

Wheel Cylinder Removal and Installation

Remove the brake drum and brake shoes. Disconnect the brake line from the cylinder and remove the bolts which secure the cylinder to the backing plate. Remove the cylinder from the vehicle.

Overhaul

Overhaul is the same as given in the "Front Drum Brake" section.

Parking Brake

Cable Adjustment

Brake cable adjustment is performed at the handbrake lever in the passenger compartment. There is a cable for each

Exploded view of rear wheel cylinder assemblies—Types 1, 3, and 4 (left) and Type 2 (right)

1. Boot   4. Cup expander   7. Bleeder valve
2. Piston   5. Spring   8. Dust cap
3. Cup   6. Housing   9. Circlip

rear wheel and there are two adjusting nuts at the lever.

To adjust the cable, loosen the locknut. Jack up the rear wheel to be adjusted so that it can be hand spun. Turn the adjusting nut until a very slight drag is felt as the wheel is spun. Then back off on the adjusting nut until the lever can be pulled up three notches.

CAUTION: *Never pull up on the handbrake lever with the cables disconnected.*

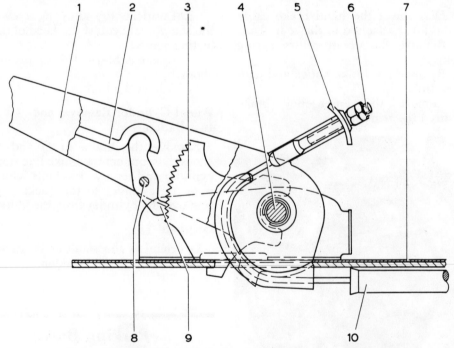

Parking brake hand lever and cable end assembly—Type 1 shown

1. Hand brake lever   6. Brake cable
2. Pawl rod   7. Frame
3. Ratchet segment   8. Pawl pin
4. Lever pin   9. Pawl
5. Cable compensator   10. Cable guide tube

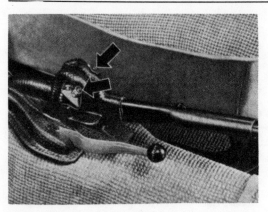

Parking brake cable adjusting nuts

Cable Removal and Installation

1. Disconnect the cables at the hand-brake lever by removing the two nuts which secure the cables to the lever. Pull the cables rearward to remove that end from the lever bracket.

2. Remove the brake drum and detach the cable end from the lever attached to the rear brake shoe.

3. Remove the brake cable bracket from the backing plate and remove the cable from the vehicle.

4. Reverse the above steps to install and adjust the cable.

Brake Specifications

(All measurements are given in in.)

Year	Model	Master Cylinder Bore	Wheel Cylinder Bore			Drum Diameter		Brake Disc	
			Front		Rear	Front	Rear	Thickness	Thickness after Machining (minimum)
			Disc	Drum					
1970–77	Type 1	0.750	1.575 ⑤③	0.874 ⑥	0.687	9.059④ + 0.008	9.055 + 0.008	0.372– 0.374	0.335
1970	Type 2	0.875	——	1.000	0.875	9.843 + 0.008	9.843 + 0.008	——	——
1971–77	Type 2	0.938	2.126	——	0.874	——	9.920 + 0.008	0.511	0.472
1970–73	Type 3	0.750	1.654	——	0.874	——	9.768 + 0.008	0.372– 0.374①	0.335②
1970–74	Type 4	0.750	1.654	——	0.874	——	9.768 + 0.008	0.433	0.393

① 1972–73—thickness 0.433
② 1972–73—thickness after machining 0.393
③ Karmann Ghia—1971–74
④ Super Beetle—9.768 + 0.008
⑤ Ate—1.575 in.; Girling 1.591 in.
⑥ Super Beetle—0.937

General Conversion Table

Multiply by	To convert	To	
2.54	Inches	Centimeters	.3937
30.48	Feet	Centimeters	.0328
.914	Yards	Meters	1.094
1.609	Miles	Kilometers	.621
.645	Square inches	Square cm.	.155
.836	Square yards	Square meters	1.196
16.39	Cubic inches	Cubic cm.	.061
28.3	Cubic feet	Liters	.0353
.4536	Pounds	Kilograms	2.2045
4.546	Gallons	Liters	.22
.068	Lbs./sq. in. (psi)	Atmospheres	14.7
.138	Foot pounds	Kg. m.	7.23
1.014	H.P. (DIN)	H.P. (SAE)	.9861
——	To obtain	From	Multiply by

Note: 1 cm. equals 10 mm.; 1 mm. equals .0394".

Conversion—Common Fractions to Decimals and Millimeters

INCHES			INCHES			INCHES		
Common Fractions	Decimal Fractions	Millimeters (approx.)	Common Fractions	Decimal Fractions	Millimeters (approx.)	Common Fractions	Decimal Fractions	Millimeters (approx.)
1/128	.008	0.20	11/32	.344	8.73	43/64	.672	17.07
1/64	.016	0.40	23/64	.359	9.13	11/16	.688	17.46
1/32	.031	0.79	3/8	.375	9.53	45/64	.703	17.86
3/64	.047	1.19	25/64	.391	9.92	23/32	.719	18.26
1/16	.063	1.59	13/32	.406	10.32	47/64	.734	18.65
5/64	.078	1.98	27/64	.422	10.72	3/4	.750	19.05
3/32	.094	2.38	7/16	.438	11.11	49/64	.766	19.45
7/64	.109	2.78	29/64	.453	11.51	25/32	.781	19.84
1/8	.125	3.18	15/32	.469	11.91	51/64	.797	20.24
9/64	.141	3.57	31/64	.484	12.30	13/16	.813	20.64
5/32	.156	3.97	1/2	.500	12.70	53/64	.828	21.03
11/64	.172	4.37	33/64	.516	13.10	27/32	.844	21.43
3/16	.188	4.76	17/32	.531	13.49	55/64	.859	21.83
13/64	.203	5.16	35/64	.547	13.89	7/8	.875	22.23
7/32	.219	5.56	9/16	.563	14.29	57/64	.891	22.62
15/64	.234	5.95	37/64	.578	14.68	29/32	.906	23.02
1/4	.250	6.35	19/32	.594	15.08	59/64	.922	23.42
17/64	.266	6.75	39/64	.609	15.48	15/16	.938	23.81
9/32	.281	7.14	5/8	.625	15.88	61/64	.953	24.21
19/64	.297	7.54	41/64	.641	16.27	31/32	.969	24.61
5/16	.313	7.94	21/32	.656	16.67	63/64	.984	25.00
21/64	.328	8.33						

Conversion—Millimeters to Decimal Inches

mm	inches	mm	inches	mm	inches	mm	inches	mm	inches
1	.039 370	31	1.220 470	61	2.401 570	91	3.582 670	210	8.267 700
2	.078 740	32	1.259 840	62	2.440 940	92	3.622 040	220	8.661 400
3	.118 110	33	1.299 210	63	2.480 310	93	3.661 410	230	9.055 100
4	.157 480	34	1.338 580	64	2.519 680	94	3.700 780	240	9.448 800
5	.196 850	35	1.377 949	65	2.559 050	95	3.740 150	250	9.842 500
6	.236 220	36	1.417 319	66	2.598 420	96	3.779 520	260	10.236 200
7	.275 590	37	1.456 689	67	2.637 790	97	3.818 890	270	10.629 900
8	.314 960	38	1.496 050	68	2.677 160	98	3.858 260	280	11.032 600
9	.354 330	39	1.535 430	69	2.716 530	99	3.897 630	290	11.417 300
10	.393 700	40	1.574 800	70	2.755 900	100	3.937 000	300	11.811 000
11	.433 070	41	1.614 170	71	2.795 270	105	4.133 848	310	12.204 700
12	.472 440	42	1.653 540	72	2.834 640	110	4.330 700	320	12.598 400
13	.511 810	43	1.692 910	73	2.874 010	115	4.527 550	330	12.992 100
14	.551 180	44	1.732 280	74	2.913 380	120	4.724 400	340	13.385 800
15	.590 550	45	1.771 650	75	2.952 750	125	4.921 250	350	13.779 500
16	.629 920	46	1.811 020	76	2.992 120	130	5.118 100	360	14.173 200
17	.669 290	47	1.850 390	77	3.031 490	135	5.314 950	370	14.566 900
18	.708 660	48	1.889 760	78	3.070 860	140	5.511 800	380	14.960 600
19	.748 030	49	1.929 130	79	3.110 230	145	5.708 650	390	15.354 300
20	.787 400	50	1.968 500	80	3.149 600	150	5.905 500	400	15.748 000
21	.826 770	51	2.007 870	81	3.188 970	155	6.102 350	500	19.685 000
22	.866 140	52	2.047 240	82	3.228 340	160	6.299 200	600	23.622 000
23	.905 510	53	2.086 610	83	3.267 710	165	6.496 050	700	27.559 000
24	.944 880	54	2.125 980	84	3.307 080	170	6.692 900	800	31.496 000
25	.984 250	55	2.165 350	85	3.346 450	175	6.889 750	900	35.433 000
26	1.023 620	56	2.204 720	86	3.385 820	180	7.086 600	1000	39.370 000
27	1.062 990	57	2.244 090	87	3.425 190	185	7.283 450	2000	78.740 000
28	1.102 360	58	2.283 460	88	3.464 560	190	7.480 300	3000	118.110 000
29	1.141 730	59	2.322 830	89	3.503 903	195	7.677 150	4000	157.480 000
30	1.181 100	60	2.362 200	90	3.543 300	200	7.874 000	5000	196.850 000

To change decimal millimeters to decimal inches, position the decimal point where desired on either side of the millimeter measurement shown and reset the inches decimal by the same number of digits in the same direction. For example, to convert 0.001 mm into decimal inches, reset the decimal behind the 1 mm (shown on the chart) to 0.001; change the decimal inch equivalent (0.039″ shown) to 0.000039″.

Tap Drill Sizes

	National Fine or S.A.E.			National Coarse or U.S.S.	
Screw & Tap Size	Threads Per Inch	Use Drill Number	Screw & Tap Size	Threads Per Inch	Use Drill Number
No. 5	44	37	No. 5	40	39
No. 6	40	33	No. 6	32	36
No. 8	36	29	No. 8	32	29
No. 10	32	21	No. 10	24	25
No. 12	28	15	No. 12	24	17
1/4	28	3	1/4	20	8
5/16	24	1	5/16	18	F
3/8	24	Q	3/8	16	5/16
7/16	20	W	7/16	14	U
1/2	20	29/64	1/2	13	27/64
9/16	18	33/64	9/16	12	31/64
5/8	18	37/64	5/8	11	17/32
3/4	16	11/16	3/4	10	21/32
7/8	14	13/16	7/8	9	49/64
1 1/8	12	1 3/64	1	8	7/8
1 1/4	12	1 11/64	1 1/8	7	63/64
1 1/2	12	1 27/64	1 1/4	7	1 7/64
			1 1/2	6	1 11/32

Decimal Equivalent Size of the Number Drills

Drill No.	Decimal Equivalent	Drill No.	Decimal Equivalent	Drill No.	Decimal Equivalent
80	.0135	53	.0595	26	.1470
79	.0145	52	.0635	25	.1495
78	.0160	51	.0670	24	.1520
77	.0180	50	.0700	23	.1540
76	.0200	49	.0730	22	.1570
75	.0210	48	.0760	21	.1590
74	.0225	47	.0785	20	.1610
73	.0240	46	.0810	19	.1660
72	.0250	45	.0820	18	.1695
71	.0260	44	.0860	17	.1730
70	.0280	43	.0890	16	.1770
69	.0292	42	.0935	15	.1800
68	.0310	41	.0960	14	.1820
67	.0320	40	.0980	13	.1850
66	.0330	39	.0995	12	.1890
65	.0350	38	.1015	11	.1910
64	.0360	37	.1040	10	.1935
63	.0370	36	.1065	9	.1960
62	.0380	35	.1100	8	.1990
61	.0390	34	.1110	7	.2010
60	.0400	33	.1130	6	.2040
59	.0410	32	.1160	5	.2055
58	.0420	31	.1200	4	.2090
57	.0430	30	.1285	3	.2130
56	.0465	29	.1360	2	.2210
55	.0520	28	.1405	1	.2280
54	.0550	27	.1440		

Decimal Equivalent Size of the Letter Drills

Letter Drill	Decimal Equivalent	Letter Drill	Decimal Equivalent	Letter Drill	Decimal Equivalent
A	.234	J	.277	S	.348
B	.238	K	.281	T	.358
C	.242	L	.290	U	.368
D	.246	M	.295	V	.377
E	.250	N	.302	W	.386
F	.257	O	.316	X	.397
G	.261	P	.323	Y	.404
H	.266	Q	.332	Z	.413
I	.272	R	.339		